Action Research in Human Services

Ernie Stringer
Curtin University of Technology

Rosalie Dwyer
Department of Community Development

PEARSON
Merrill
Prentice Hall

Upper Saddle River, New Jersey
Columbus, Ohio

Library of Congress Cataloging-in-Publication Data

Stringer, Ernest T.
   Action research in human services / Ernie Stringer, Rosalie Dwyer.
      p. cm.
   Includes bibliographical references and index.
   ISBN 0-13-097423-4
    1. Human services—Research. 2. Action research. I. Dwyer, Rosalie. II. Title.

HV11.S835 2005
361'.0072—dc22

2004044621

Vice President and Executive Publisher: Jeffery W. Johnston
Publisher: Kevin M. Davis
Editorial Assistant: Amanda King
Production Editor: Mary Harlan
Production Coordinator: Lea Baranowski, Carlisle Publishers Services
Design Coordinator: Diane C. Lorenzo
Text Design and Illustrations: Carlisle Publishers Services
Cover Design: Robin Chukes
Cover Image: SuperStock
Production Manager: Ann Castel Davis
Marketing Manager: Autumn Purdy
Marketing Coordinator: Tyra Poole

Copyright © 2005 by Pearson Education, Inc., Upper Saddle River, New Jersey 07458.
Pearson Prentice Hall. All rights reserved. Printed in the United States of America. This publication is
protected by Copyright and permission should be obtained from the publisher prior to any prohibited
reproduction, storage in a retrieval system, or transmission in any form or by any means, electronic,
mechanical, photocopying, recording, or likewise. For information regarding permission(s), write to:
Rights and Permissions Department.

Pearson Prentice Hall™ is a trademark of Pearson Education, Inc.
Pearson® is a registered trademark of Pearson plc
Prentice Hall® is a registered trademark of Pearson Education, Inc.
Merrill® is a registered trademark of Pearson Education, Inc.

Pearson Education Ltd.   Pearson Education Australia Pty. Limited
Pearson Education Singapore Pte. Ltd.   Pearson Education North Asia Ltd.
Pearson Education Canada, Ltd.   Pearson Educación de Mexico, S.A. de C.V.
Pearson Education—Japan   Pearson Education Malaysia Pte. Ltd.

ISBN: 0-13-097423-4

Preface

Introduction

Action Research in Human Services presents an approach to action research that assists human service professionals to improving their practice. Though the action research processes articulated in this book may be used effectively with individuals, they are particularly relevant to work with groups, families, and communities. Action research is suited to a wide range of human services work—child protection, family support, domestic violence, juvenile justice, corrections, youth work, aged care, rehabilitation, community work, community development, services to the disabled, and others. Ultimately, action research enables human service professionals to work in partnership with clients, community groups, colleagues, and others to explore significant issues and to take therapeutic action to resolve problems.

The general orientation of this book is toward a participatory approach to research. It is a style of investigation grounded in the belief that effective solutions to significant problems are more likely to emerge where all "stakeholders"—those who are affected or have an effect on an issue—are involved in the processes of inquiry. Further, it enhances possibilities for connecting people to multiple networks of support within local organizations, neighborhood clubs, sports groups, schools, churches, and friendship groups. Though individual counseling and therapy continue to have an important place in this process, action research provides the basis for long-term, effective, and efficient measures to remedy problematic situations. Procedures described in this book not only build people's capacity to resolve issues effectively, but also provide long-term outcomes that strengthen families and communities, reduce dependency, and create healthier family and community environments.

Approaches to Research

Action Research in Human Services does not pretend to provide a comprehensive rendering of all the forms of action research, but rather presents a distinctive approach that has currency in many academic, professional, and community settings. The text offers an essentially qualitative approach to research that can be modified to accommodate researchers oriented toward other modes of inquiry. Qualitative research now encompasses a broad array of orientations and approaches, many of which are described in Denzin and Lincoln's *Handbook of Qualitative Research* (2000). They are complemented by a range of approaches to action research presented by Reason and Bradbury in the *Handbook of Action Research* (2001) and by Susan Noffke (1997).

The approach presented in this book derives from the need to be sensitive to the diverse perspectives and experiences now evident in most modern communities—to give voice to those perspectives and empower people to develop more effective ways of dealing with their professional, personal, family, or community lives. This orientation emerges from recent developments within postmodern, feminist, and critical scholarship, so that issues of positioning, knowledge, and power are embedded in the research practices presented herein.

Action Research on the Run

One reviewer of a draft version of this book commented, "My students would never have time to do all this." The text is necessarily detailed, providing specific guidance for many of the skills that may be required for the different contexts and problems to which action research can be applied. The Look-Think-Act routine included in Chapter 1, however, has been used in planning or problem-solving sessions covering a period of only two hours. Though complex and endemic problems may require more extensive and detailed work, a simpler research process may be applied "on the run" for daily work issues. Professional practice is enhanced by the development of a culture of inquiry that helps people gain greater clarity in thinking about their work.

Structure of the Book

The purpose of this book is to provide human service practitioners with an understanding of the nature of action research (Chapters 1 and 2) and the procedures and applications of action research (Chapters 3 through 7). In addition, it provides practical resources that add to the fund of knowledge available to action researchers (Chapters 8 through 10).

Chapter 1 presents an overview of action research, describing its characteristics and accentuating the research relationships that are integral to this methodology.

Chapter 2 provides readers with a deeper understanding of the epistemology (system of meaning) that drives action research. It describes theoretical positions that inform the practice of action research, focusing on the interpretive processes now central to much professional and social scientific research.

Chapters 3 through 7 describe in detail the stages of one cycle of an action research process—research design, data gathering, data analysis, reporting, and taking action. Each chapter features both processes and skills, providing readers with clear guidance for enacting action research routines.

Chapter 8 provides a set of tools that are useful adjuncts to research. As research participants engage complex contexts, issues, and interactions, they will enhance their capacity to work effectively if they can manage conflict productively, conduct meetings efficiently, use their time effectively, facilitate the work of diverse individuals and groups, and manage the complexity and stress that come from work in complex organizational settings.

Chapter 9 presents a number of case studies that are indicative of the broad range of ways in which action research can be applied to professional and community life. Stories and reports drawn from diverse settings describe ways that human service practitioners and community groups have enhanced their work by the use of action research.

Finally, Chapter 10 offers a small sample of the proliferating resources now available on websites throughout the world, providing a rich resource for human service professionals, community groups, agencies, programs, and services.

Acknowledgments

This book could not have been written without the input and support of many people. We would particularly like to acknowledge the influence and support of many of our colleagues and friends, especially Tony Kelly, Doug McCauley, Darryl Kickett, Carol Martin, Bill Genat, and Susan Young. We are also grateful to Kevin Davis, Mary Harlan, and Autumn Crisp Benson of Merrill/Prentice Hall and to Lea Baranowski of Carlisle Communications for their consistent support during the development and production stages of this text. Our reviewers likewise deserve our thanks: Steve Anderson, University of Illinois; Patrick Bordnick, Georgia University; James Hall, University of Iowa; Nancy Larson, Arizona State University; and Sabrina Williams, Indiana University. They provided many useful comments, and their keen insights ensured that this book has gained greatly in clarity and usability.

Ernie Stringer
e.stringer@exchange.curtin.edu.au
erniestringer@hotmail.com

Rosalie Dwyer
rosalid@dcd.wa.gov.au

Research Navigator:
Research Made Simple!

www.ResearchNavigator.com

Merrill Education is pleased to introduce Research Navigator—a one-stop research solution for students that simplifies and streamlines the entire research process. At www.researchnavigator.com, students will find extensive resources to enhance their understanding of the research process so they can effectively complete research assignments. In addition, Research Navigator has three exclusive databases of credible and reliable source content to help students focus their research efforts and begin the research process.

How Will Research Navigator Enhance Your Course?

- Extensive content helps students understand the research process, including writing, Internet research, and citing sources.
- Step-by-step tutorial guides students through the entire research process from selecting a topic to revising a rough draft.
- Research Writing in the Disciplines section details the differences in research across disciplines.
- Three exclusive databases—EBSCO's ContentSelect Academic Journal Database, *The New York Times* Search by Subject Archive, and "Best of the Web" Link Library—allow students to easily find journal articles and sources.

What's the Cost?

A subscription to Research Navigator is $7.50 but is **free** when used in conjunction with this textbook. To obtain free passcodes for your students, simply contact your local Merrill/Prentice Hall sales representative, and your representative will send you the Evaluating Online Resource Guide, which contains the code to access Research Navigator as well as tips on how to use Research Navigator and how to evaluate research. To preview the value of this website to your students, please go to www.educatorlearningcenter.com and use the Login Name "Research" and the password "Demo."

Brief Contents

Contents

4   Gathering Data: Tools and Techniques   54

5 Giving Voice: Interpretive and Qualitative Data Analysis 87

6 Representation: Communicating Research Processes and Outcomes 116

NOTE: Every effort has been made to provide accurate and current information in this book. However, the Internet and information posted on it are constantly changing. It is inevitable that some of the Internet addresses listed in this textbook will change.

Purposes and Processes of Action Research

1

Contents of This Chapter

The purpose of this chapter is to provide readers with an understanding of the nature of action research and the practice frameworks that guide its application in family, community, and organizational settings.

The chapter begins by describing how action research is relevant to the work of human service practitioners. The sections that follow discuss the nature of action research, focusing on:

- Action research as a *systematic process of inquiry*
- *Models of action research* that provide frameworks guiding processes of inquiry, including:
  - An action research *cycle*
  - An action research *helix*
  - An action research *sequence*
  - An action research *spiral*
- The *participatory research relationships* required for effective action research
- The *working principles* of action research—relationships, communication, participation, and inclusion
- *Further reading* that presents action research literature relevant to human service professionals

---

Action Research and Professional Practice

We spoke recently with a young social worker who had been appointed to a government welfare agency in a large rural town. He talked enthusiastically about his work, which included child abuse investigations, work with juveniles in contact with the justice system, and at-risk families. He not only was engaged and excited, but also enjoyed putting his recently learned professional skills into practice and having the authority to do so. He was somewhat perplexed, however, with the complexities of some of his

1

casework. "To begin with I couldn't believe the situations people get themselves into," he said. "But I enjoy working carefully through problems and coming up with solutions with them. It's why I went into social work."

Some of his work with clients was very difficult, relating to social problems deeply ingrained in the history of the community and the economic situation of some groups. There were families with generations of members who were largely unemployed often with drug or alcohol as an inherent part of their lifestyles, and with a common litany of low educational achievement, poor health status, and frequent brushes with the justice system. "Some of these cases are really difficult," he declared as he reflected on particularly complex aspects of his work. "I try to think my way through—to figure out what to do—but sometimes it seems hopeless, and I'm left with a standard routine response that really doesn't change anything. The people just continue to grind their way through the same old mill! These cases have even started to affect my sleep. I wake up at 2:00 A.M. going over them in my mind."

Another aspect of his situation became apparent as he talked. He realized the need to be systematic and thorough in his work, ensuring that his investigations took into account all relevant information and all aspects that might impact on the situation of his clients. Not only did he need to get the best outcomes possible, but he sometimes found that he needed to be able to provide detailed justifications for his decisions, recommendations, and actions. He needed a really thorough analysis, especially when he wanted to do something that differed from practices commonly accepted in the office where he worked. "Some of the older workers get that look in their eye that says 'Ah, yes! The new social worker who knows it all.' I really need to have it carefully mapped out when I go outside of the box. My supervisor, especially, really grills me."

As we reflected on our experiences in similar situations, we realized that the work we now envisage as action research had its genesis in attempts to come to grips with these types of situations—developing systematic ways of dealing with highly problematic situations and finding effective ways to resolve problems. It is not that action research is different from common practice frameworks that guide the work of professional practitioners in human services—investigation, analysis, recommendations, and so on. Action research provides a means for strengthening or enhancing existing work practices.

This is evident in situations where social workers and counselors have a counseling role whose particular function is to enable clients to talk through, reflect on, or explore a problematic issue. The purpose of this process is to provide clients with greater clarity and understanding that leads them to engage in actions to resolve the situation. This is a clear analogy to action research—a process of inquiry enabling participants to gather information, analyze it carefully, and use the understandings that emerge as the basis for therapeutic action. By framing these activities as action research, we seek to consciously enhance professional practices by engaging in systematic processes of inquiry that provide the means to make a real difference in people's lives.

Action Research: A Systematic Process of Inquiry

Research may be defined as a process of systematic investigation leading to increased understanding of a phenomenon or issue of interest. The distinctive feature of action research is that increased understanding is used to formulate effective action to resolve a problem or issue. Though research is ultimately quite an ordinary process for looking again at an existing situation (researching it) and seeing it in a different way, systematic investigation provides the means for ensuring strong and effective processes of inquiry. While action research may be used by human service professionals to enhance their casework practices, its greatest potential is realized in family, community, agency, and organizational settings.

Action research has a long history, one often associated with the work of Kurt Lewin, who viewed action research as a cyclical, dynamic, and collaborative process in which people addressed social issues affecting their lives. Through cycles of planning, acting, observing, and reflecting, participants used action research to address problems of assimilation, segregation, and discrimination, assisting people to resolve issues, initiate change, and study the impact of those changes (Lewin, 1938, 1946, 1948; Lewin & Lewin, 1942). Lewin's approach to action research is reflected in the definition given by Bogdan and Biklen (1992): "the systematic collection of information that is designed to bring about social change."

Kemmis and McTaggart (1988) suggest action research is "a form of collective, self-reflective enquiry undertaken by participants in social situations in order to improve the rationality and justice of their own social or educational practices, as well as their understanding of these practices and the situations in which these practices are carried out" (p. 6). For Kemmis and McTaggart, research is carried out by any group with a shared concern, and it is only action research when it is collaborative.

Reason and Bradbury (2001) extend this vision by describing action research as "a participatory, democratic process concerned with developing practical knowing in the pursuit of worthwhile human purposes, grounded in a participatory worldview which we believe is emerging at this historical moment. It seeks to bring together action and reflection, theory and practice, in participation with others, in the pursuit of practical solutions to issues of pressing concern to people, and more generally the flourishing of individual persons and their communities" (p. 1). For them, action research requires skills and methods to enable researchers to foster an inquiring approach to their own practices, to engage in face-to-face work with others to address issues of mutual concern, and to create a wider community of inquiry involving whole organizations.

The need for approaches to research that enable social workers, counselors, youth workers, and other human service professionals to formulate appropriate service delivery practices, along with an increasing emphasis on understanding the way that laypeople may contribute to the development of appropriate service delivery and developmental strategies, has extended the use of practioner-friendly research methodologies (Abbott & Sapsford, 1997; Fuller & Petch, 1995; Winter & Munn-Giddings, 2001).

Action research might usefully be distinguished from practitioner research, insofar as human service practitioners may make use of a variety of approaches to research to assist them in their work. When they stand back from their clients and use a variety of small experiments or surveys, engage in observations, or apply reflective analysis to obtain objective, factual information related to their intervention or service delivery strategies, they are doing **practitioner research.** When they engage in *collaborative* processes of inquiry, however, that incorporate the views, perspectives, and experiences of their clients, with the intent of solving a problem related to program or service delivery practices, they are doing **action research.**

It takes only a brief perusal of the action research literature to recognize that both the growth and the salience of work in this area in recent years have been marked not only by an increase in volume of references but also by a proliferation of varied usages of the term. Noffke (1997) quotes a generic definition of action research as "research designed to yield practical results that are immediately applicable to a specific situation or problem" (p. 306).

The model of action research described herein derives from a participatory approach to action research that focuses on:

1. **Change:** People changing and improving their own practices and behaviors
2. **Reflection:** People thinking, reflecting, and theorizing about their own practices, behaviors, and situations
3. **Inclusion:** Starting with the agendas and perspectives of the least powerful and widening the circle to include all those affected by the problem
4. **Sharing:** People sharing their perspectives with others
5. **Understanding:** Achieving clarity of understanding of the different perspectives and experiences of all involved
6. **Practice:** Testing emerging understandings by using them as the basis for changing practices or constructing new practices
7. **Community:** Working toward the building of a learning community

Models of Action Research

Action research has much in common with the regular problem-solving and planning routines used by human service practitioners in their daily work in family, organizational, agency, and community settings, but its strength lies in the systematic execution of carefully articulated processes of inquiry. As action researchers, practitioners:

- **Design a study,** carefully defining the issue to be investigated, formulating a research question, planning systematic processes of inquiry, and checking the ethics and validity of their work
- **Collect data,** including information from a variety of sources
- **Analyze the data** to identify key features of the issue investigated
- **Communicate** the outcomes of the study to relevant audiences
- **Take action** to resolve the issue investigated

Figure 1.1
Action Research Cycle

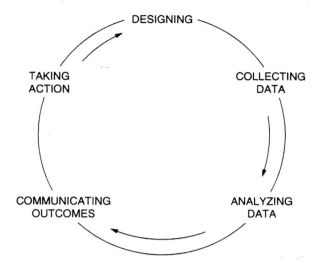

Figure 1.2
Action Research Helix

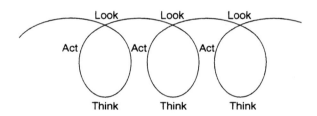

Action research usually is envisaged as cyclical in nature, participants continuously cycling through processes of investigation and working toward effective solutions to a research problem. It is often depicted as illustrated in Figure 1.1.

Action research is sometimes presented as a spiral helix Look-Think-Act routine (Figure 1.2) that provides a simple way of typifying a research process. It has been used to great effect in family, community, and institutional settings, providing the means for people to work toward resolution of significant problems in their day-to-day lives. The iterative process enables participants to check the effectiveness or appropriateness of information gained in the initial phases of inquiry by "putting it to the test" in immediate action.

Action research may be used as an integral part of professional practice, providing a framework that assists practitioners to increase the rigor of their regular professional routines. Action research processes are similar in structure to counseling or case management routines. Framing an investigation as an action research routine, with implications of systematic, skilled inquiry, serves to provide practitioners with a checklist they can use to review their work processes with the intent of making them more rigorous and effective. This is demonstrated in the following case, a summary version of a considerably longer report:

STRENGTHENING FAMILIES: AN ACTION RESEARCH PROCESS

Introduction

Social worker Edith Prince was given a case of two teenage boys whose single-parent mother had recently died and who were in the care of an aunt, Heather_____. Initial reports from a complainant suggested that the boys were at risk since the aunt had a history of drug addiction and prostitution and was known to consort with men with criminal histories. Edith's task was to investigate the situation and make a determination whether there was need for formal intervention from her agency.

Investigation: Collecting Information (Look)

Edith sought information from a variety of sources. She first read thoroughly the case history file that indicated considerable problems with the aunt. Information in the file indicated that the aunt had been involved with prostitution, and there was a suggestion she had introduced her now deceased sister into the profession. She had mental health problems and had suffered a breakdown requiring the need for psychiatric services. Further, she was known to associate with a gang with links to criminal activities and associated drug use. In addition, the children suffered from a number of mild conditions, including developmental delay, ADHD, mild epilepsy, and mild autism. There were also complaints that one of them failed to attend school regularly and created problems within his classroom.

Edith then initiated an interview with the aunt (Heather), with follow-up interviews in the days following as a broader picture emerged. With Heather's permission, Edith then consulted with a Mental Health Services physician who provides Heather with weekly psychotherapy sessions, a local police officer who had previous dealings with her, and teachers at the local school attended by the boys.

The picture that emerged was much more positive than suggested by the information in the file. In person, Heather presented as a very straightforward no-nonsense person who appeared extremely protective of the children and, despite obvious difficulties, provided thoughtful care. Not only was she aware of the children's mental and physical health, but had taken active steps to ensure that they acquired relevant treatment for their conditions. She was adamant that she had not used drugs for some years, except medication prescribed for her own condition, and that drugs would in no way be allowed in her home or near the children. She cared deeply for the children, made sure they dressed well, though conservatively, kept to regular routines, and ate healthy meals. She had a regular session with the children each week in which they had an hour's "mother-time" during which they could talk about their memories of their mother.

Her story was corroborated by the other sources interviewed. Mental Health Services indicated that Heather continued to maintain weekly visits to a counselor and had sought and gained treatment for the boys. The police officer confirmed that though Heather had a previous history of drugs and prostitution, she had been "clean" for the previous four years. Moreover, none of her current associates were known to engage in criminal or drug-related activities. He confirmed that the children's father led an itinerant and troubled lifestyle and had shown no interest in providing or caring for them. Teachers indicated that Heather contacted them regularly to check on the boys' schooling, and though the younger child had fairly severe problems following the death of his mother, his behavior and attendance had improved dramatically in recent weeks. One teacher attributed this fact to the stability of the home and the care shown the children by their aunt.

Analysis/Assessment (Think)

Edith was able to make a favorable assessment, based on the information acquired from these sources. Her report indicated that the family was going through an extremely difficult and emotional time, due to the death of the children's mother. They were coping well, however, given the traumatic circumstances of the mother's death. Though the aunt suffered mild mental health problems, she was seeking regular treatment for her condition and presented herself as a stable person showing great concern for the two boys. Indications were that her level of care for the boys was of a good standard, that she was assisting them to work actively through a grieving process, and that she was providing them with services required for mild mental and physical health conditions. Though the boys had troubled times immediately following the death of their mother, one of them was coming to terms with the situation and accepting changes, so that his schoolwork and behavior had not suffered in the long term. The other boy was more problematic, and though he had improved quite dramatically, his behavior and academic performance had not yet returned to their previous levels.

Reports and Actions (Act)

Based on her analysis, Edith wrote a report to the manager of the Family and Children's Services office. A copy of this report was placed in the office file and another copy forwarded to the state office that had initiated the original inquiry. She indicated that in light of her investigation of the circumstances, the safety of the children did not appear to be at risk. She recommended that:

The children remain in the care of their aunt, Heather _____
That they be classified for Family Support by the agency office for a period of six months
That a social worker visit the family regularly to provide assistance and support as required
That the agency office endorse the need for an ongoing program of treatment of the children through the local school and Mental Health Services

(continued)

(continued)

Edith informed the school, the police, and the Mental Health Services of the steps being taken and touched base with them from time to time in the following months. She also presented the aunt and the two boys with a note outlining these steps so that they were fully informed of the outcomes of their conversations. Edith was assigned to visit the family on a weekly basis for two months and on a monthly basis for the following four months to provide assistance and support. During this time, she worked with the children and other family members to review their situation and to help them formulate appropriate actions when they were needed, thus engaging in continuing cycles of the Look-Think-Act process.

Investigating Complex Problems and Issues

A more complex model of action research is provided in Figure 1.3, a model that is particularly suited to the more complex problems confronted by people working in professional, organizational, or university environments. The following chapters of this book use this framework as the means of describing detailed features of a systematic process of inquiry. This more detailed framework not only provides the basis for more formalized research practices, but gives guidance for professional practitioners to systematically investigate practical problems related to problems and issues in agency and community contexts. As with other models of action research, it is a cyclical, reiterative process, but it is presented here in linear form for purposes of clarity.

Figure 1.3 illustrates the relationship between action research and other approaches to qualitative research. While qualitative research studies are generally complete when the report is written, action research engages participants in the process of developing and implementing actions that resolve the problem on which the research has focused. The final box of the figure, therefore, includes the action planning that is a necessary part of action research and specifies the types of common practices to which action research might be applied.

Working Developmentally: Building Family and Community Capacities

Rosalie: Workers really need to develop positive relationships with their clients. Often, the only connection that people in troubled families have with the world is through role- and rule-bound relationships with service delivery professionals. The isolation of modern families doesn't always provide people with the type of social relationships they need when they have problems or confront crises. To develop supportive relationships with all individual clients would be an overwhelming task. That, to some extent, is the problem with much of the work we do now. When abuse or neglect or violence occurs within

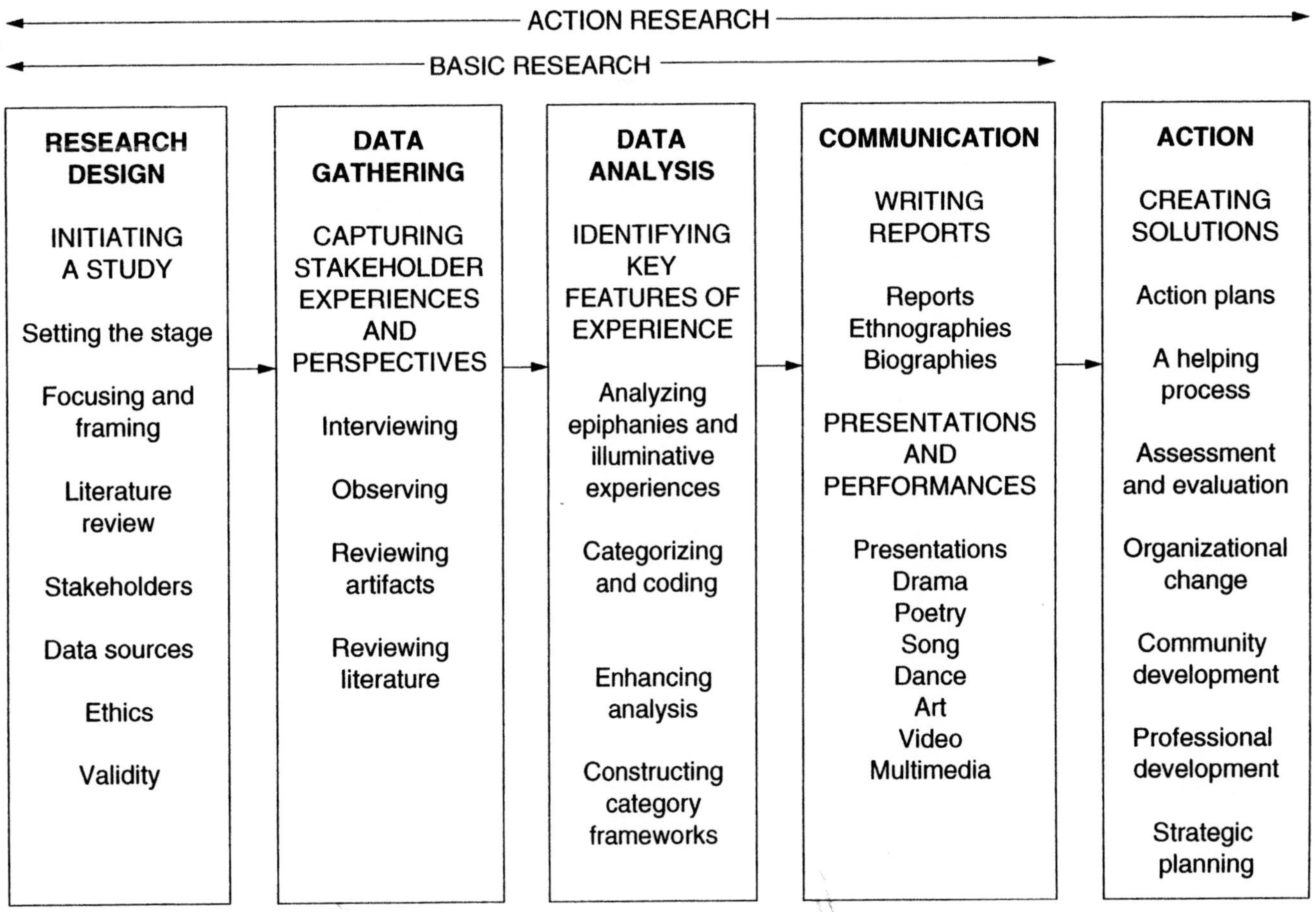

ACTION RESEARCH

BASIC RESEARCH

RESEARCH DESIGN

INITIATING A STUDY

Setting the stage

Focusing and framing

Literature review

Stakeholders

Data sources

Ethics

Validity

DATA GATHERING

CAPTURING STAKEHOLDER EXPERIENCES AND PERSPECTIVES

Interviewing

Observing

Reviewing artifacts

Reviewing literature

DATA ANALYSIS

IDENTIFYING KEY FEATURES OF EXPERIENCE

Analyzing epiphanies and illuminative experiences

Categorizing and coding

Enhancing analysis

Constructing category frameworks

COMMUNICATION

WRITING REPORTS

Reports
Ethnographies
Biographies

PRESENTATIONS AND PERFORMANCES

Presentations
Drama
Poetry
Song
Dance
Art
Video
Multimedia

ACTION

CREATING SOLUTIONS

Action plans

A helping process

Assessment and evaluation

Organizational change

Community development

Professional development

Strategic planning

Figure 1.3
Action Research Sequence

9

a family, it's quite often because the family is not only experiencing problems, but also is isolated—not connected to a network of supportive relationships. People don't get input to their situation, have no one to go to or talk to, no one who can provide information or suggest ways to deal with the situation. By the time people come to the attention of authorities or agencies, they're often mired in a deeply problematic situation.

Ernie: So are you suggesting there are limits to working with individual clients to try and have them conform to a set of prescribed behaviors? To stop them from abusing a child, or being violent with a spouse, or whatever?

Rosalie: Exactly. This way of working individually or with families soaks up huge amounts of resources. In many situations it just isn't working, and many workers are feeling the stress of increasingly large caseloads. We need to be able to spend time with families to reconnect them to their communities and the supportive relationships there. Community center programs and activities, for instance, provide a context for families to initially link for a specific purpose, but then develop a network of relationships that sustains and supports them, and helps them get through difficult times. We need processes to assist people to connect with their communities. Otherwise we'll continue to pour huge resources into sustaining institutions or foster care services that are often poor substitutes for a child's own family and often lead to greater problems in the long run.

Ernie: Are you advocating a greater emphasis on community work, then?

Rosalie: There definitely needs to be a place for human service professionals to take a community-oriented approach to their work with clients. It's certainly not the only way, but in the long run services will be just swamped if workers can't work developmentally—to assist people to determine the strengths within their families and identify the assets in their communities, and to incorporate that into case management processes. Further, unless professional workers can utilize part of their time and resources to build the capacity of communities to provide for people's needs, they'll continue to be the only resource available for many people. A focus on individual service delivery is self-defeating in the long run.

As human service professionals work with their clients, therefore, effective practice not only will engage individual therapeutic outcomes, but will assist them to connect more effectively with the community. By engaging clients and their families in processes of exploration and by assisting them to make appropriate connections, human resource professionals will increase their understanding of the resources available in the community.

They will not do this in isolation, however, since they will often work as part of a team or in conjunction with other professionals—health, education, legal, accommodation, etc.— who will be able to contribute to this knowledge base. Further, they will be able to detect gaps in community resources and to identify individuals, groups, agencies, or businesses that might assist in appropriate developments. In some circumstances they might engage in systematic community development processes, such as those suggested by Kretzmann and McKnight (1993), that identify individual capacities, take advantage of local associations, organizations, and institutions, and mobilize people to engage in appropriate developments.

Action research, therefore, may be engaged effectively for discrete problems and issues with clients, but it has the potential for more extended applications across organizations or within the community. As human service and social workers cycle through a research process with their clients, increased understandings may point to productive possibilities that might emerge by increasing the scope of inquiry. Investigation of specific problems often reveals the multiple dimensions of the situation requiring attention. Investigation of each of those dimensions further illuminates the situation, revealing other possibilities for action.

The process of "starting small" and increasing the breadth and complexity of activity is called "working developmentally." Though somewhat different from developmental psychology or child development, there are some conceptual similarities. In each, it is important to engage clients at the level they are capable of comprehending and achieving, according to their stage of "development." In participatory action research, a study may start with limited objectives, but the scope of the study may be extended as understanding and awareness increase. The potential for positive change and development increases exponentially as increasing numbers of people and issues are included (Figure 1.4).

Figure 1.4
Action Research Spiral

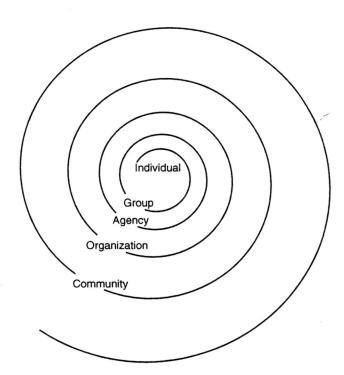

> **Rosalie:** I once worked with women in a new rural housing project, discussing problems they were experiencing settling into their new homes. Many of them were concerned about lack of furniture, for with limited income and no used-furniture stores in the vicinity, their families were, in some instances, sleeping and sitting on the floor. The women held a meeting, and I assisted them to develop a plan to raise funds to visit a city that had a number of used-furniture stores. They arranged transport for themselves by using vehicles within the community and a truck to transport furniture. Over a period of days, men and women from the community visited the city, bought furniture, and transported it to their homes.
>
> This project was so successful that the women continued to meet to work on other issues that had arisen in their initial discussions. They gained use of a local building for a women's center as a base for their continuing activities, and a number of initiatives emerged. They outfitted their houses with curtains, started a schoolchildren's meal program, and eventually raised funds for a bus. This decreased the isolation of people in the housing project and linked them with resources, services, and activities in nearby communities.
>
> An ever-widening circle of activities emerged from what initially had been a limited project. Through one small project, people within the community built their capacity to solve problems and to initiate desired activities and services that increased the quality of community life.

Research Relationships: Participatory Processes of Inquiry

Human service practitioners often work with clients who are in crisis or are in need of long-term assistance and support. In difficult circumstances and with limited resources, they face complex problems requiring a wide range of professional "tools." In any circumstance, they may find themselves engaged in an integrated set of problems related to child protection, family support, domestic violence, accommodation, drug and alcohol abuse, and/or juvenile justice. The complexity of these issues may require them to take on a variety of roles—broker, counselor, advocate, mobilizer, and/or caregiver.

When human service practitioners work with clients in action research mode, they enact a set of relationships that is quite different from that imposed by the demands of traditional scientific research. Action researchers are positioned quite differently, engaging in empathetic relationships with clients, colleagues, and other people involved in the situation. They do not wear the "mask of authority," but come to the table, as it were, as a facilitator of people's exploration. Their task is not to impose a regimen of prescribed requirements to which clients must conform, but to assist clients and other stakeholders to work toward the best possible solution to their situation. Action research enables clients, their families, and others to investigate their situation systematically, with dignity and with a therapeutic end in mind. It is a relationship-driven process that assists individuals and groups to become engaged in and take ownership of systematic processes of inquiry into issues affecting their lives.

Participatory action research therefore provides the technical means not only for accomplishing sound behavioral practices, but also for developing a sense of community and living democracy. Its purpose is to bring people together in a dialogic and productive relationship, enabling the development of a sense of togetherness through the sharing of perspectives, the negotiation of meaning, and the development of collaboratively produced outcomes. These processes should not be interpreted in idealized, touchy-feely, romantic terms, but utilized as pick-and-shovel, bread-and-butter issues that engage the hard realities of people whose lives are often shattered or in a state of high conflict.

The essential features of a participatory approach to inquiry do not merely focus on the technicalities of service provision. They also include contextual factors that need to be taken into account in producing effective and humanized service practices. The search for harmony, peace, and happiness needs to become an integral part of the daily processes of work with clients. Human service work is not just about technical or clinical efficiency, but also about the construction of a healthy lifestyle, an effective workplace, and a viable community.

The clear message of a participatory approach to action research, therefore, is that all stakeholders whose lives are affected by an issue need to be incorporated in the search for solutions to that issue. The process of collaboratively working toward that goal not only provides a wide range of expertise, both professional and cultural, but also generates positive working relationships. By including clients and families in the search for solutions to problems, we create the possibility of making use of their wisdom and acknowledge the concrete realities affecting client behaviors and lifestyle outcomes. Moreover, by engaging them in processes of inquiry that recognize their competence and worth, we provide the basis for developing productive relationships engendering trust and understanding. Even the most disadvantaged family or community has a store of experience and knowledge that can be incorporated into exciting and meaningful activities that have the power to transform the behavioral or lifestyle outcomes desired by professionals and their clients. Building stronger families and communities starts with people's strengths, extending their capacity to take responsibility for their own lives and to develop stable lifestyles.

This orientation does not deny the reality that clients sometimes are deliberately deceptive, uncooperative, or even aggressive, engaging in a variety of tactics and techniques to evade responsibility. If we *start* from the assumption that clients will respond in these ways, however, there is likely to be a built-in failure in our interactions—we often get what we expect.

Action research, therefore, seeks to enhance people's feelings of competence and worth, involving them in processes that provide an affirmation of themselves, their friends, their families, and their communities. By working collaboratively with others—clients, colleagues, families, and people in their community—we assist them to attain a constructive vision of themselves, anchoring them in a positive perspective of their worlds and enabling them to work confidently and comfortably with those around them. "Engaging the heart" means connecting people with those facets

Figure 1.5
The Human Dimensions of
Action Research

Pride Feelings of personal worth
Dignity Feelings of competence
Identity Acknowledging the worth of social identities: female, mother, person of color, parent
Responsibility Acknowledging people's ability to be responsible for their actions
Space Feelings of comfort from working in non-threatening physical environments
Place Feelings of having a legitimate place in the social context

of human experience that make a difference in the quality of their day-to-day lives. When we talk of the "heart" of the matter, or of engaging the "heart" of the people, we are talking of their feelings of pride, dignity, identity, responsibility, and locatedness (see Figure 1.5).

Working Principles of Action Research

Stringer (1999) presented a group of key concepts holding the principles of action research. The key principle is that of **relationship,** for when relationships are wrong, it is hard to accomplish the desired outcomes of any project. **Communication** also is a central feature of action research, enabling all participants to remain informed and in harmony with the different activities in which people are engaged. The principle of **participation** signals the need to ensure that people are actively engaged in the work of the project, gaining energy from the resulting feelings of ownership and accomplishment. Finally, the principle of **inclusion** speaks to the need to ensure that all people whose lives are affected or who have an effect on the issue investigated are included and that all significant factors having an effect are taken into account.

Many of these principles are part of the repertoire of human service workers and are incorporated into professional preparation programs in social work, leadership, and counseling. The same processes, therefore, also need to be incorporated into action research to provide the means to accomplish the desired therapeutic outcomes. The technical aspects of research must stand alongside the professional behaviors and interactional styles that facilitate the work we wish to accomplish.

Relationships

Effective working relationships enable individuals and groups to trust each other. These relationships provide high levels of motivation and form the basis for continuing research activities over the sometimes long periods required to deal with significant issues. Action research participants work together in ways that:

- Promote feelings of equality for all people involved
- Maintain harmony
- Avoid conflicts where possible
- Resolve conflicts that arise, openly and dialogically
- Accept people as they are, not as some people think they ought to be
- Encourage personal, cooperative relationships, rather than impersonal, competitive, conflictual, or authoritarian relationships
- Are sensitive to people's feelings

Communication

Maintaining good relationships depends, to a significant extent, on the ability of people to communicate effectively. The quality, consistency, and correctness of communication have a vital effect on interactions between individuals and groups. Their work together is likely to be short-lived or ineffectual if people talk to each other in disparaging or demeaning ways, if they fail to provide information about their activities, or if they distort or selectively communicate information.

Effective communication occurs when all participants:

- Listen attentively to each other
- Accept and act upon what is said
- Can understand what has been said
- Are truthful and sincere
- Act in socially and culturally appropriate ways
- Regularly advise others about what is happening

Participation

It is usual practice for professional practitioners to take responsibility for all that needs to be done in their sphere of operation. They either do things themselves or find someone to do it for them. While this is quite necessary for many activities related to professional practice, one of the purposes of action research is to involve the natural expertise and experience of all participants. When people are able to see that their worth is acknowledged by the activities in which they are able to engage, high levels of personal investment—in terms of resources, time, and emotion—often result. Active participation is very empowering, especially for people who have a poor self-image. Another of the key features of action research, therefore, is for facilitators to provide opportunities for people to demonstrate their competence by participating in research-related activities themselves. Sometimes people may start with quite simple tasks, taking on increasingly complex activities as their confidence increases. Although this can require more time and considerable patience on the part of research facilitators, the long-term benefits easily outweigh the initial outlay of time and effort.

Participation is most effective when it:

- Enables significant levels of active involvement
- Allows people to perform tasks themselves, rather than having it done by others
- Provides support for people as they learn to act for themselves
- Encourages plans and activities that people are able to accomplish themselves
- Deals personally with people rather than with their representatives or agents

Inclusion

Often people are tempted to carve out a piece of "territory" or to "take charge" of an issue. In professional life, service providers and administrators almost automatically take responsibility for any actions required to deal with issues within their professional realm. Further, there is often pressure to find short-term solutions to complex problems with a long history of ineffective outcomes, providing practitioners and administrators with the temptation to engage in simplistic responses that fail to deal with the underlying issues. Usually these actions fail to take into account many of the factors contributing to the problem or to include people who are an integral part of the context or whose lives are substantially affected by the problem.

Inclusion requires participants to:

- Involve all relevant groups and individuals whose lives are affected by the issue investigated
- Take into account all relevant issues affecting the issue
- Cooperate with related groups, agencies, and organizations where necessary
- Ensure all relevant groups benefit from activities

Further Reading

The literature on action research is voluminous. Though action research has become widely used in education, it is now emerging as a significant tool for human service providers. More general texts on action research include Berge and Ve (2000), Bray, Lee, Smith, and Yorks (2000), Carr and Kemmis (1986), Carson and Sumara (1997), Coughlan and Brannick (2001), Fals-Borda and Rahman (1991), Heron (1996), McNiff (1995), McNiff, Lomax, and Whitehead (1996), McTaggart (1997), and Schmuck

(1997). The *Handbook of Action Research* (Reason & Bradbury, 2001) provides an excellent resource for those doing an in-depth study of the theory, principles, and practices of action research.

Hart and Bond (1995) provide a guide to research in health and social care that seeks to demystify some of the research thinking processes. Winter and Munn-Giddings (2001) offer a guide to action research as a strategy for inquiry and development in health and social care. Mienczakowski and Morgan (2001) describe how they apply action research with health care patients and professionals to such issues as schizophrenia, drug and alcohol abuse, and sexual assault recovery. Hills (2001) shows how cooperative inquiry, a form of action research, was used to create methods of evaluating students that are compatible with the new human science, caring paradigm. Wadsworth (2001) describes how action research was used to facilitate the development of mental health services in a large central-city psychiatric hospital.

Benner (1994) presents another related methodology—interpretive phenomenology—that explores embodiment, caring, and ethics in care practices. She gives examples of ways this approach to research has been used in working with teenage mothers (Smithbattle, 1994), living with chronic illness (Benner, Janson-Bjerklie, Ferketich, & Becker, 1994), and doing disaster recovery work (Stuhlmiller, 1994). Van Willigen (1993) provides case studies of ways that action anthropology has been applied to health and welfare issues in low-income and urban contexts. Stringer (1999) presents a simple Look-Think-Act model that has been adopted by human service practitioners in a range of community and organizational contexts.

There is an increasing focus on action research on alcohol and drug abuse. small sample of the literature includes Graham and Chandler-Coutts (2000), who describe lessons learned about community action research, drawing upon papers presented at a recent international conference on community action research and the prevention of alcohol and other drug problems. Casswell (2000) comments on the past decade of research and community action on alcohol abuse. Holder and Moore (2000) identify characteristics of successful drug and alcohol community action programs that outlived their original funding. Dedobbeleer and Desjardins (2001) present the outcomes of an ecological and participatory approach to prevent alcohol and other drug "abuse" among multiethnic adolescents.

The literature incorporates diverse orientations that derive from the different theories used by the writers, the assumptions drawn from these theories about what should or could be accomplished, and the set of appropriate practices that are therefore entailed. Noffke (1997), for instance, defines differences in action research according to their personal, professional, and political dimensions. Some authors present a naturalistic approach to research, seeking to engage practitioners in reflective processes that will illuminate significant features of their professional practice and will enable them to understand the experience and perspective of other participants in agency and community contexts (Taylor, 2000).

The action research literature continues to proliferate as it becomes accepted as a legitimate tool for human service practitioners. Still, there is a wide range of approaches, some of which seem to neglect the carefully articulated processes of investigation that are the hallmark of a rigorous action research process. Readers would do well to keep this in mind as they continue their professional explorations.

SUMMARY

This chapter has explored the nature of action research and the practice frameworks that guide its application in family, community, and organizational settings.

It has described how action research is relevant to the work of human service practitioners:

- The nature of action research as *a systematic process of inquiry*
- *Models of action research* that provide frameworks guiding processes of inquiry, including:
  - An action research cycle indicating the need for repeated activity
  - An action research *helix* suitable for work with lay participants
  - An action research *sequence* that guides complex investigations
  - An action research *spiral* relative to developmental action research
- The *participatory research relationships* required for effective action research
- The *working principles* of action research—*relationships, communication, participation,* and *inclusion*
- *Further reading* that presents action research literature relevant to human service professionals

Understanding Action Research: Exploring Issues of Paradigm and Method

2

Contents of This Chapter

The purpose of this chapter is to clarify the relationship between action research and scientific research. The chapter:

- Distinguishes positivistic science (often described as quantitative research) that seeks to provide objective explanations for events from naturalistic inquiry (often called qualitative research) that constructs understandings of people's everyday cultural worlds.
- Describes how naturalistic inquiry seeks to reveal socially constructed life-worlds that enable individuals to live in a social world according to systems of meaning deeply embedded in their everyday conduct.
- Shows how a phenomenological approach to inquiry assists research participants to gain insight into other people's life-worlds.
- Presents postmodern perspectives that focus on the political nature of everyday interaction—the intimate relationship between the systems of knowledge embedded in professional practice and the exercise of social control and domination.
- Describes the nature of relationships within an action research orientation. The purpose is to acknowledge the legitimacy of knowledge that people have of their own lives and to enable a participatory approach to research and professional practice that is more democratic, empowering, and life-enhancing.

Distinguishing Between Different Approaches to Research: Objective Science and Naturalistic Inquiry

Research assists human service practitioners to find workable solutions to problematic events occurring on a day-to-day basis in their work. Action research, however, is quite different in many ways from forms of inquiry historically associated with the scientific method. Where the purpose of scientific research is to establish verifiable facts as the basis for **explanations** of events, action research is oriented toward qualitative or naturalistic studies designed to develop **understandings** of people's everyday cultural worlds.

As a hallmark of modern achievement, scientific experiments and quasi-experiments provide a rich body of substantive explanations that supplies the basis for powerful understandings of the physical and social worlds that humans inhabit. The purpose of the scientific method is to describe with precision the features of the universe and the stable relationships that hold between those features. Scientific work is therefore often associated with accurate measurement of "variables" to determine the nature and extent of those relationships, the ultimate goal being to establish causal connections between different features of the physical world and social life. The high degrees of certainty engendered by these explanations provide the basis for much of the miracles of modern life—clothing, vehicles, computers, structural steel, medicines, and so on—which have the potential to dramatically enhance our lives.

Naturalistic or **qualitative inquiry** provides a different approach to research based on a different set of assumptions about ways of acquiring knowledge. As revealed in the following sections, naturalistic inquiry gives greater insight into the ways people perceive, interpret, and act in their everyday, culturally constructed worlds. Human service practitioners therefore need to keep in mind the essential differences between positivist and naturalistic approaches to research, as both provide information that assists people to engage in effective and productive therapeutic activities. Each has a distinctive mode that should be consciously engaged to ensure appropriate outcomes for the purposes required.

Understanding Human Social Life: Naturalistic Inquiry

The problem with applying science to human affairs lies in the nature of humanity. We are at once physical, biological, and sociocultural beings, and attempts to understand our behavior need to take into account each of these facets. While the methods of positivistic science are powerful ways of understanding our physical being, and offer deep insights into some aspects of our social and biologic nature, they are limited as vehicles for providing explanations for the culturally derived aspects of human life. Ultimately, positivistic explanations must fail to encompass some of the fundamental features of human life—the creative and willful construction of meaning that is at the center of every social activity. Investigating meaning is at the heart of naturalistic inquiry.

While experimental science has provided much useful information, any experimentally derived theory of human behavior can only be a tentative, partial explanation of the acts or behaviors of any particular individual or group. The cultural nature of human experience intervenes in attempts to describe scientific laws of human behavior. As cross-cultural studies have demonstrated convincingly, people perceive the world and respond to it in many different ways. Given the same sets of "facts," people will give their own interpretations to both what they are seeing and what that means. No amount of explanation or clarification can provide a set of foundational truths about the way people should behave since behavior is predicated on sets of beliefs that are not, in principle, verifiable. Any "truth" of human experience is true only within a given framework of meanings.

This becomes increasingly clear if we consider some of the fundamental conditions of human social life and the way they impact the lives of individuals. The concept of the life-world from the work of sociologist Peter Berger (Berger, Berger, & Kellner, 1973; Berger & Luckmann, 1967) suggests that people construct reality as an ongoing social process in their everyday lives. The term "life-world" refers to the consciousness of everyday life carried by all individuals that provides coherence and order to their existence. The life-world is not a genetically inherited view of the world, but is learned by individuals as they experience everyday events and interactions within the compass of their families and communities. The life-world is therefore socially constructed, so that individuals learn to live in a social world according to sets of meaning, deeply embedded in their everyday conduct, that are shared by others living in that particular place and time.

The life-world is not a random set of events. It is given order and coherence by a patterned, structured organization of meaning that is so "ordinary" that people literally do not see, or are usually not conscious of, the depth and complexity of the worlds they inhabit. A child learns to associate with parents and siblings in certain ways, to communicate using a specific language, to act in particular ways, to participate in events like meals, conversation, play, and work, using appropriate behaviors and routine ways of accomplishing his or her everyday life. Like fish in the sea, people cannot see the "water" of this patterned, structured everyday life. They live in a taken-for-granted social world that provides order and coherence for every aspect of daily living—the interactions, acts, activities, events, purposes, feelings, and productions that constitute their lives.

> We get some idea of what this means when we visit a place for the first time, especially if it is in a foreign country. We feel uncomfortable to varying degrees until we learn the "rules" that enable us to operate in the new setting—what words are appropriate, how to sit or stand, how to eat, how to dress appropriately, and so on. We become aware of a myriad of small behaviors that those living in the context take for granted because it is so much an ordinary part of their life-world.
>
> **Ernie:** I remember people's consternation when I visited an indigenous community for the first time and sat with my wife in church, not realizing that the sexes had been strictly segregated and that I was sitting with the women. I've also inadvertently entered a female restroom and felt embarrassed by the surprised exclamations of the women there and my flustered retreat. Small and apparently inconsequential behaviors can sometimes have quite dramatic impact on our ability to interact comfortably with other people.

The anthropologist Goodenough (1971) conceptualized this life-world in terms of the concept of culture, which he defines as the socially learned rules and boundaries that enable a person to know what *is* (how the world is *defined,* structured, made up), what *can be* (what is *possible* in the world, whether it be ancestral ghosts, the existence of God, or faster-than-light travel), what *should be* (the system of values enabling the individual to distinguish between good and bad, appropriate and inappropriate), *what to do* (what acts or behaviors are required to accomplish a purpose), and *how to do it* (the steps required to accomplish that purpose). Individuals, therefore, inhabit a life-world that consists of taken-for-granted rules and boundaries giving order and coherence to their lives. Without these patterns and structures of meaning, people would live in a bewildering, chaotic world of sensation and events that would make human life, as we know it, impossible. It is this cultural cradle that enables us to live together in harmony, to accomplish day-to-day tasks like eating meals, dressing, communicating through talk and discussion, working, resolving disputes, and mowing the lawn.

Though we live within a particular life-world made of sets of meaning deeply embedded in our life histories, we are usually not conscious of the rules, boundaries, routines or recipes giving meaning and coherence to our lives. The taken-for-granted world is not seen, or apprehended, but *lived*. Recent anthropological explorations focus on the primacy of experience (Bruner, 1986; Jackson, 1996), using Dilthey's (1976) notion that reality exists only in the facts of consciousness given by inner experience. We can understand the social world, however, only through recognizing the cultural "texts" (Barthes, 1986; Ricoeur, 1979) or discourses through which people communicate their experience. Often we become aware of the personal or shared nature of our taken-for-granted world when we come in conflict with another "discourse"—where disjuncture occurs in our interactions with others.

The distinctive aspect of our cultural life-world, therefore, is that we share it with people who have learned similar sets of meanings and who act according to corresponding patterns and structures of meaning. But beneath the apparent order and coherence of the social life-world is a deeply chaotic system of meanings that continually threatens the possibility of an ordered and productive daily life. This is so because each person has had somewhat different experiences, and each has built a system of meanings that works superficially to accomplish ordinary tasks but that has slightly different nuances and interpretations. At any one time, these can be magnified and distorted, causing confusion or conflict as people try to accomplish their everyday lives. This is readily apparent when people get married and discover that the person with whom they thought they shared deeply consonant views of the world evinces acts and behaviors not in accord with their own. Small acts like the dropping of a sock or tissue, the use of a word, can trigger discomfort, discordance, and even conflict. The art of marriage requires people to learn new sets of meaning, to negotiate acts and behaviors consonant with a partner's existing habits and values, in order to accomplish a life together. It is a process that is sometimes astonishingly difficult, even for people deeply committed to each other.

Social scientists have long studied the intricacies of interaction between people. Ethnomethodologists (e.g., Garfinkel, 1967) provide us with glimpses into the ways that people negotiate these worlds of meanings to accomplish everyday social life, constantly constructing activity and behavior together, negotiating meaning, trialing behavior, repairing disjuncture in perspective, and so on. The French writer Lyotard (1984) speaks of a social world atomized into flexible networks of "language games," with individuals selecting from a number of possible games depending on the context in which they are operating. Similarly, Derrida (1976) views social life as being lived at the intersection of a large body of "discourses," or "texts."

We get some idea of how this operates if we were to follow a teenager into a classroom, a schoolyard, the teen's home, or a sports team practice. Both behavior and language change from context to context—"What's happenin'" becomes "Hello," "Hi," or "How are you?" with accompanying changes in body language and "attitude." In a similar vein, Toombs (1993) reveals that "in discussing my illness with physicians, it has often seemed to me that we have been somehow talking at cross-purposes, discussing different things, never quite reaching one another." This arises, she suggests, not from insensitivity or inattentiveness, but from a fundamental disagreement about the nature of illness. The same is true for human service professionals who work with clients whose realities appear to fly in the face of concrete evidence that lies before their very eyes.

Since research revolves around a search for solutions to problematic issues and events, one of its major tasks is to uncover the meanings implicit in the acts and behaviors of interacting individuals. By exploring the world of others in a setting or during events, we seek to understand what they experience and the meaning they give to that experience. In other words, through an increased understanding of people's divergent life-worlds, we attempt to redo, reenact, and reconceptualize events in ways that will make sense to all those involved.

Ernie: This lesson is deeply inscribed in my consciousness. As a young teacher I worked with the children of Australian Aboriginal people who lived a very traditional hunter-gatherer lifestyle. It soon became evident to me that they literally lived in a different universe—that the way they viewed the world, the way they acted toward each other, their aspirations and responses were so dramatically different from my own that my teaching made absolutely no "sense" to their everyday world. I became aware of the need to learn more about that world in order to provide a bridge of understanding between their world and the curriculum that I was teaching.

Even the simplest aspects of the syllabus entailed elements that were deeply enmeshed with the different visions of the world and the lifestyles attached. As I watched the people engaged in the simple act of gathering seeds and fruit from the plants in the desert to provide for their immediate needs, I became aware of how deeply embedded I was in the world of technological production when I cut a slice of bread for my lunch. Behind that simple act lay the mining and production of metals needed for the knife, as well as that required for the manufacturing of the machinery needed to grow and process the wheat and to fabricate the ovens and other machinery needed to make the bread. What I had seen as a simple loaf of bread became a complex technological production.

My eyes began to see a different world when I asked the question, "What do I need to know in order to understand where this bread came from?" A very different order of understanding came to mind when I asked, "What do Aboriginal people need to know when they ask a similar question about their own foodstuffs?" Not only does the actual world of technological production intrude, but the web of work and economic relationships enabling me to acquire that loaf of bread are likewise complex, and very different from the web of relationships surrounding Aboriginal meals.

This experience changed forever the way I interact with other people, including my circle of friends. I now realize the need to find ways of making connections between what others know—how they perceive and understand the world from the standpoint of their own history of experience—and what I need to know to interact with them harmoniously and successfully. That fundamental perception has been recently reinforced as I've worked in the United States, where the experiences and perspectives of Hispanic and African American people have enriched and challenged my professional endeavors. As I worked in the South Valley in Albuquerque and the poorer suburbs of Columbia and Richmond, I had much learning to do before I could frame my knowledge in ways that made sense to people in those places. The same dynamic operated in my work with youth in London, where I had to engage in some on-the-spot research to enable me to work effectively.

Differences in cultural perspective do not relate to ethnic differences alone, however. We have only to look at the differences in the way teenagers and their parents interpret events to realize the extent to which age differentials create differences in cultural experience and perspective in everyday life. Parents listening to their children's music often shake their heads in wonder that *anyone* could find the experience pleasurable, a response mirrored by teenagers listening to their parents' music. They all are hearing the same sounds emanating from the instrument or recording, but they have very different experiences of the sounds, and associate very different meanings to them.

Phenomenology: Exploring Everyday Experience

The perspectives from sociology and anthropology presented in the previous section are clearly associated with phenomenology, a philosophical standpoint that explores subjective dimensions of human experience. Schutz's phenomenological insights provide useful ways of conceptualizing the human social world and, in turn, help provide ways of understanding the complex phenomena of human behavior that professionals meet in their everyday work.

Extending Husserl's (1970) ideas, Schutz (1964, 1970) explored the ways in which ordinary members of society constitute and reconstitute the world of everyday life. He argued that the social sciences should focus on the ways that the life-world—that is, the experiential world every person takes for granted—is produced and experienced by its members. He suggested the need to safeguard the subjective point of view in order to guarantee that the world of social reality was not replaced by a fictional, nonexisting world constructed by a scientific observer.

Schutz proposed, therefore, that we acknowledge the veracity of an individual's "stock of knowledge," composed as it is of commonsense constructs and categories—images, theories, ideas, values, and attitudes—that are social in origin and that enable an individual to make aspects of experience meaningful. It is this stock of common-sense knowledge that permits individuals to interpret experience and to interact and coordinate their actions with others.

Dreyfus (1994) suggests the value of acknowledging this stock of knowledge for those in the caring professions. He defines caring as "a way of helping people by entering their world, . . . a higher kind of knowledge, which we can call understanding [that uses] the potential of . . . practical wisdom." He further proposes that "experts in caring know they cannot be guided by principles or any pseudo-sciences of the psyche, but must enter into the situation of the patient" (p. x).

This does not mean that science does not have a place in caring. As Benner (1994) points out, only by combining technological and existential skills can we approach the healing of an embodied person. This perspective has direct implications for the way human service practitioners position themselves vis-à-vis their patients. A similar viewpoint is expressed by Van Manen (1984, 1990), who emphasizes the need for contact rather than control, thus modifying the traditional, detached, and observational standpoint taken by professional practitioners and placing them in the position of active participant in the process of investigating problems and issues in people's lives.

Extrapolating from Van Manen's ideas (1984), we can say that the purpose of research is not to put human service practitioners in *command* of their clients, but in *touch* with them. The emphasis is on "seeing" or "insight" rather than explanation, to reveal meanings and experiences associated with people's vision and experience of their own life-world. To gain phenomenological insight we do not just ask "What is the cause of this person's condition?" but also "What is the nature of the person's experience of his or her condition?" with the intent of better understanding how the *person* is experiencing events.

It will sometimes be appropriate for practitioners and researchers to stand back and observe a situation objectively, assessing and evaluating events in unemotional and disengaged terms. At other times, however, they need to enter the life-world of their clients to understand how to construct processes or practices that make sense within their everyday lives. These practitioners and researchers will also need to understand the bigger picture—how overarching, collective representations and discourse structures, such as scientific knowledge, might be productively linked to local interpretive procedures. The processes of action research provide the means to transact these seemingly incommensurable, incompatible "stocks of knowledge," enabling people to collaboratively and interactively seek ways of understanding that make sense to all involved.

Postmodern Thought and the Helping Professions: The Power of Meaning and Interpretation

Much of the above discussion is associated with a postmodern perspective or frame of reference. The postmodern mind is described by Tarnas (1991) as an open-ended, indeterminate set of attitudes that has been fashioned by a great diversity of intellectual and cultural currents. Shaped by increasing sensitivity to the limitations of a highly deterministic view of science, postmodern thought is based on a few widely shared working principles:

> There is an appreciation of the plasticity and constant change of reality and knowledge, a stress on the priority of concrete experience over fixed abstract principles, and conviction that no single a priori thought system should govern belief or investigation. It is recognized that human knowledge is subjectively determined by a multitude of factors; that objective essences, or things-in-themselves, are neither accessible nor positable; and that the value of all truths and assumptions must be continually subjected to direct testing. The critical search for truth is constrained to be tolerant of ambiguity and pluralism, and its outcome will necessarily be knowledge that is relative and fallible rather than absolute or certain. (Tarnas, 1991, p. 395)

Postmodern thought also highlights the essentially political nature of knowledge production. The tendency toward bureaucratically centralized operations inherent in modern institutions is characterized by high degrees of control—"accountability"—that promise efficiency but, instead, often deliver high levels of stress and questionable outcomes. Because highly prescriptive plans and practices provide little opportunity for practitioners and administrators to adapt their work to the realities of particular environments, these plans and practices create, in the process, increased levels of anxiety and inefficiency.

The French scholar Foucault (1972, 1979) suggests, on the basis of his studies of modern institutional life, that there is an intimate relationship between the systems of knowledge—discourses—by which people arrange their lives and the techniques and practices through which social control and domination are exercised at the local level. At each site, he proposes, a professional elite defines the language of the discourse, and in doing so, controls the systems of knowledge that form the operating frameworks and procedures of institutional life. Foucault contends that feelings of alienation, stress, and oppression that appear to be an increasingly prominent feature of modern institutional life can be understood by building our understanding of the micropolitics of power at the local level. He suggests the need to conduct an ascending analysis of power, starting from the infinitesimal techniques and tactics that have extended ever more general mechanisms and forms of domination.

The means by which people are subjugated, according to Foucault, is not through the imposition of centralized domination and control by unfeeling autocrats, but through the very codes and discourses of unconsciously accepted, routine practices enacted in everyday professional life. Foucault suggests that:

> the only way to eliminate this fascism in our heads is to explore and build on the open qualities of human discourse and, thereby, intervene in the way knowledge is constituted

at particular sites where a localized power-discourse prevails. . . . To prefer what is positive and multiple, difference over uniformity, flows over unities, mobile arrangements over systems. (Foucault, 1984. Quoted in Stringer, 1999, p. 198)

Denzin (1989b) suggests that the problem with many human services is that programs, policies, and practices are based on the interpretations and judgments of the people responsible for their development and delivery. In child care agencies, for instance, faulty or incorrect understandings arise when agency workers mistake their own experiences and perspectives for their clients' experiences and perspectives. A consequence of this dynamic, however, is that case management often doesn't work adequately because interventions or management strategies bear little relationship to the client's meanings, interpretations, and experiences.

Action research employs qualitative processes of interpretation as a central dynamic of investigation. Its purpose is to describe and give meaning to events, showing how a set of events or phenomena is perceived and interpreted by actors in the setting. By studying events in this way, we are able to better understand or comprehend other people's experience. This reflective, reflexive (feeding back) process also assists in untangling and clarifying the meanings embedded in any set of experiences, leading those who have experienced the events and other audiences to gain greater or extended understanding of the issues investigated. Interpretive research therefore:

- Identifies different definitions of the problem
- Reveals the perspectives of the various interested parties
- Suggests alternative points of view from which the problem can be interpreted and assessed
- Identifies strategic points of intervention
- Exposes the limits of statistical information by furnishing materials enabling understanding of individual experiences

Understanding, in an interpretive sense, enables us to project ourselves (enter) into the experience of "the other," to understand what others think and feel about particular acts and events. As Denzin (1989b) says, "The goal of interpretation is to build true, authentic understandings of the phenomena under investigation" (p. 123). More particularly, the goal is to reveal how significant experiences—epiphanies—are embedded in the taken-for-granted world of everyday life. Interpretive studies record the agonies, pains, tragedies, triumphs, and peaks of human experience—the actions, activities, behavior, and deeply felt emotion: love, pride, dignity, honor, hate, and envy of people's lived experience.

Qualitative, interpretive approaches to inquiry provide the principal means for enabling human service practitioners to engage in action research to devise strategies more attuned to the realities of peoples' lives. While it is useful in some contexts to think of those strategies in objective terms, there will be times when the collaborative construction of care processes or the formulation of socially and culturally appropriate programs will be enhanced by the interpretive processes explored in the coming chapters.

Ernie: When I first entered university life, I was the sole arbiter of the content and processes of teaching in my courses. I formulated the syllabus from the content of my professional expertise and ensured that I maintained carefully controlled instructional processes in order to ensure that students in my class learned systematically.

Because of my experiences in many different cultural contexts, my preparation for classes and my teaching is much more flexible and participatory. I engage students in the process of assisting me to formulate a syllabus and, in the process, try to accommodate the diverse backgrounds and learning styles with which they come to my classes. That doesn't mean that I do not prepare thoroughly, or that classroom management is never an issue, but preparation and management have necessarily become a collaborative process.

At first, as I learned how to do this, it seemed like extra work, but having become more skilled, I can now accomplish it easily. Further, I've learned that by engaging students in these processes, they not only become more interested and enthusiastic about their learning, but also have some wonderful ideas about both the content and the processes of learning.

While I still appreciate and make use of the information acquired from my studies of educational psychology, sociology, and anthropology—much of it gained through experimental or quasi-experimental research—I am able to place that alongside the knowledge I acquire of my students' experience using naturalistic techniques of inquiry. Each has its place. Each provides tools for acquiring knowledge.

Distinguishing Different Types of Research

As practitioners read research reports and engage in investigative activities related to their ongoing work, they need to clearly distinguish between the different types of information presented or required. They will be confronted with a variety of different types of information, some derived from experimental studies based on fixed measurements of carefully defined variables and some consisting of descriptive information related to the sociocultural and interactive dimensions of people's experience. None of it will be right or wrong, or good or bad. It will simply be used for different purposes and provide different types of input to professional practice and client outcomes. Practitioners need to be clear about the type of information being used and the suitability of the information for their particular purposes.

As Figure 2.1 indicates, objective and naturalistic approaches to inquiry have quite different purposes, processes, and outcomes. The objective approach is used to acquire objective, factual information about a limited number of variables, and the naturalistic approach is used to understand more clearly the multiple dimensions of socially constructed human behavior.

Figure 2.1
Objective
Science and
Naturalistic
Inquiry

OBJECTIVE SCIENCE	NATURALISTIC INQUIRY
Purposes Studies events and behaviors *objectively* *Hypothesizes* a relationship between variables of interest	**Purposes** Studies people's *subjective* experience *Explores perspectives* on an issue or problem
Processes Precisely *measures* quantities of variables Carefully *controls* events and conditions within the study Uses *statistical analysis* of data	**Processes** *Describes* people's experience and perspective of the issue or problem Allows events to unfold *naturally* Uses *interpretive methods* to analyze the data
Products Seeks *explanations* for events and behaviors Describes *causes* of events and behaviors *Generalizes* findings to sites and people not included in the study	**Products** Seeks to *understand* events and behaviors Constructs *detailed descriptions* of events and behaviors Findings are *setting-* and *person-specific*

Distinguishing between different research paradigms is not always straightforward. The problem partially relates to rather loose use of associated terminology, where the literature often refers to *quantitative* and *qualitative* methods as equivalent to the distinction between objective science and naturalistic inquiry and fails to differentiate between the research *paradigm* and the research *methods.* There is a difference, for instance, between qualitative *research* and qualitative *methods.* It is possible to use qualitative methods to acquire and partially analyze data in experimental science—to use qualitative data objectively. Conversely, it is possible to use numerical or quantitative data within a naturalistic study to clarify emerging perspectives.

The use of qualitative methods, however, does not necessarily constitute qualitative research, nor must the use of quantitative methods result in a quantitative study. The way the data are manipulated and applied to research outcomes provides an indication of the appropriate use of the terminology. Objective studies seeking causal explanations and generalizable results are appropriately named quantitative or positivistic research, while interpretive studies resulting in detailed descriptive accounts of people's subjective experiences are appropriately identified as naturalistic or qualitative research.

While we can mix methods and data, it is difficult to mix research paradigms within the same study without damaging the utility and integrity of the research. Quantitative studies without a random sample, for instance, cannot generalize results. Similarly, qualitative studies that measure fixed variables limit the extent of holistic understanding emerging from a study. Neither paradigm is right or wrong, better or worse. Each seeks to attain different purposes, using different processes to achieve different types of outcome. Each is evaluated by a different set of criteria to determine the strength, quality, or rigor of the research. (See the section on validity in Chapter 3.)

We need to be wary of setting up boundaries that rigidly fix the distinctions between the two paradigms. Qualitative research does, for instance, sometimes make use of numerical data to extend or clarify information emerging in the research process. Conversely, quantitative researchers sometimes engage in preliminary qualitative studies to identify the variables to be included in their research. To ensure that their research does not become caught in the muddy waters between the different paradigms, however, researchers need to frequently ask themselves, "What is the purpose or objective of this part of the research? How can I accomplish that purpose, and what type of methods should I use to achieve my purposes?" Answers to these questions help us to assess the nature of the information we have at hand and to determine the uses to which it might be put.

Democracy, Status, and Power

Professional life is constrained by role relationships that sometimes become directive and controlling and hinder the development of productive relationships. A common assumption built into interactions between professionals and their client groups says, in effect, "I'm the expert here. I know what needs to be done." The supposition here is that training and experience have provided professionals with special knowledge enabling them to make definitive judgments about the nature of problems experienced and to formulate appropriate solutions. While this works in some instances where the clients are culturally and socially similar to the professional, there are many instances where the "expert" knowledge of the professional does not provide the basis for an effective solution to a problem. Some of the deep-seated and long-standing problems in human services relate to the imposition of Eurocentric, middle-class-oriented systems of understanding onto people—clients, community groups, and sometimes fellow professionals—whose social and cultural orientations are quite different.

Interpretive action research starts from a different position. It says, in effect, "Although I have professional knowledge that may be useful in exploring the issue or problem facing us, my knowledge is incomplete. We will need to investigate the issue further to reveal other relevant (cultural) knowledge that may extend our understanding of the issue." Expert knowledge, in this case, becomes another resource to be applied to the issue investigated, and stands alongside the knowledge and understandings of other people whose deep and extended experience in the setting provides knowledge resources that might usefully be applied to the solution of the problem investigated.

This change in status of the researcher also signals a change in relationships since the researcher is no longer "boss" or director of the investigation, but acts more like a consultant. In this latter case, research participants may be seen as "employers" or "customers" with the right to determine the nature of the research as well as the research processes. As a good business principle, "The customer is always right" signals the nature of the change in relationship between researcher and participants. As John Heron (1996) indicates in *Co-operative Inquiry*, "Self-directing persons develop most fully through fully reciprocal relations with other self-directing persons. Autonomy and co-operation are necessary and mutually enhancing values of human life. Hence experiential research involves a co-equal relation between two people, reversing the roles of facilitator and agent, or combining them at the same time" (p.3). As the anthropologist George Marcus (1998) noted, "[Social] affiliations and identities give [research participants] an immense advantage in shaping research . . . . There is control of language and a well of life experience that are great assets for achieving the sort of depth [of understanding] that anthropologists have always hoped for from one- to two-year fieldwork projects" (p. 246).

Wadsworth (2001) describes the complex and highly integrated experience required to investigate mental health services at a large central-city psychiatric hospital. The study incorporated the perspectives of patients, staff, and a consumer organization. The study used multiple sources of information and a reiterative, participatory approach to inquiry that provided deep insight into the experienced reality of people providing or being provided services. It supplied the means to effect systematic change, including the use of consumers to act as quality improvement consultants in mental health services. Wadsworth writes of the many microskills required to enact this type of work and describes the major areas of activity required to successfully facilitate collaborative inquiry. The message is clear. Just as carefully controlled and rigorous procedures provide the basis for sound scientific experimentation, so the work of action research requires different, but equally rigorous, activity to translate multiple perspectives and experiences into practical, effective outcomes.

Participatory action research, therefore, enacts systematic inquiry in ways that are:

- Democratic
- Participatory
- Empowering
- Life-enhancing

These changes highlight the potential of action research to enable practitioners, clients, colleagues, families, and other stakeholders to engage in exciting and sometimes exhilarating work together. Processes of investigation not only provide information and understanding as key outcomes of a process of inquiry, but enable people to develop a sense of togetherness, the basis for productive relationships that contribute to the success of their work. As they participate in action research, people develop high degrees of motivation and are often empowered to act in ways they never thought possible. Action research not only is empowering, therefore, but provides the basis for building democratic learning communities that enhance the life of agencies, organizations, and institutions.

Ernie: Recently I engaged in an action research project with a neighborhood group in a poorer part of town. Debriefing participants in the latter stages of the process, I was struck by their excitement, evident in their lively talk, their shining eyes, and the enthusiasm with which they reviewed their experience. "You know, Ernie," said one, "it was such an empowering experience for us." Asked how it had been empowering, she responded, "Because we were able to do it ourselves, instead of having experts come and do it and tell us. We learned so much in the process, and now we know how to do research." She and another woman who participated in the project wanted to extend their understanding of research processes and to extend their skills. Enrolled as extension students, they sat in on my graduate research class, participating actively and providing class participants with great insight into effective ways of practicing action research in community contexts.

This is not an isolated instance, as I've shared the excitement and experienced the feelings of accomplishment of young children, teenagers, administrators, parents, graduate students, and university professors in large cities, small country towns, and remote communities. My experience encompasses a wide range of social and cultural contexts on two continents, and the power of participatory processes to engender enthusiasm and excitement continues to motivate me. Action research is not a dreary, objective, mechanistic process, but a vital, energizing process that engages the mind, enhances the spirit, and creates unity, enabling people to accomplish highly significant goals. At its best, it is a transformational experience that lets people see the world anew, and in some cases, literally changes their lives.

There is another side to action research, however, that continues to sustain me professionally: the ability to provide the means to accomplish exciting work in the most difficult of circumstances. In a world that has become increasingly alienating by the forces of economic rationalism and accountability, where every activity must be justified in terms of a prespecified "benchmark" and justified in dollar terms, the spiritual and artistic side of worklife can easily be lost in a maze of technical, mechanistic, and clinical procedures that too easily dull and nullify the creative, life-enhancing outcomes of a truly professional experience. The energy and excitement generated by collaborative accomplishment provides the means not only to accomplish the technical, profesional goals of our work, but to do so in ways that are truly meaningful and enriching, not only for ourselves, but also for the people with whom we work.

SUMMARY

This chapter clarifies the relationship between action research and scientific research. The chapter:

- Distinguishes positivistic science (often described as quantitative research) from naturalistic inquiry (often called qualitative research).
- Describes how naturalistic inquiry seeks to reveal socially constructed life-worlds that comprise systems of meaning deeply embedded in people's everyday conduct.
- Shows how a phenomenological approach to inquiry assists research participants to gain insight into other people's worlds.
- Presents postmodern perspectives that focus on the political nature of everyday interaction—the intimate relationship between the systems of knowledge embedded in professional practice and the exercise of social control and domination.
- Describes the nature of relationships within an action research orientation. The purpose is to acknowledge the legitimacy of knowledge that people have of their own lives and to enable a participatory approach to research and professional practice that is more democratic, empowering, and life-enhancing.

Initiating an Action Research Study: Research Design

3

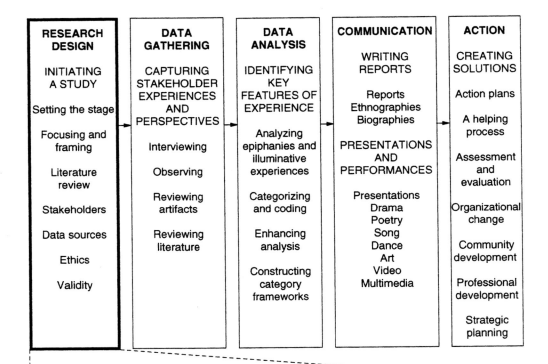

RESEARCH DESIGN	DATA GATHERING	DATA ANALYSIS	COMMUNICATION	ACTION
INITIATING A STUDY	CAPTURING STAKEHOLDER EXPERIENCES AND PERSPECTIVES	IDENTIFYING KEY FEATURES OF EXPERIENCE	WRITING REPORTS	CREATING SOLUTIONS
Setting the stage			Reports Ethnographies Biographies	Action plans
Focusing and framing	Interviewing	Analyzing epiphanies and illuminative experiences	PRESENTATIONS AND PERFORMANCES	A helping process
Literature review	Observing			Assessment and evaluation
Stakeholders	Reviewing artifacts	Categorizing and coding	Presentations Drama Poetry	Organizational change
Data sources	Reviewing literature	Enhancing analysis	Song Dance Art	Community development
Ethics			Video Multimedia	Professional development
Validity		Constructing category frameworks		Strategic planning

Contents of This Chapter

This chapter presents the first iteration of an action research cycle—designing the study. Research participants *formulate a research plan* by:

- *Building a preliminary picture* for the study
- *Focusing* the study and stating it in researchable terms
- *Framing* the scope of the inquiry
- Engaging in a preliminary *review of the literature*
- *Sampling*—identifying participants
- Identifying *sources and forms of data*
- Describing methods of *data gathering and analysis*
- Taking account of *ethical* considerations
- Establishing the *validity* of the study

Formulating the Research Plan

As human service professionals engage in action research, they become not only practitioner researchers, but also research facilitators assisting other stakeholders to become research participants. Initially they construct a preliminary picture of the project, working with participating stakeholders to refine this picture and incorporate more detailed research activities.

As they begin the work of inquiry, they will design the research, detailing an action plan that lists the steps to be taken. The plan will include:

- **Building a preliminary picture:**   Identifying the research problem and the people affected by or having an effect on the problem
- **Focusing the study:**   Refining the statement of the research problem, the research question, and the research objectives
- **Framing the study:**   Establishing the scope of the inquiry
- **Preliminary literature review:**   Exploring perspectives in the literature.
- **Sampling:**   Stipulating procedures for identifying project participants
- **Identifying sources and forms of information—Data gathering:**   Identifying sources and procedures for gathering information pertinent to the research question
- **Analyzing the data:**   Describing ways of distilling information to identify key features, concepts, or meanings—e.g., event analysis, categorizing, and coding
- **Ensuring ethical conduct:**   Outlining steps to make certain that no harm is done to people through their inclusion in the research
- **Assuring validity:**   Specifying procedures to ensure the strength of the research

Building a Preliminary Picture: The Reflective Practitioner

Reflective human service practitioners are curious about their work, wish to learn from it, and consciously engage in cycles of observation, reflection, and new action—conscious trial and error—to improve their practice. Their professional education and experience provides a "toolkit" of concepts and frameworks enabling them to systematically reflect upon their complex and inspirational professional craft. Action research extends the possibilities for engaging this professional repertoire. It outlines systematic methods of investigation and conceptual frameworks that enable practitioners to manage the more difficult and long-term problems in agency and community and to formulate effective programs and services with individuals and groups.

While investigations by individual researchers can provide an effective means to solve human service problems, the power of research is greatly enhanced when practitioners undertake exploration with clients, families, colleagues, administrators, and others affected by the issue. By participating in dialogue and discussion with others, not only do collaborative researchers engage a larger pool of knowledge, but they also begin to establish learning communities that have a truly transformative potential.

One of the first difficulties confronting researchers is to acquire clarity about the nature and purposes of the research. Agencies, clinics, homes, and other community

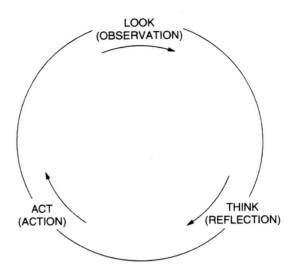

Figure 3.1
The Look-Think-Act
Research Process

situations are highly complex social contexts, containing myriad interactions among a wide range of people, each enacting a number of social roles—e.g., social worker-woman-caregiver-parent-partner. In their day-to-day work, professional practitioners deal with a vast array of interrelated issues and problems that have a continuing impact on their work. The initial processes of focusing, framing, and designing an action research study constitute the first of a number of cycles of observation, reflection, and action—depicted in Figure 3.1 as a Look-Think-Act sequence of activity.

Initiating an action research project may be seen as the first cycle of investigation, as practitioners carefully observe relevant settings and then reflect on their observations to clarify the nature of the research problem. They systematically identify the people who will be affected by the issue, and they begin to engage them in conversations to clarify the issue, formulate the research question upon which the study will initially focus, and delineate the scope of inquiry. Continuing cycles of the Look-Think-Act process enable the practitioner-researcher and other participants to further refine the details of their investigation.

> ***Look*** entails building a preliminary picture of the situation, enabling the researcher to describe *who* is involved, *what* is happening, and *how, where,* and *when* events and activities occur. Information is acquired by observing, interacting, and talking informally with people.
> ***Think*** requires researchers to reflect on the emerging picture. It is essentially a preliminary analysis of the situation, enabling researchers to develop a clearer understanding of what is happening, how it is happening, and who is involved in the stakeholding groups affected by or affecting the issue. It enables practitioners to identify potential participants in the study.
> ***Act*** defines the actions emerging from reflection. It requires people to *plan* their next steps and *implement* appropriate activity.

Focusing the Study

In the everyday world, agency, organization, or community, professional practitioners are confronted with an ongoing series of small crises and problems to which they apply a repertoire of skills and knowledge acquired through their professional training and experience. More systematic research becomes necessary when they are unable to find an effective solution to a persistent or serious problem. Identifying where to begin a study is sometimes a delicate matter since problems tend to occur as an interrelated series of events. Specific social or behavioral problems may be associated with family relationships, inadequate living conditions, unemployment, drug abuse, and so on. Trying to define what is *the* problem can easily become a "chicken-and-egg" process, having no particular beginning or end or no clearly defined cause-and-effect relationships. Where to begin, where to focus initial attention, becomes part of the research process.

> ***Ernie:*** Sometimes our first analysis of a situation focuses on related events that prove to be peripheral to the problem about which we are concerned. A recent meeting of a community organization I attended focused on the "problem" of lack of community participation, with the executive committee discussing ways of increasing the levels of involvement of local people. Eventually I asked committee members whether, in fact, participation was the "real" problem, and asked them to consider "the problem behind the problem." They spoke of a number of issues, including the failure of people to do the tasks required to solve the problem. In this case, the "problem" upon which the community initially focused—participation—turned out to be multidimensional, with participation being one facet of more deep-seated problems. Once the underlying problems were identified, the committee members were able to reflect more broadly on the issues about which they were concerned. The "problem" of participation, in fact, was eventually suggested as a solution to the underlying problems. In the first stages of research, therefore, research participants need to carefully reflect on the nature of the "problem" about which they are concerned.

One of the major strengths of action research is its emergent quality—its ability to allow researchers to tentatively state the problem and then refine and reframe the study by continuing iterations of the Look-Think-Act research cycle. In a study instigated by managers of a local human service agency, for instance, the researcher was told that alcohol was a major problem for the community. The researcher facilitated a discussion among managers and employees guided by the question, "What do we want to know about alcohol?" A specific question emerged from the group discussion, "What effects does alcohol have in our community?" The group then decided to investigate people's experience of alcohol use in a sample of households. The human service workers who conducted the study first needed to find a way to contact people in the community in a respectful manner to explore this question. After a series of role plays in which they rehearsed the scenario for contacting people in their homes, the workers framed their research question within the rationale of their professional role. The research question became, "What suffering is experienced in your household as a result of alcohol?"

The initial stages of focusing the research and formulating a research question are essentially reflective processes, requiring practitioners to engage in conversations with other stakeholders and to think carefully through all the dimensions of the issue causing concern. The first step is to reflect carefully on what is happening that is problematic and what issues and events are related to that problem. To focus the research, the issue or problem is stated in the form of a researchable question, and the objective of studying that issue is identified. The question and objective should be clearly stated, as follows[1]:

- The **issue or topic to be studied:** Defining which issues or events are causing concern
- The **research problem:** Stating the issue as a problem
- The **research question:** Reframing that problem as a question—asking, in effect, "What is happening here?"
- The **research objective:** Describing what we would hope to achieve by investigating this question[2]

The preliminary reflective process for developing the focus of the study is assisted by dialogue with the potential participants, including clients and colleagues. While it is possible that the research focus may later change as other participants pose their own questions, the initiator of the project should be clear about the original research question and the significance of the question to the participants. The initial development of the research question should focus on *how* participants and other stakeholders experience the problematic issue and *how* they interpret events and other information. How is it that these problems occur? How do people respond to case plans? In action research the focus is largely on events and their interpretation, rather than factual information of strongly developed causal connections explaining "why" events occur.

By developing a clear, precise, and focused research question, research participants take an essential reference point into their inquiry. As investigations proceed, the participants are able to evaluate the emerging data with reference to the research question. The initial research question should be shared by all participants and reiterated consistently throughout the research cycles as a constant guide to investigation.

---

[1] Since this is a qualitative research study, a research hypothesis—a suggested answer to the research question—is not part of the design. Qualitative or interpretive inquiry is hypothesis generating, rather than hypothesis testing. "Testing" the "answers" generated by an action research process is accomplished through continual cycling through the Look-Think-Act routine, so that actions put into place as a result of the first cycle of investigation are subject to evaluative processes through further observation and analysis—Look and Think.

[2] Qualitative studies usually focus on *understanding* people's experience and perspectives as a common outcome of the research process. Quantitative or experimental studies, on the other hand, more often focus on *causal explanations* that explain how one group of variables is "caused" by the effect of preceding variables. "How" questions are therefore more appropriate since "why" questions may lead toward clinically oriented explanations.

Sheila Jones's analysis of case management plans was defined in the following terms:

Issue: Some clients are consistently refusing to comply with their case plans, resulting in failure to progress.
Problem: Some clients are failing to carry out their case plans.
Question: How do those clients experience and understand their case plans?
Objective: To understand how the clients experience and understand their case plans.

Framing the Study: Delimiting the Scope of the Inquiry

As research participants identify and clarify the research issues and questions, they will also need to define the broad parameters of the study, determining whether it will be limited in scope, involving a small number of people over a small time period, or whether more extended study is required. Sometimes it is a relatively simple matter to work with clients within an agency to formulate successful plans or strategies. At other times it may be necessary to also work in conjunction with colleagues in other agencies or organizations, with agency administrators, and/or with a client's family. Before starting the research, therefore, participants will make decisions about the number of people to be included in the study, the sites or settings in which the research will take place, and the times the research activities will take place. Decisions will also be made about the extent of participation by those involved in the study, defining who will be involved in the various aspects of the research and who will monitor and support people in the process.

These considerations run hand in hand with the need to consider the breadth of issues to be incorporated into the study as they emerge. Too many issues may make the study complex and unwieldy, but restricting the study may cause issues to be neglected that have an important bearing on the problem. In the community women's project, for instance (see p. 12), a group of women in the community initially explored a broad range of issues. As the study developed, however, the women focused more particularly on ways to furnish their new dwellings. In this instance, they were able to identify specific strategies for acquiring furniture, thus improving the quality of their families' lives. They were then able to move on to other issues, related to children's nutrition and so on.

Researcher participants therefore will initially broadly identify:

- **What:**   What are the problems requiring investigation? What is the initial research question?
- **Who:**   Who are the likely stakeholders? Which people are affected by or have an effect on the issue being studied? Clients? Social workers? Lawyers? Administrators? Family members? Others?
- **Where (place):**   Where will the research take place? Which sites or settings will be included in the study? Agency? Offices? Homes? Schools? Other locations?

- **When (time):**   When will the research begin? How long might it take?
- **How broad is the scope:**   What is the likely scope of the investigation? What issues will be included? Will interventions or activities be confined to one person? Or will others be included? Etc.

Once research facilitators have assisted participants to clarify the focus, frame, and scope of the research, they will undertake a preliminary search to identify other perspectives on the issue embedded in the literature. This may assist to further clarify the nature and extent of their investigations.

Preliminary Literature Review

Literature reviews for qualitative research have different purposes than do those in quantitative research (Creswell, 2002). While quantitative studies make substantial use of the literature review as the basis for formulating a study, qualitative studies use the literature review quite minimally in the earlier phases of planning an investigation. Because qualitative studies are based on emergent processes of inquiry, preformulations of the issue according to concepts and analyses in the literature weaken the strength of the research. Because qualitative research seeks to conceptualize and describe phenomena in "local" terms, initial conceptions are always assumed to be provisional, thus negating the appropriateness of an exhaustive review of the literature prior to the commencement of a study. The preliminary literature review serves three main purposes: It alerts research participants to a range of perspectives on the issue studied, assists to refine the research question, and provides insights into appropriate methods of investigation.

Understandings and information emerging from the literature, however, may eventually augment, complement, and challenge stakeholder perspectives. As a study progresses, research participants may increase the power of their investigation by reviewing literature that speaks to evolving concepts and issues. In some cases the participants may identify solutions to the problem that have been successfully enacted in other contexts, or they may acquire information that clarifies issues surfacing in the study. Frequently, however, unanticipated issues arise as the study progresses, sometimes altering the direction of the investigation and causing participants to pursue different but related questions. Hence, the literature search will evolve as an ongoing feature of the research process, emerging in accordance with the directions and agendas arising from participant descriptions and interpretations.

Literature Search

The first phase of a search requires researchers to identify relevant literature. This task is greatly enhanced by the capabilities of computer-assisted search engines available in most libraries. Three to four key concepts related to the research issue are identified and fed into the search routine. When large numbers of items are identified, it may be necessary to delineate further key concepts to narrow the search to the most relevant sources of information. Perusing annotated collections that give a brief description of the content of the reading may enhance this process.

An increasing body of material is available on the internet, providing researchers with useful resources for their study. Sole reliance on websites, however, is not recommended, as the information available from this source tends to be incomplete and patchy. As in library searches, researchers will need to identify key concepts to feed into the search process.

Researchers often distinguish between:

- **Primary sources** that provide direct reports of original research
- **Secondary sources** that report on or summarize primary source material
- **Professional literature** based on the perspectives of experienced professionals
- **Official reports** from government or institutional authorities
- **Practice literature** that present or advocate particular techniques or procedures

University and professional libraries provide a wide variety of relevant literature, including theses and dissertations, journals, books, handbooks, abstracts, and encyclopedias. Library staff can often assist in identifying initial reading pertinent to the problem being investigated, but a review of any material will identify other sources of information, so that a review of the literature becomes an ever-expanding search. Researchers should note sources cited in journal articles, research reports, and texts and then review those for further information.

Identifying Different Perspectives in the Literature

The initial literature review extends the Think (reflect) part of the research cycle, providing new possibilities for conceptualizing or interpreting the issue. The preliminary search, therefore, should be sufficiently broad to give researchers an understanding of the different perspectives and types of information presented within the literature. These will differ not only according to the disciplines of the authors—psychology, sociology, cultural studies, etc.— but also according to different theoretical positions from within each discipline. The literature may also vary according to the formal and informal reports from a variety of educational sources, including agency, district, state, and national documents. It may include video and television documentaries, as well as information on projects and activities available on internet websites.

As the project progresses, participants will select, review, and evaluate relevant literature as part of the process of data collection, identifying pertinent information to enhance the understandings emerging from other sources (see Chapter 4). Studies within the literature become other perspectives (or stakeholders) to be incorporated into the process of data collection and analysis. The preliminary review of the literature within the first iteration of the action research cycle is conducted through the lens of the initial research question, alerting participants to other studies about similar problems, assisting with the refinement of the research question, and providing insight into research methods.

Sampling: Selecting Participants

The purpose of sampling is to ensure that the particular assumptions and under-standings of people involved in a specific context are illuminated and taken into ac-count in seeking effective solutions to the issue studied. In most studies, limits on time and resources make it impossible to include *all* people who might potentially in-form the research process, and so it is necessary to select a smaller group to provide the information (data) on which the research is grounded. A technique called *purposive, or purposeful, sampling* seeks to ensure that the diverse perspectives of people likely to affect the issue are included. Creswell (2002) suggests that pur-posive sampling can be used to select participants for a variety of purposes. Those chosen might include:

- People who represent the diverse perspectives found in any social context (max-imal variation sampling)
- Particularly troublesome or enlightening cases (extreme case sampling)
- Participants who are typical of people in the setting (typical sampling)
- Participants who have particular knowledge related to the issue studied (theory or concept sampling)

In all cases, researchers need to purposively select a sample of participants that represents the variation of perspectives and experiences across all groups and sub-groups who affect or are affected by the issue under investigation—the stakeholders in the study.[3]

The first task is to identify the primary stakeholding group[4]—that is, the group most centrally involved or affected by the issue studied. If a study is concerned about youths engaging in risky behaviors, the youths themselves would be a primary stake-holding group, while a study of client participation in the development of a case man-agement plan would have the client as a primary stakeholder. Sometimes the primary stakeholding groups are complementary groups. A study of a youth support issue might include clients, friends, and families, while a study to develop a new program might include clients and people in associated professional services and community organizations.

The next task is to identify other stakeholders who affect the issue but are not principally involved. Researchers need to include all the different groups of people likely to have an effect on or be affected by the issue studied. Issues of gender, class, race, and ethnicity are paramount since these factors are likely to be related to sig-nificant variation in experience and perspective. Researchers may need to ensure

---

[3] Purposive sampling differs in nature and purpose from random sampling used for experi-mental studies. A random sample drawn from a larger population enables experimental re-searchers to use statistical procedures to generalize from that sample to a larger population. Rather than seeking to generalize, action research seeks solutions to problems and questions that are context-specific.

[4] In some literature the *primary stakeholding group* is referred to as the *critical reference group*. The intent, however, is similar—to focus on those primarily affected by the issue studied.

An action research study of the activities of a child care agency identified agency professional staff as the primary reference group. During initial investigations, professional staff identified clients, families, transport drivers, administrative staff, and workers in other agencies as stakeholders to be included in the study.

that men and women are included in their sample, that poorer clients are represented as well as those from more middle-class backgrounds, and that each racial and ethnic group in the client group is included. Depending on the context, it may be necessary for researchers to include members of different social cliques, religious affiliations, sporting groups, or other types of groups represented in the social setting.

An older woman attended an action research project discussion group focusing on drug abuse in a rural town. While more articulate middle-aged people readily presented their viewpoints on the nature and scope of the problem, she remained silent. However, in a quiet moment, she spoke of her own anguish and suffering caring for grandchildren who seemed to have lost respect for their elders. Her story added considerably to the group's understanding of the situation, contributing previously unrecognized dimensions of the issue.

While it is not always possible to include people from *all* groups in any setting, it is important to select participants from groups likely to have a significant impact on the issue studied or likely to be impacted most by the issue. To fail to include participants because it is not convenient, because they show little interest, or because they are noncommunicative is to put the effectiveness of the study at risk. The previous chapter talked of the need to establish research relationships to maximize the possibility of including everyone likely to affect the issue studied.

Researchers will need to nominate in advance those who should be part of a study. A technique called "snowballing" enables researchers to extend their work to relevant people as the study progresses. They may ask participants to nominate others with quite different perspectives or experiences who could be included. In this way, researchers begin by defining likely participants, but extend their sample to more widely embrace the diverse and significant perspectives embodied in the study.

Any group, however, is likely to include people who are natural leaders or people who in some way are able to sway the opinions or perspectives of others in their group—sometimes referred to as opinion leaders. Researchers should try to ensure that the sample selected has both natural leaders or opinion leaders. A general rule of thumb in this process is to ask, "Who can speak for this group? Which people will group members acknowledge as representing their perspective?"

The research design may not specify a particular sample, but it will describe the procedures for identifying those who will be active participants in the study.

Identifying Sources and Form of Information—Data Gathering

Research participants will need to identify the types of information that will enable them to work toward a resolution of the issue on which they have focused. Participant perspectives, experiences, and events will constitute a significant portion of the data, captured in the form of accounts that describe qualities of the problem or the issue being investigated. The major source of information in action research, therefore, is acquired from interviews with stakeholding research participants—the "sample" described above.

Other sources of information that complement participant accounts include information acquired by observations of settings or reviews of other relevant information sources. Thus data from observations of sites and settings (places), events, and activities, as well as from reviews of materials, equipment, work samples, documents, records, reports, and relevant literature, may be incorporated into the study (see Chapter 4). Data are collected from these sources by observing settings and events or by reviewing documentary and other recorded information.

The research plan, therefore, should stipulate the type of data to be acquired and the methods employed to gather different types of information, including interviews, focus groups, observations, reviews, photographs, videotapes, and audiotapes. Because of the emergent nature of qualitative research, it is not possible to signal precisely all sources of information in advance, but the research plan should provide participants with guidance about *where, when, how,* and *from whom* initial information will be acquired. An indication of the number and duration of interviews and observations enables participants to clarify their research processes.

Distilling Information: Analyzing the Data

A research design informs participants and other readers of the data analysis methods to be used in the study. The research design should clearly signal the type of data analysis to be employed and the way analyzed data might be applied to actions emerging in the latter stages of the study (see Chapter 5).

Ensuring Ethical Conduct: Research Ethics

The research plan also will include ethical protocols that protect the well-being and interests of research participants. Punch (1994) suggests that "the view that science is intrinsically neutral and essentially beneficial disappeared with the revelations at the Nuremberg trials." Some well-known studies have shown that researchers are not always aware of the potential harm that may come to those who participate in research studies (e.g., Horowitz, 1970; Milgram, 1963). Most public institutions and professional organizations have formal procedures to ensure that researchers do not knowingly or unknowingly put research participants at risk. The research design needs to specifically address situations of potential harm and include procedures ensuring the safety of participants. As Sieber (1992) indicates, sound ethics and sound methodology go hand in hand.

Confidentiality, Care, and Sensitivity

When people talk for extended periods, they may speak of very private matters, reveal highly problematic events, or even disclose potentially harmful information. A prime directive of social research is to protect the anonymity of participants, and in practice, it is best to assume that *all* information acquired is highly confidential. Where researchers wish to share information with other participants or audiences, they must first ask relevant participants for permission to do so. When I read back my field notes, or share analyzed information with participants, I ask, "Is there anything here you would not like to reveal to other people in this project?" If they appear unsure, I inform them that it may be possible to present the information in a way that disguises its source. I can do this by using fictitious names, or by reporting the information generally—"Some people suggest that . . . " "Other participants provide a different perspective . . . ."

Along with confidentiality, researchers have a related obligation of duty of care to participants. They need to ensure that information is stored securely so that others do not inadvertently see it. They certainly should not share recorded information with others without permission of the persons concerned, even if that information points to apparently harmful events in a person's life—drug abuse, physical abuse, and so on. This points to another possibility occasionally arising in the processes of the extended interview, where the recall of distressing events creates a deep emotional response. Duty of care requires researchers to provide sufficient time for the person to "debrief." Either the researcher and the participant can talk through issues or events to a point of comfort, or the researcher can put the participant in contact with a family member or counselor who can assist the person to resolve the situation.

Permissions

Permission is not usually required when professionals engage in research directly applied to their own work. However, when they engage in more extended studies involving work with colleagues, other clients, families, or other agencies or services, they may need to obtain formal permission before beginning the project. To the extent that the research becomes a public process, therefore, where people's privacy or personal well-being is "at risk," written permission from individuals themselves is warranted. This also is the case in agencies and organizations, where permission from a person in a position of responsibility—a manager, director, or other relevant authority—must be gained. In these circumstances it is necessary to provide information about the nature of the research, the significance of the study, and the ways in which ethical considerations will be taken into account. It is useful to attach a copy of the research design to the request for permission to pursue the study.

Where research is associated with a university course or program, the institution itself will usually have processes for reviewing research through an ethics committee. Though these procedures are sometimes unwieldy and time-consuming, they provide a means of ensuring that people's privacy is not violated and that research processes do not put their well-being at risk.

Informed Consent

In many contexts, protocols require those people facilitating research to obtain informed consent. This means that the research facilitator and others engaged in data gathering must:

- Inform each participant of the purpose and nature of the study
- Ask whether the participants still wish to participate
- Ask permission to record information they provide
- Assure them of the confidentiality of that information
- Advise them that they may withdraw at any stage and have their recorded information returned
- Ask them to sign a short document confirming their permission

Figure 3.2 provides an example of how these processes are presented to participants and documented. A consent form not only provides information, but is a record of consent, so copies should be given to each signatory.

Assuring Validity in Action Research: Establishing Trustworthiness

When human service professionals engage in research directly related to their work, they can usually ascertain the worth of research according to its usefulness in helping them accomplish their professional tasks. Wider studies involving official approval or requests for funding, however, often need to satisfy more stringent requirements. People want assurance that poorly devised, or inappropriate research will not result in inadequate or potentially damaging outcomes. In these circumstances they often require that research plans and reports include assurances of the rigor or strength of procedures.

Procedures for evaluating the rigor of experimental or survey research evolve around well-formulated processes for testing reliability[5] and establishing the validity[6] of a study. Because qualitative methods are essentially subjective in nature and local in scope, procedures for assessing the validity of action research are quite different

---

[5] Reliability is estimated by measures of the extent to which similar results may be expected from similar samples within the population studied, across different contexts, and at different times. Reliability focuses on the stability of results across time, settings, and samples.

[6] Experimental validity is defined in two ways—external validity and internal validity. Measures of external validity estimate the probability that results obtained from the sample differ significantly from results we would expect. Internal validity focuses on the extent to which results obtained might be attributed to the dependent variables included in the study, and not some other cause. Researchers ask, "Do our instruments actually measure what we wish them to measure?" and "Are the results attributable to the dependent variables we have stipulated, or to some other related variable?" Internal validity focuses on careful research design and instrumentation. Both reliability and validity are verified by statistical and other techniques.

Agreement to Participate

Research Study: Services Provided by the Alderton Child Care Agency

Researcher: Jeanette Williams   **Phone:** 555-1713

Background

Since 1978, the Alderton Child Care Agency has assisted families experiencing a crisis to maintain adequate care of their children. The agency provides many services, including a family support team that works alongside psychologists, therapists, and other professionals to assist families in working their way through crises. Although the agency continues to supply other much needed services, some confusion has arisen in client families and the agency about the role and responsibilities of the family support team.

This research seeks to discover:

- What are the principal tasks of the family support team?
- Are there specialist tasks which are the responsibility of the family support team?

Knowing about these things will provide information about:

- How to organize the duties and responsibilities of the family support team.
- The qualifications and training needed by family support team members.

The information in this project will largely be collected by observing team members and talking with them, their clients, and their colleagues about their work. Reports will be written and shared with participants and agency staff, but all names and place names will be changed to avoid identification of individuals. Participants will be asked to engage in two interviews of about one hour's duration each. The researcher also will have a follow-up session with each person to check the accuracy of the information.

Names will be kept confidential. Tape recordings and field notes always will be stored in a secure place by the researcher and not used for purposes other than the current study. Photographs will only be used with written permission.

If you wish to withdraw from the study at any time, you are free to do so and, if you wish, all information you have given will be shredded or returned. If you wish to contact the research coordinator at any time, you may contact her at the above phone number.

I _____ have read the information above, and questions I have asked have been answered to my satisfaction. I agree to participate in this activity with the understanding that I may withdraw at any time without prejudice. I agree the research data generated may be published provided my name is not used or that I am not otherwise identified.

Signed _____ Date _____
             (participant)
Signed _____ Date _____
             (facilitator)

Figure 3.2
Informed Consent Protocol

from those used for experimental studies. A common set of criteria for establishing the validity of research has been provided by Lincoln and Guba (1985). They suggest that because there can be no objective measures of validity, the underlying issue is to identify ways of establishing *trustworthiness*—the extent to which we can trust the truthfulness or adequacy of a research project. They propose that trustworthiness can be established through:

- **Credibility:** Is the study plausible, and does it have integrity?
- **Transferability:** Can the results be applied to contexts other than the research setting?
- **Dependability:** Are research processes clearly defined and open to scrutiny?
- **Confirmability:** Can the outcomes of the study be demonstrably drawn from the data?

Trustworthiness is obtained by recording and reviewing the research procedures themselves to establish the extent to which they ensure that the phenomena studied are accurately and adequately represented. The following procedures are adapted from those suggested by Guba and Lincoln.

Credibility

Qualitative research is easily open to sloppy, biased processes that merely reinscribe the biases and perspectives of those in control of the research process. By reviewing and recording the following features of the research process, researchers minimize the extent to which their own viewpoints intrude, and provide evidence of rigorous procedures that enhance the plausibility of their findings (Lincoln & Guba, 1985).

Prolonged Engagement

Brief visits to a research site provide only superficial understandings of events. A rigorous study requires researchers to engage in extended periods of investigation to achieve relatively sophisticated understandings—to learn the intricacies of cultural knowledge and meaning that sustain people's actions and activities in a setting. Prolonged engagement in a setting also enables researchers to establish relationships of trust with participants, allowing them greater access to the "insider" knowledge that surpasses in quality and value the often superficial, distorted, or inaccurate information given to strangers. Researchers therefore add to the credibility of a study by recording the time spent in the research context.

Persistent Observation

Being present in the research context for an extended time period is not a sufficient condition to establish credibility, however. Sometimes researchers mistake their presence in the field for engagement in research. In a recent study one researcher indicated he had worked with a group of human service professionals for some months. He had, however, not engaged in systematic research at that time, and his "observations" were undirected, unfocused, and unrecorded. Participants need to consciously engage in data collection activities to provide depth to their inquiries. This is particularly true of interviews, as a single interview lasting 15 to 20 minutes produces very superficial understandings that lack both detail and adequacy. Persistent observation signals the need for repeated, extended interviews to establish the adequacy, accuracy, and appropriateness of research materials. Researchers therefore need to record the number and duration of observations and interviews.

Triangulation

Triangulation involves the use of multiple and different sources, methods, and perspectives to corroborate, elaborate, or illuminate the research problem and its outcomes. It enables the inquirer to clarify meaning by identifying different ways the phenomenon is being perceived (Stake, 1994). In action research we include all stakeholders relevant to the issue investigated, observe multiple sites and events, and review all related materials and resources—reports, records, research literature, and so on. These multiple sources and methods provide a rich resource for building adequate and appropriate accounts and understandings that enhance the credibility of the study.

Participant Debriefing

This process is similar to the *peer debriefing* proposed by Lincoln and Guba (1985). It differs because of the change in the status of the researcher in an action research process. It is not only the research facilitator who is in need of debriefing, but other participants in the process as well. Debriefing is a process of exploring and challenging aspects of the inquiry that might otherwise remain only implicit within a participant's mind (Lincoln & Guba, 1985). The purposes of debriefing are to review the appropriateness of research procedures and to clarify ways of describing and interpreting participant experience and perspectives. Debriefing also provides participants with an opportunity for catharsis, enabling them to deal with emotions and feelings that might cloud their vision or prevent relevant information from emerging. Research facilitators often provide debriefing sessions with research participants, but may themselves require an interested colleague to debrief them on the processes of research they are guiding. The credibility of a study is enhanced when researchers record opportunities given to participants to debrief.

Diverse Case Analysis

In all research it is necessary to ensure that all interpretations of the data are fully explored. Sometimes there is a temptation to include in a research process only those people who are positively inclined toward the issue under study or who interpret the information in particular ways. Diverse case analysis seeks to ensure that all possible perspectives are taken into account and that interpretations of important, significant, or powerful people do not overwhelm others. Diverse case analysis enables participants to constantly refine interpretations so that all participant perspectives are included in the final report and all issues are dealt with. The credibility of a study is enhanced if researchers can demonstrate that all perspectives affecting the study have been included. A clear statement of sampling procedures assists in this process.

Referential Adequacy

Referential adequacy refers to the need for concepts and structures of meaning within the study to clearly reflect the perspectives, perceptions, and language of participants. When participants' experiences and perspectives are reinterpreted through the lenses of official reports or academic theories, or in terms derived from existing practices, procedures, or policies, research outcomes are likely to be distorted. One of the key features of qualitative research is the need to ensure that interpretations are experience-near, grounded in the language and terminology used by participants to frame and describe their experience. Where it is necessary to use more general terms to refer to a number of phenomena, those terms should adequately reflect the phenomena to which they refer. The credibility of a study is enhanced to the extent that researchers can demonstrate that outcomes of a study have a direct relationship to the concepts, terminology, and language used by participants.

Member Checks

In experimental inquiry, research subjects rarely have the opportunity to question or review the information gathered and the outcomes of the study. The practical nature of action research, however, requires that participants be given frequent opportunity to review the raw data, the analyzed data, and reports that are produced. This process of review is called "member checking" and provides the means for ensuring that the research adequately and accurately represents the perspectives and experiences of participants. Member checking is one of the key procedures required to establish the credibility of a study.

Transferability

Unlike quantitative research that assumes the need to generalize the results of the study, qualitative research by its very nature can only apply results directly to the context studied. Nevertheless, it is possible that outcomes from one study might be used in other settings that are sufficiently similar for results to be applicable. A study from rural Mexico, for instance, may or may not be relevant to suburban Canada. Qualitative research seeks to provide sufficiently detailed reports of the context and the participants to enable others to assess the applicability of a study to their own situation. Thickly detailed descriptions contribute to the trustworthiness of a study by enabling other audiences to clearly understand the nature of the context and the people participating in the study.

Dependability

Trustworthiness also depends on the extent to which observers can decide whether research procedures are adequate for the purposes of the study. When there is insufficient information about research procedures, audiences will have limited trust in the dependability of the study. Dependability is therefore achieved through an *inquiry audit* that presents details of research activities, including processes for defining the research problem, collecting and analyzing data, and constructing reports.

Confirmability

Confirmability is a process that enables audiences to confirm that research processes were scrupulously followed and that outcomes were appropriately and adequately derived from the data. Confirmability is achieved through an *audit trail,* the inquirer having retained recorded information that can be made available for review. The information includes raw data such as field notes, photographs, diary entries, original and annotated documents, copies of letters, and materials generated at meetings. It also includes data reduction and analysis products, as well as plans and reports derived from the study. By enabling reviewers, at least in principal, to "audit" the research processes, the researchers enhance the trustworthiness of the study.

Participatory Validity

The strength of qualitative research derives from the methodological intent to build accounts that more clearly represent the experience, perspective, and voice of those people included in the study. The credibility of accounts, to some extent, is derived from the degree to which researchers can enact the procedures delineated in the previous section. Throughout the process, however, researchers constantly run the risk of observing and interpreting events through the lens of their own history of experience, thus putting the validity of the study at risk (Stringer & Genat, 1998).

A much greater degree of credibility, however, is gained through the use of participatory processes. When research participants engage in the processes of collecting and analyzing data, they are in a position to constantly check and extend the veracity of the material with which they are working. As participants read the data of their interviews, they not only see themselves more clearly (the looking glass-self), but are drawn to extend and clarify the events they describe. As they engage in data analysis, they are able to identify more clearly and correctly the significant experiences, features, and elements that make up events. As they assist in the construction of reports, they help formulate accounts that use familiar language to represent their experience and perspective.

Participatory processes are consonant with recent developments in qualitative research (Altheide & Johnson, 1998) that point to the multiple means now used to establish validity, according to the nature and purposes of the study and the theoretical frames of reference upon which the research rests. In a very direct way, engaging people as direct participants in the research also enables a study to take into account such issues as emotionality, caring, subjective understanding, and relationships in research (Lather, 1993; Oleson, 1994) that are important features of feminist research. These not only enhance the validity or trustworthiness of a study, but also improve the chance of effective action.

Pragmatic Validity

One of the greatest sources of validity in action research is the utility of the outcomes of research. When participants are able to construct ways of describing and interpreting events that enable them to take effective action on the issue they demonstrate the validity of the meaning-making processes incorporated into their research. Effective actions clearly demonstrate success in identifying concepts and meanings. High degrees of credibility are evident since the understandings that emerge from the processes of inquiry are successfully applied to actions within the research setting. It becomes immediately evident that descriptions and interpretations emerging from the research are adequate to account for the phenomena investigated.

SUMMARY

The Research Plan

An action research design includes:

1. *Focus:*   **A statement of the issue, the research problem, the research question, and the research objectives.**
2. *Framing* **the scope of inquiry: The place, the time, the stakeholding groups, and the scope of the issues included in the study.**
3. *Preliminary literature review:*   **Processes for reviewing the literature.**
4. *The sample:*   **Identifying stakeholding research participants.**
5. *Sources of information and data gathering processes:*   **The sources from which information will be acquired and ways information will be gathered.**
6. *Data analysis processes:*   **Procedures used for distilling information.**

Research Ethics

Ethical procedures are established by:

1. *Confidentiality:*   **Privacy is protected by ensuring confidentiality of information.**
2. *Permissions:*   **Permission is obtained to carry out the research from people in positions of responsibility.**
3. *Informed consent:*   **Participants are informed of the nature of the study and provide formal consent to be included.**

Assuring Validity: Establishing Trustworthiness

The *trustworthiness* of action research is verified through procedures establishing credibility, transferability, dependability, confirmability, degrees of participation, and practical utility.

Credibility is established by reporting on:

1. *Prolonged engagement:* The duration of the research processes.
2. *Persistent observation:* The number and duration of observations and interviews.
3. *Triangulation:* All sources of data, including the settings observed, the stakeholders interviewed, and materials reviewed.
4. *Participant debriefing:* Processes for reviewing research procedures.
5. *Diverse case analysis:* Processes for ensuring the exploration of a diversity of interpretations.
6. *Referential adequacy:* How terminology within the study is drawn from participant language and concepts.
7. *Member checks:* Procedures for checking the accuracy of data and the appropriateness of data analysis and reporting.

Transferability is established through the inclusion of detailed descriptions of the participants and the research context.

Dependability is established through detailed description of the research process.

Confirmability is established by having the data available for review.

Validity is enhanced by *participation*—the extent of stakeholder participation in the research process.

Validity is also enhanced by the extent to which *practical outcomes* are achieved.

Gathering Data: Tools and Techniques 4

RESEARCH DESIGN	DATA GATHERING	DATA ANALYSIS	COMMUNICATION	ACTION
INITIATING A STUDY	CAPTURING STAKEHOLDER EXPERIENCES AND PERSPECTIVES	IDENTIFYING KEY FEATURES OF EXPERIENCE	WRITING REPORTS	CREATING SOLUTIONS
Setting the stage			Reports Ethnographies Biographies	Action plans
Focusing and framing	Interviewing	Analyzing epiphanies and illuminative experiences	PRESENTATIONS AND PERFORMANCES	A helping process
Literature review	Observing			Assessment and evaluation
Stakeholders	Reviewing artifacts	Categorizing and coding	Presentations Drama Poetry	Organizational change
Data sources	Reviewing literature	Enhancing analysis	Song Dance Art	Community development
Ethics		Constructing category frameworks	Video Multimedia	Professional development
Validity				Strategic planning

Contents of This Chapter

This chapter presents procedures for systematically gathering information. It focuses on:

- The *purposes* for gathering information
- Participant *interviews*
- *Observation of* settings and events
- The review of *artifacts*—records, documents, and materials
- *Statistical and numerical data*, including those obtained from *surveys*
- Review of the *literature*

Introduction

Action research is based on an assumption that people, even very young people, have deep and extended understandings of their lives, enabling them to negotiate their ways through an often bewildering and unpredictable life-world. It is the willingness to acknowledge both the legitimacy of people's world views and the wisdom that enables them to survive and often thrive in difficult circumstances that is at the heart of the participatory processes described in this book. The use of interviews as a central component of action research enables researchers to listen carefully to people, to record and represent in their own terms the events people describe, and to use people's perceptions and interpretations in formulating plans and activities. The task is not to convince them of the inadequacies of their perspective, but to find ways of enabling them, through sharing one another's perspectives, to formulate more productive understandings of their own situation. We may also acquire other information that extends, enhances, or challenges the viewpoints and perspectives that different participants bring to the research process. This chapter presents the tools and techniques for these purposes.

Building a Picture: Gathering Information

In the previous chapter, we explored the first movement of the Look-Think-Act research cycle in which participants defined the research problem and question, along with a plan for enacting the investigation. In this chapter, we explore the next iteration of the cycle, as both the research facilitators and the other participants begin to "build a picture" of the problem they are investigating, focusing on the Look step that entails gathering information from a variety of sources (see Figure 4.1). Ultimately,

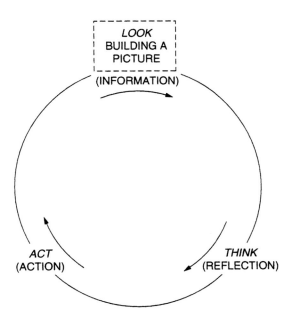

Figure 4.1
Gathering Information

this information will be used to develop detailed accounts that clarify and extend people's understanding of the acts, activities, events, purposes, and emotions that make up their everyday lives and become the basis for therapeutic action.

Qualitative, interpretive processes of inquiry seek to understand the experience of interacting individuals. When we work with individuals or groups who appear unaware of factors affecting their well-being, who seem reluctant to engage the services of qualified professionals, or who have difficulty managing their own affairs, we wonder, "What is happening for this person? What is this person's experience? What is this person's understanding of the situation?" Action research seeks to understand the experience and perspective of clients and other stakeholders—parents, friends and relatives, supervisors, employers, and other significant actors such as service professionals. The information acquired enables research participants to understand and interpret events in ways that mesh with their different experiences and perspectives.

> *Ernie:* There are many situations where considerable investment in community facilities, programs, or services has had negligible use by groups for whom they were intended. In one instance I spoke with the principal of a school that had explicitly been set up as a "community school." He was perturbed by the almost total lack of parent participation in his school. In other locations I've seen community centers that have been barely used at all, or youth programs that have failed to attract any of the young people that had been the target population. In almost all instances those responsible had spent considerable time and resources setting up the center or program, and were frustrated by their apparent failure. One youth worker exploded, "These kids are just a lazy bunch of no-hopers. All they want to do is lay around watching TV and smoking dope. I don't know what you have to do to make them get active!"
>
> Often agency or organization staff explain such situations as a lack of gratitude, or negative personal qualities of people concerned. Our experience suggests, however, that systematic research focused on the experiences, perceptions, and needs of the primary stakeholders—those primarily concerned with the issue or problem—becomes the basis for development of programs and services. There is a clear need for professionals to engage local knowledge to ensure that desired social outcomes are achieved in appropriate ways.

In action research, *interviews* are the principal means of understanding people's experiences and perspectives. Information is also gathered by systematically *observing* settings and events, *reviewing relevant documents and records,* and examining related *materials and equipment. Numerical and statistical information* may complement other data. Relevant *literature,* including academic research reports, professional publications, and official reports, may further illuminate the issue being studied. Each of these types of information—records of interviews, observations, and reviews of documents, artifacts, and literature—has the potential to increase the power and scope of the research process. If we not only listen to people describe and interpret their experience, but observe and participate in events and read reports of those or similar events, then we enrich the research process. Multiple sources diminish the possibility that one perspective alone will shape the course or determine the outcomes of investigation; and in addition, multiple sources provide a diversity of materials from which to fashion effective solutions to the matter being investigated. This *triangulation* of data adds depth and rigor to the research process.

Interviewing: Guided Conversations

This section presents detailed procedures for enacting interview techniques that suit the purposes of action research, focusing on the sensitive process of initiating interviews, describing detailed questioning techniques, and suggesting methods for recording information. Although interviews are an integral part of the tools of the trade of social workers and other human service professionals (e.g., Kadushin & Kadushin, 1997; Murphy & Dillon, 1997), they often are used for the purpose of developing case materials, formulating assessments, and planning interventions. Assessment interviews, for instance, tend to be highly structured and to focus attention on the wide range of factors that are likely to affect the case.

Interviews in action research tend to be more ethnographic in intent, assisting participants to describe a situation in their own terms and to reveal their own interpretation of issues studied. Action research interviews enable research facilitators and other participants to "enter the world" of the person interviewed and to understand events from that person's perspective (Denzin, 1997; Spradley, 1979a; Spradley & McCurdy, 1972). Interviews not only provide a record of interviewees' views and perspectives, but also symbolically recognize the legitimacy of their point of view. Interviews are the principal means by which we can "hear the voice of the other" and incorporate others' perspectives into the inquiry process. Interviews also provide opportunities for participants to revisit and reflect on events in their lives, and in so doing, extend their understanding of their own experience. This double hermeneutic—meaning-making—process serves as the main powerhouse of the research process, enabling all participants to extend their understanding of their own and others' experience.

Interviewing is best accomplished as a sociable series of events, not unlike a conversation between friends, where an easy exchange of information takes place in a comfortable, friendly environment. Although some people envision interviewing as a form of authentic dialogue, we need to be wary of the way this "dialogue" emerges. When interviewers engage in exchanges of information or experience, as in a normal conversation, they unwittingly inscribe their own sets of meanings onto the dialogue, constructing descriptions and interpretations that distort the experience or perspective of the participant being interviewed. Authentic dialogue is more likely where a research facilitator is a natural participant in the setting and where other participants have had opportunities to explore their own experience prior to engaging in dialogue. The following protocols provide ways to engage the interview process comfortably, ethically, and productively.

A wide range of literature provides information about interviewing for qualitative research purposes (e.g., Chirban, 1996; Holstein & Gubrium, 1995; Kvale, 1996; Mc-Cracken, 1988; Rubin & Rubin, 1995). Researchers should use these materials selectively, however, since some interview techniques are used for clinical purposes or hypothesis-testing processes but are not suited to action research. The key issue guiding selection of technique is whether it is used to reveal the perspective of the participant. Ultimately, interviewing is the means whereby people "tell their stories" and thus reveal important elements of their lives.

FAMILY SUPPORT SERVICES: A MANAGER'S STORY

[This message was received following a manager's participation in an action research training workshop. It typifies how action research processes can provide the means to enhance the everyday work of service delivery in human service contexts.]

A team of support workers that I manage are continually in turmoil with each other and often at loggerheads with the families of the people that they, as a team, support. I have tried all of the standard "scientific" methods to improve the situation, such as team development strategies and meetings, and conflict resolution with each other and the families. Sometimes this works for a while and then it's back to the same old ways.

During our action research course I realized I had never really asked any of them for "their stories" and had only focused on the job that needed to be done to provide quality service. Since returning from the workshop, I have started the process of asking stories of both staff and families, and the results have been surprising. I actually had one parent drive 200 kms just to tell me her story face to face as, she said, "It is the first time anyone has actually asked me [for my story]."

I can see the light at the end of the tunnel—it is not to say that it will be a miracle cure, [but] we may find enough common ground/threads/ideas to enable everyone to finally work together and provide a service that not only enhances the lives of the clients we support, but empowers all of the stakeholders.

Initiating Interviews: Establishing Relationships of Trust

Initial stages of an interview process can be a little uncomfortable for both interviewer and interviewee, and the interviewer must establish a relationship of trust in order to enable the person interviewed to feel able to reveal his or her experience, either to a stranger or to a colleague. Chapter 3 suggests using initial contacts with people to inform them of the issue being studied and to explore the possibility that they might participate. The researcher:

- Identifies himself or herself
- Identifies the issue of interest

- Asks permission to talk about that issue
- Negotiates a convenient time and place to meet

An actual conversation may sound something like:

"Hi! My name's Rosalie Dwyer. I'm a social worker for the state child care agency. I've heard that some mothers in this community are concerned about what children around here are doing after school. I'd like to hear your views. Could we talk about that?" If the response is affirmative: "Can we talk now, or would you like to set another time?"

The primary consideration in interviewing is for the interviewee to feel comfortable and safe talking with the interviewer. The above information is best presented in ways that are appropriate to the people and the setting and that enable respondents to feel in control of the situation—so that they feel they're not being put upon. Research facilitators should provide people with opportunities to determine both the time and the place of interviews. The facilitators should ask them to suggest places to meet where they are comfortable. An office may not be the best place to interview clients, the site itself having possible negative connotations affecting a participant's state of mind. As noted in Chapter 1, action research is a sociable process, rather than a clinical procedure, and should, wherever possible, be enacted in contexts where action is to take place. According to the circumstances, people may be comfortable in their own homes, in a community center, in cafes or fast-food outlets, or in a park or other public place. A meeting over coffee enables interviewer and interviewee to chat about general events and establish a conversational tone in their interactions. This provides a context to move easily to the issue of interest.

Initiating interviews sometimes is a sensitive process. Initially, you might manage short, informal conversations, which open possibilities for more extended dialogues (interviews). It's important to keep these initial occasions low key and informal, so people feel they aren't being imposed upon. After an initial interaction, you might indicate your desire to have them speak at greater length about issues arising in your conversation.

"This has been interesting, Jack. I'd like to be able to explore this issue further. Could we meet somewhere and continue this conversation?"

This provides a context for commencing more in-depth "conversations" that provide the basis for a continuing research relationship.

Questioning Techniques

Spradley (1979a) provides a useful framework of questions derived from his attempts to elicit natural structures of meaning used by people to describe and organize their social worlds. His essentially ethnographic methodology suggests the use of neutral, nonleading questions that minimize the extent to which participant responses will be governed by frameworks of meaning inadvertently imposed by the researcher. A modified form of this framework provides the means to engage in extended interviews revealing detailed descriptions of events and interactions in participants' lives, and providing opportunities to explore significant issues in depth on their own terms.

A major problem is that the researcher's perceptions, perspectives, interests, and agendas often bias the questions asked and the direction of the interview. Interviews based on extended lists of predefined, highly structured questions therefore are seen as inappropriate for the purpose of this type of research. Ethnographic interviews are quite different from clinical interviews that focus on specific details of the situation. This detracts from the ability of participants to define, describe, and interpret experience in their own terms, and it can sometimes alienate audiences central to the study. The following questioning techniques illustrate ways to minimize the intrusion of researcher perspectives in interviews.

Phase One: Grand Tour Questions

Interviews should be scheduled for a place and time convenient and comfortable for the interviewee. It is helpful if participants are relaxed and comfortable and are in a familiar setting. Generally, avoid formal settings, with participants sitting behind desks. And also try to avoid noisy, crowded places, where privacy cannot be guaranteed.

An action research interview begins with one general "grand tour" question taking the form:

> *"Tell me about. . ."*—"Tell me about your situation." "Tell me about what happened last night."

Though there are many extensions of this fundamental query, the simple format enables respondents to describe, frame, and interpret events, issues, and other phenomena in their own terms. The grand tour question is not asked in bald isolation, but emerges contextually when sufficient rapport has been established. It is also necessary to *frame* or contextualize the question:

> "I haven't been here for long, and I'm not sure what's happening for you. Can you *tell me about* your situation?"

Often it is best to contextualize the issue by starting with a more general question:

> "You live in Avalon, don't you? I'm not very familiar with this part of town. Can you *tell me something about* it?"

In most cases, people are able to talk at length on an issue about which they are concerned. It merely requires a listener with an attentive attitude to enable them to engage in an extended discourse, sometimes encouraged by prompts (see below) to extend their descriptions. In some instances, however, participants may be unable to answer such a general question, tempting the researcher to insert more specific questions that undermine the intent of the research process. Spradley (1979a) suggests alternative ways of asking grand tour questions when respondents can give only limited responses to a more general question:

- **Typical grand tour questions.** These enable respondents to talk of ways that events usually occur. For example, "What do you usually do in Avalon?" "Can you describe a typical day for you in Avalon?"

- **Specific grand tour questions.** These focus on particular events or times. For example, "Did you do anything (in Avalon) yesterday?" "Did you do anything last week?"
- **Guided tour questions.** These kinds of questions are requests for an actual tour that allows participants to show researchers (and, where possible, other stakeholders) around sites associated with the issue being investigated. (For example, "Could you show me around Avalon?" "Could you show me your home?") As they walk around, participants may explain details about the people and activities involved in each part of the setting. Researchers may use *mini-tour* or *prompt* questions (see below) to extend the descriptions provided. For example, "Tell me more about what happens in this part of town." "Can you tell me more about the people you've mentioned?"
- **Task-related grand tour questions.** These aid in description. For example, "Could you draw me a map of Avalon?" Maps are often very instructive and provide opportunities for extensive description and questioning. You can also ask participants to demonstrate how things are done. For example, "Can you show me how you fix things for the kids?" "Can you show me how that works?"

Grand tour questions serve as prompts to participants to initiate descriptions of their experience. Information acquired in this way provides the basis for more detailed descriptions, elicited by similar types of questions, but emerging from ideas, agendas, concepts, and meanings implicit in the respondents own descriptions.

Phase Two: Expanding the Interview—Mini-Tour Questions

Interviews emerge and expand from responses to initial grand tour questions. As people respond to the initial grand tour questions, a number of details begin to surface, revealing events, activities, issues, concerns, etc., that constitute their experience and perspective. Sometimes the information is limited or somewhat superficial, and interviewers need to probe further to enable the respondents to dig deeper into their experience. At this stage, further questions emerge from concepts, issues, and ideas embedded in respondent answers to the first grand tour questions (Figure 4.2). The interviewer asks *mini-tour* questions that use the concepts and language of the respondents and enable them to extend their responses in their own terms.

Mini-tour questions are similar in form to the general, typical, specific, guided, and task-related grand tour questions, but the focus of the questions is derived from information revealed in initial responses. They take the form:

"You talked about visiting your children. Can you tell me more about those visits?" (general)

Or "Tell me what you usually do during a visit to your children." (typical)

Or "Tell me what happened during your last visit." (specific)

Or "Can you draw me your child's home and tell me what happens there during a visit?" (task related)

Or "Can you show me or demonstrate what you do during a visit?

Novice researchers sometimes find interviewing an uncomfortable experience. The process of working through structured questioning processes often feels awkward and unnatural, and they tend to fall back on "conversation" as a means of engaging participants. Practice and experience, however, show how it is possible for interview questions to be used freely and easily to develop a conversation. In its best formulation, questions should emerge in a friendly, informal manner, echoing informal talk amongst friends—"What's happening?" "What's up?" "What's going on?"

Novice researchers can prepare for interviewing processes by memorizing the forms of questioning described herein and practicing mock interviews with friends and colleagues. Such role plays can assist interviewers to translate seemingly formal interview formats into conversational language of participating groups. Like any set of skills, practice may not make perfect, but it certainly increases effectiveness.

An interesting outcome of the acquisition of these questioning skills is their more general application to human services contexts. Practitioners will find them wonderful tools for client interviews, and administrators will find them useful in refining aspects of their managerial work—consultation, planning, leadership, and organization. A youth worker wrote of a research process in a message to a colleague:

"Spradley's format is very helpful when I apply it for talking with young people in my area. I use the visual cues, have them write stuff out on paper, make drawings, maps of the district. The work is shared. We physically walk the area—a guided tour. I first thought the idea was dumb, but it's a great success. It's engaged, it's shared, we are walking together. The movement stops the 'tape in my head.' The experience is shared. It's generative."

Mini-tour questions can also reveal meanings embedded in the language of participant groups:

"Earlier you talked about being a 'support' to your daughter. Tell me more about being a 'support.' "

Or ". . . you talked about having to 'hang out' after you have seen your daughter. Tell me more about having to 'hang out.' "

Or ". . . you mentioned that you encourage young people to 'take control of their lives.' Tell me more about young people 'taking control of their lives.' "

Or ". . . you mentioned that you encourage young people to 'take control of their lives.' Can you tell me about a young person who has 'taken control of his or her life?' "

Responses to these questions may lead to further mini-tour questions, eventually providing extended detailed descriptions of the issue and context being investigated.

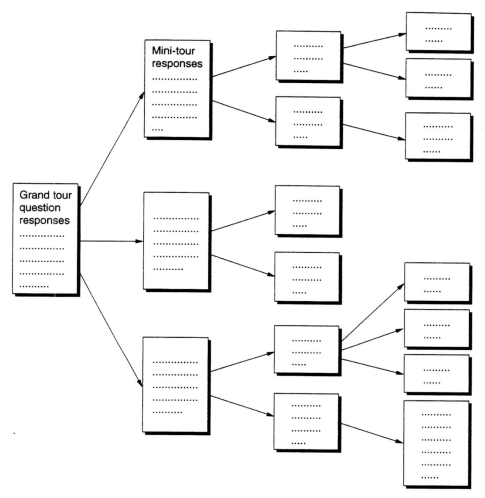

Figure 4.2
Mini-Tour Questioning Processes

Extending Participant Responses: Prompt Questions

Further information may be acquired through the skillful use of prompts, enabling participants to reveal more details of the phenomena they are discussing:

- **Extension questions.** For example, "Tell me more about. . . " "Is there anything else you can tell me about.'. . ?" "What else?"
- **Encouraging comments and questions.** For example, "Go on." "Yes?" "Uh-huh?" "Mmmm?"
- **Example questions.** For example, "Can you give me an example of how you usually begin a visit?"

Prompt questions are not designed to elicit particular types of information the interviewer might see as desirable, but merely to enable the interviewee to think more closely about events or perspectives described.

Avoid criticizing the perspective presented by the interviewees, and do not suggest alternative viewpoints or explanations, even when faced with information that appears limited, biased, wrong, or potentially harmful. Interviewers should avoid discussion or debate about information presented and should not attempt to correct or extend the participants' responses by pointing out inconsistencies—"Don't you think that . . . ?" or "That's just not true, Jim. Our records show that . . . "

Challenges to viewpoints presented will occur naturally as actions are devised on the basis of information given or as differing perspectives are presented by other participants. Varying perspectives and interpretations will be subject to reinterpretation and negotiation as the research progresses, but at this stage the principal task is to grasp a person's point of view, to realize the person's vision of his or her world (Malinowski, 1922/1961).

Ernie: In the course of some work with senior government department managers, Aboriginal colleagues and I sometimes faced people whose perspectives were fundamentally racist. I would converse with them with barely controlled rage, fuming at the insensitive nature of their remarks. On one occasion an Aboriginal colleague later said, "Take it easy, Stringer. He doesn't understand," to which I responded, "But I get so angry. How can you stand it?" He looked at me quizzically and said, "You just get used to it." In many of these situations, by engaging in nonconfrontive behavior, we developed productive working relationships with these government departments that, in the longer term, sensitized people to their inappropriate behavior and/or perspectives. I learned at that time that immediate confrontation is not always an appropriate response to inappropriate speech or behavior.

Prolonged Engagement

The intent of action research is to assist people to develop new insights into issues or problems. Merely asking them to "explain" why and how an issue affects them often elicits only taken-for-granted responses or perspectives that produce superficial understandings. Such responses provide little basis for revealing implicit meanings and underlying features of their experience. Interview processes can give people an opportunity to carefully reflect on their experience, examining how events and issues are embedded in the complexity of events that constitute their everyday lives.

The questioning techniques described in previous pages helps to facilitate this descriptive process, but they are only effective if sufficient time is allocated to enable participants to explore the issue in depth. While some problems or issues may require relatively small investments of time, larger or long-standing issues often require prolonged periods of reflection and analysis. Thus a single 15- to 20-minute interview may suffice for a simple issue, but significant problems may require multiple interviews of 30 to 60 minutes each, enabling participants to explore issues in depth, engaging multiple dimensions of their experience, and, in the process, extending their understanding of the complexity of problems they face.

Repeat interviews are an essential feature of good action research. They not only enable participants to reflect on issues more extensively, but provide opportunities to review and extend information revealed in previous interviews. Extended engagement, therefore, suggests the need for a significant time commitment and repeated interaction with or between research participants. Merely being in the context is not sufficient—researchers must be engaged in the systematic inquiry required to *research* an issue.

> ***Ernie:*** When I queried the apparently inadequate interview procedures of one researcher, she replied, "Oh, I was working with those people for months."
>
> Unfortunately, the intensive nature of the work in which the people and the researcher were engaged provided little opportunity for them to discuss the nature of their experience as most of their attention was focused on the provision of technical issues related to the project. The single 15-minute interview of each person in the project was a poor vehicle for revealing the complex nature of their experience, providing only superficial comments that were uninformative and uninspiring.

Recording Information

Although action research processes often are informal, especially in small-scale or localized projects, it is important to keep a record of the information acquired. This is especially vital when different groups are involved, when personality differences are likely to create discord, or when sensitive issues are investigated. Participants acquire a degree of safety when they know that their perspectives are not forgotten or distorted over time. For reasons of accuracy and harmony, an ongoing record of information is a central feature of research. Field notes and tape recordings provide the two major forms of recording information, though increasing use is being made of videotape.

> On numerous occasions I have been involved in action research projects which threatened to be disrupted by disputes about things people had said or decisions that had been made. Referring back to the recorded data and reading the actual words people had used usually restores order when disputes threaten to erupt. In numerous instances a mollified participant has acknowledged his or her error by saying "Did I say that?" or "I forgot that we'd decided that."

Field Notes

Verbatim Record: Wherever possible, interviewers should make an immediate record of responses. Ask the respondent's permission to do so before the interview, or in some cases, after the first few minutes, when the person has begun talking. You might say, "This is very interesting. Do you mind if I take notes as you talk?" Handwritten field notes provide the means to obtain a written verbatim record of people's actual words. This requires researchers to record what is *actually said* by the person being interviewed, rather than a condensed or "tidied-up" version. It is a "warts-and-all" procedure, where colloquialisms, incorrect grammar, or even blatantly incorrect information is precisely recorded. Scribes recording information need to be wary of paraphrasing or abstracting since this defeats the purpose of interviewing, i.e., capturing the voice of participants and describing things as they would describe them. At later stages of the interview (see "Member Checking," below) the interviewee will have opportunities to correct or add to the information given.

The following example is a record of an interview with a social worker:

Interviewer: Some clients have told me they'd like greater family participation in the preparation of case plans. Can you tell me what you think of this idea?

Client: Well, my family feel they are part of the situation. If they could have, like, some information on things like the court orders, tests, visits. . . you know. . . .

It would help my family to assist me, especially when I'm struggling. They could have information sessions. It'd be low pressure, low key. You could bring along people with special skills, special expertise.

It would help establish good relationships with my family. Give them greater ability to communicate about what's happening. They'd be able to talk more easily.

Interviewer: Are there other ways we can help to increase family participation?

Client: I like having people who can guide and help me, but not do what has to be done. Some people help, but they end up doing things themselves. That's not on. But if they support me in what I have to do, it's a great help.

A handwritten record requires practice in writing quickly and the concomitant development of personal "shorthand" writing protocols—"&" for "and," "w/" for "with," "t" for "the," "g" for "ing," omission of consonants such as "writg" or "wrtg" for "writing," and so on. It takes practice, but it is essential if researchers are to record the respondent's actual words. Sometimes it may be necessary to ask the person interviewed to repeat information or to pause momentarily so the interviewer can catch up on the notes.

Member Checking: Once an interview has finished, the interviewer should read back the recorded notes, giving the respondent an opportunity to confirm their accuracy or to extend or clarify information. In some cases it may also be possible to identify key features of the interview to use in data analysis (see Chapter 5). Some people type their notes and have the respondent read them to check for accuracy. It may also be appropriate, in some instances, to provide a copy of the field notes to the respondent for his or her own information.

Tape Recorders

Using a tape recorder has the advantage of allowing the researcher to acquire a detailed and accurate account of an interview. Researchers acquire large quantities of information from multiple sources, and so a careful record of tapes should be maintained, noting on each tape the person, place, times, and dates of the interviews.

Tape recordings have a number of disadvantages, however, and researchers should carefully weigh the merits of this technology. Technical difficulties with equipment may result in loss of data and can damage rapport with respondents. People sometimes find it difficult to talk freely in the presence of a recording device, especially when sensitive issues are discussed. A researcher may need to wait until a reasonable degree of rapport has been established before introducing the possibility of using a tape recorder. When using a recorder, the researcher should be prepared to stop the tape to allow respondents to speak "off the record" if they show signs of discomfort.

The sheer volume of material obtained through tape recording also may inhibit the steady progress of a research process. Researchers should be wary of accumulating tapes for later transcribing. Frequently this becomes a lengthy and tedious process that can detract from the power of the research. If tape recordings are used, they should be transcribed immediately so that relevant information is available to participants. This is particularly useful when contentious or sensitive issues are explored since a person's own words may help resolve potentially inflammatory situations.

Using Focus Groups to Gather Data

In recent years, focus groups have emerged as a useful way to engage people in processes of inquiry. They enable research participants to share information and experiences that trigger new ideas that provide greater insight into events and activities. A focus group may be envisioned as a group interview, where questions provide a stimulus for capturing people's experiences and perspectives. It offers the means for including relatively large numbers of people in a research process, an important consideration in larger projects.

Traditional research practices focus largely on gathering data from individuals and using the information as the basis for a process of analysis. Data gathering and analysis in action research often go hand in hand as people explore their experiences interactively. Although it is important for people to have opportunities to explore issues individually in the early stages of inquiry, joint processes of collaborative description and analysis considerably enhance the power of a research process. Focus groups can provide the context for people to identify and name shared categories of experience *or to identify different ways they have interpreted events.* Individual interviews followed by focus group exploration provide a context for participants to share information and extend their understanding of issues.

Action research, therefore, increases in power when undertaken as a *participatory* process that fosters the interactive engagement of participants. The power increases exponentially when such participatory processes become collaborative, when respondents begin to ask questions of other respondents and the research

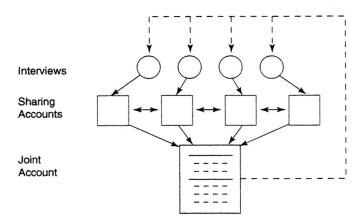

Interviews

Sharing Accounts

Joint Account

Figure 4.3
Focus Group Processes

facilitator. When participants work together, share ideas, and explore their collective experience and perspectives, the productive, creative, and innovative possibilities of action research emerge strongly.

A cyclical process of investigation emerges, depicted in the concept map shown in Figure 4.3. Interviews lead to individual accounts, which are shared and then formulated into joint accounts that record both commonalities and divergences of experience and perspective.

When we bring diverse groups together, however, we need to carefully manage the dynamics of interaction and discussion to ensure the productive operation of focus groups. Too easily they sometimes degenerate into "gabfests" or "slinging matches" where unfocused discussions or argumentative interchanges damage the harmonious qualities characteristic of good action research. Helpful literature for facilitating focus groups includes Barbour and Kitzinger (1998), Greenbaum (2000), Krueger (1994, 1997a, 1997b), Krueger and Casey (2000), Morgan (1997a, 1997b), and Morgan and Krueger (1997).

Bringing People Together

To initiate focus group explorations, the research facilitator should seek opportunities to convene forums where participants can discuss issues of common interest. You might say, "I've spoken with a number of people about this issue, and some of them have similar views to yourself. Would you be willing to meet with them to talk about the issues you've raised?" Or "As you know, I've been speaking with some other people who are concerned about the way these things are happening in this part of town. Would you be willing to meet with some other people to discuss this issue?"

As with interviews, the time and the place must be conducive to the process. People should have adequate time to explore the issue in a place where they are comfortable and feel they can express their views and experiences freely. A rushed meeting—say, during a coffee break or in a cafeteria where others can overhear—is likely to limit the information shared and is unlikely to generate the positive working relationships required. These matters are especially important when working with clients or their families. As with interviews, meetings away from offices or formal settings may be more conducive to the production of an easy and communicative atmosphere, providing a basis for the ongoing development of productive action research processes.

Initially, research facilitators may arrange focus group meetings for small groups of stakeholders, but as the processes of inquiry develop, it may be fruitful to work with larger groups of participants. Larger meetings are especially productive when all individuals have opportunities to share their perceptions and experiences, and focus groups may be used to enable greater active participation. The size of groups is important, four to six people being the optimal number in each group to enable everyone to participate effectively. When dealing with large groups, then, it is usually best to form subgroups, each subgroup recording its exploration and reporting back to the whole group. Since information gathering is often concomitant with information processing (analysis or interpretation), processes for facilitating focus groups will be discussed in greater depth in following chapters.

Focus groups can be used in many contexts large and small. When working with staff from a community training program to facilitate an internal review of implementation, a research facilitator interviewed each staff member separately. He then wrote a short report describing the issues that emerged from these interactions. After staff had read the report, he facilitated a focus group meeting enabling them to clarify issues in the report and to identify and prioritize issues on which they wished to take action. Because it was a small work unit, they completed this process within a week.

On another occasion, a group of community workers and administrators at a small rural community center were concerned about the use of alcohol in the community and the associated trauma to families. The community workers were interested in community perceptions of the issue, but were conscious of the difficulty of approaching households where alcohol use was known to be high. After experimenting with ways to approach households using role-play methods, the community workers presented themselves to households as professionals concerned with suffering in the community and seeking community perceptions about the suffering caused by alcohol. After analyzing the interview data, the workers presented the results at a community meeting where the issues were ascribed different priorities. Over a period of six months, community workers and community members met to seek further information, to clarify concerns, and to develop and implement action plans to address the issues.

Focus Group Processes

Focus group sessions must be carefully planned and facilitated to ensure the productive use of time. It is all too easy for poorly prepared groups to degenerate into gossip sessions, to be dominated by a forceful person, or to create antagonisms derived from intemperate debates. As with data gathering, research facilitators may engage single focus groups, but multiple groups may be used productively when meeting with diverse groups of stakeholders. The following steps provide a basic procedure for running focus groups:

1. Set ground rules. For example:
   - All persons will have opportunities to express their perspective.
   - All perspectives will be accepted nonjudgmentally.
2. Provide clear guidance:
   - Provide and display focus questions.
   - Designate a time frame for each section or question.
3. Designate a facilitator for each group to:
   - Ensure each person has an equal chance to talk.
   - Keep discussions on track.
   - Monitor times.
4. Record group talk in each group:
   - Designate a person to record proceedings.
   - Record the details of each person's contribution, using the person's own words.
   - Where appropriate, have each group summarize its discussions, identifying and recording the key features of participant experiences and the significant issues or problems.
5. Get feedback and clarification:
   - Bring groups together, ensuring adequate time is available for feedback and discussion.
   - Have each group present the summary of its discussions.
   - Provide opportunities for individuals within each group to extend or clarify points presented.
   - Ask each group questions designed to have them clarify and extend their contribution.
   - Ensure that new information emerging from this process is recorded.
6. Analyze combined information:
   - Identify common features across groups.
   - Identify divergent issues or perspectives.
   - Rank issues in order of priority.
7. Make a plan for action:
   - Define what is to happen next—determine what actions are to be taken, who will be responsible for them, where and when they will be done, what resources are required, and who will organize them.
   - Designate a person to monitor these actions.
   - Designate a time and place to meet again to review progress.

These seemingly bland procedures mask the exciting and rewarding possibilities emerging from dialogue, discussion, and personal interactions common in these types of processes. The benefits gained by providing participants with the space and time to engage in open dialogue on issues about which they are deeply concerned include increased clarity and understanding, and the development of productive personal relationships that are so important to the effective enactment of action research.

Focus Questions

Focus groups require careful facilitation to ensure people can accomplish productive tasks in the time they spend together. The purpose for meeting should be clearly described by the facilitator, and discussion should be focused on specific issues related to that purpose. As with individual interviews, the major purpose of focus groups is to provide people with opportunities to describe and reflect on their own experiences and perspectives. A general statement by the facilitator contextualizing and framing the issue is followed by a series of *focus questions* similar in format to those provided for individual interviews:

Grand Tour Questions

These kinds of questions enable people to express their experiences and perspectives in their own terms: "We're meeting today to think about ways we might more effectively link with families living in this community. I'd like you to talk in groups about ways you currently link with families and then extend our discussions from there. Please focus initially on the first question, 'How do I currently link with families?'"

Mini-Tour Questions

As people explore these topics, further questions may arise from their discussion. "There's not enough time," "There are some families who don't wish to have contact with us," and so on. These statements are reframed in question form and allow for further sharing of information: "How do we currently make time to link with families?" "How do we try to link with families who don't appear to want to have contact with us?" Sharing information in this way not only enables people to benefit from each others' experience, but also provides possibilities for directly formulating solutions to issues as they emerge.

Guided Tour Questions

Focus groups may engage in a *guided tour,* in which people tour a neighborhood, community center, or some other facility, sharing their experiences or perspectives of events related to those environments.

Task-related Questions

Groups may also benefit from *task-related* questions, so that members can demonstrate how they go about achieving some purpose. "Could you show us how you organize the program you've been talking about?" "Could you show the group how you conduct an initial interview with a client?" "Could you demonstrate how you show groups how to put a plan together?" Facilitators may ask people, either individually or as a group, to draw a picture, a map, or a diagram illustrating their experience of the issue on which they are focused. When people express their perspectives *artistically* or *visually,* they often provide very evocative accounts of their experience, and *maps and diagrams* may be similarly productive. These productions then become the focus for more discussions, further extending participant understandings of other people's experiences and perspectives.

Activities and physical demonstrations or representations of experience are well-known techniques in human service reviews and have been documented in the literature on participatory rural appraisal (Chambers, 1992; Mascarenhas, 1992). Participants use drama, diagrams, maps, models, inscriptions, natural materials, and objects to represent their experience, rank preferences, draw comparisons about wealth and well-being, or represent time lines and seasonal variations. Providing the means for participants to represent their experience in a variety of media is crucial when working in situations where diverse cultural traditions operate.

Facilitators should ensure that each group keeps an ongoing record of its discussions. This may take the form of notes, recorded by a volunteer in the group, but sometimes the discussions may be recorded in summary form on charts. Where multiple groups are engaged in discussions, a plenary session provides opportunities for participants to share the results of their exploration.

Overview: Interviews and Focus Groups

Interviews and focus groups are the principal entry points into an action research process. They provide the means for all stakeholders to reveal their experiences and to further explore their understanding of the issues investigated. Through continued cycles of questioning, participants seek to uncover the often-unquestioned assumptions embedded in their world views and to make explicit the taken-for-granted knowledge inscribed in their everyday activities. Human service professionals, as stakeholders in the process, also should have opportunities to disclose their perspectives and experiences, thus enabling clients and client groups to understand the possibilities and restrictions that encompass their work. All participants thus gain greater clarity in understanding the complexities of the situation and set the groundwork for developing solutions to the problems they are studying. Interviews, however, are not the sole means of acquiring information. As the following sections describe, participants can extend their understanding by carefully observating what is going on and by reviewing information from other sources.

Participant Observation

The principal purposes of observation are to familiarize research participants with the context in which issues and events are played out and to provide opportunities for them to stand back from their everyday involvement and observe purposefully as events unfold. Such observation extends participants' awareness and understanding of the everyday features of their life-world and provides information for constructing more complete accounts of their situation. Careful observation enables participants to "build a picture" of the context and of the activities and events within the context, revealing details of the setting as well as the mundane, routine activities that constitute the life-world of clients, colleagues, and the community. Sometimes, however, the observation is revelatory, providing keen insights or illuminating important but taken-for-granted features of agency, institution, or community life.

Observation in action research is very different from the highly structured types of observation required in experimental research, where the researcher records the frequency of specific types of behavior, acts, or events using a highly structured observation schedule. Participant observation in action research is much less structured and more open-ended, its purpose being to provide more detailed descriptions of people's actions and the context in which they occur. Participant observation seeks a deeper level of understanding through extended immersion in the context and interaction with associated people and events within that context.

While research facilitators may engage in observations of their own, they may also engage in collaborative observation processes using questions to elicit participant descriptions of the context. As with interviews, observation requires focus, so that relevant features of the scene are recorded. Spradley (1979b) suggests observations should always be accompanied or preceded by relevant questions for this purpose. A research facilitator may ask participants for a guided tour, while keeping in mind the underlying questions, "What do I need to know about this place to understand the situation here? What do I need to know about the neighborhood (the family, community groups, etc.)?" Participant observations will be enriched as they focus on:

- **People:** Clients, family members, community groups, administrators, allied and support staff, and others
- **Places:** Reception rooms, offices, homes, community contexts, locations of activities and events, physical layouts
- **Acts:** Single actions that people take (e.g., handing a report to a colleague)
- **Activities:** Sets of related acts (e.g., writing a report, an activity that comprises a number of acts)
- **Events:** Sets of related activities (e.g., a case management conference, which includes a series of activities)
- **Objects:** Buildings, furniture, equipment, reports, and so on
- **Purposes:** What people are trying to accomplish
- **Time:** Times, frequency, duration, and sequencing of events and activities
- **Feelings:** Emotional orientations and responses to people, events, activities, situations, and settings

Participant descriptions enable research facilitators to check the veracity of their own observations as well as provide useful primary data. This is important to note since it is all too easy for a researcher to focus on irrelevant issues or to misinterpret events when guided by his or her own perspective.

In an inquiry into the practice of youth workers, a researcher carefully recorded features of the households they visited. He observed the decorations and family photographs on the wall, the type of furniture, the activities of the grandchildren, and the interaction amongst family members. When these observations were reported to the youth workers, they were able to elaborate on these taken-for-granted features of the context. For example, they described how parents were affected by the presence and behavior of children at consultations in the home, and also focused on the poverty evident in households. Both were features of the situation the researcher had failed to note in his observations.

Recording Observations

Field Notes

Research participants should record their observations as field notes that provide on-going records of important acts, activities, events, and so on. Field notes serve as the vital repository of data that will both guide further inquiry and provide the material from which research outcomes will emerge. Field notes enable research participants to record detailed descriptions of places and events as they occur in their natural settings. While it is not always possible to record field notes immediately, observers should record events as soon as possible after they occur.

The task may appear quite daunting, as any context contains huge amounts of information that could be recorded. Research participants should therefore focus on that information that enables people to understand the *context* and *social processes* related to the issue being investigated. The recorded information provides material that will later be used to describe the context of the research or to relate events and activities.

Hand-drawn maps or pictures may supplement written descriptions to give increased clarity. A map of a building, housing complex, or neighborhood, for instance, provides a pictorial representation that may be used later to increase understanding and clarity. Observers may "set up" their observations by describing and drawing the setting, recording pertinent events and activities as they occur over a period of time, and then member-checking to ensure appropriate renditions of both setting and events.

Transcripts

Transcripts of tape-recorded information present a detailed text of all that is said in a given situation. This type of record provides clear evidence of what is actually said by participants and can help research participants describe and clarify events recorded. Tape recordings of naturally occurring conversations enable researchers to check the accuracy of their observations and analysis. The recordings also provide the means to ensure that language and concepts used in analysis and reporting match those of the participants.

Rosalie: On one particular occasion during fieldwork, I became acutely conscious of the way I had skewed interpretation of events. On this occasion, as is evident in the transcript below, I was challenged directly by the person concerned.

Rosalie: "What you have been saying is that the problem is that people have to pay and that a lot of people *don't want to pay.* Is that right? . . . "
June: "Quite often *they haven't got money.*"
Rosalie: "Yeah."
June: "Not that they *don't want to pay.*"
Rosalie: "Oh no—but I mean—yeah, they don't have money."

Photographs

Photographs provide a graphic record that enables future audiences to more clearly visualize settings and events. Photographs are a particularly useful means of stimulating discussion during focus groups, and they may provide the basis for focusing or extending interviews. A mini-tour question, "Tell me what's happening in this photograph," can provide richly detailed descriptions, proving especially useful when working with children or elderly clients. Photographs may also be used to enhance reports presented to participants or to other research audiences.

Videotapes

Videotapes are also an important research resource. Written descriptions are necessarily limited, being highly dependent on the skills of the writer and providing inadequate and rudimentary understanding of events and contexts. Videotapes have the advantage of making the scene immediately available to viewers, providing a far greater depth of understanding of the acts, activities, events, interactions, behaviors, and nature of the context. While videotapes have their own limitations, they can provide highly informative pictures easily viewed by large audiences.

Careful consideration needs to be given to the specific settings and events to be recorded. Schouten and Watling (1997) suggest a process by which participants "beacon out" their fields of concerns, exploring the extent of their investigations through dialogue and then focusing on salient features to be taped. They suggest the following basic procedures:

- Leave a 10-second gap at the beginning of each tape.
- Make a trial recording to ensure equipment is working.
- Enable people time to "warm up" before taping.
- Check the material immediately after taping.
- Stick to a designated time limit.
- Allow time for people to comment after recording.

Videos, however, do not reveal the "facts" or the "truth." They still provide only partial information since only small segments of time may be recorded and since the lens focuses only on particular features of the context or events, according to the interest or interpreting eye of the videographer. A useful way of using this tool is to record events identified by preliminary analyses of interview data. The camera then focuses on features of the scene identified as significant by participants in the process.

Artifacts: Documents, Records, Materials, and Equipment

In traditional anthropological investigations, understanding a cultural context sometimes required an intensive study of artifacts related to the daily social life of the setting. This is also true to some extent in action research, though the focus on artifacts is somewhat different in nature. Voluminous information related to cases and services can be found in the documents and records of any agency and organization, and useful insight may be gained by investigating associated books, materials, and equipment. A survey of physical facilities—furniture, buildings, homes, offices, and so on—may also be instructive.

Research participants, however, need to be selective and focused since huge and unwieldy masses of information, much of which has little relevance to the issue being explored, may overwhelm an investigation. In action research, participant accounts provide a frame of reference to focus further observation. Preliminary analysis of interview data reveals the features and elements of experience or context that might benefit from the gathering of additional information. Comments like "I hate the way we're supposed to report in. It's so frightening" or "These new procedures are the best thing since sliced bread" may lead to a review of reporting or other procedures used in the office.

Researchers should be wary of gathering information just for the sake of it or of gathering information indicated by common practice or traditional formulations. One of the strengths of action research is its ability to work by or through common everyday practices and taken-for-granted knowledge to reveal underlying dynamics or features that are central features of the problem being investigated. Participant perspectives as revealed in interviews, therefore, provide the central point of reference for reviewing artifacts. Ultimately, however, material is collected according to whether or not it appears pertinent to the issue being studied. Researchers do not determine which artifacts are to be reviewed prior to the start of the study, however, since their pertinence or relevance to the research question is revealed as participant perspectives emerge. Whether case plans, organizational activities, furniture, community facilities, or other items are included becomes evident when they are suggested by participant interview responses. Reviewing interview field notes or transcripts, therefore, enables researchers to identify the artifacts to be included in the study.

Documents

Researchers can obtain a great deal of significant information by reviewing documents in the research context (see Figure 4.4). Client files and records, organizational procedural manuals, and duty statements may contain crucial information about factors involved in the delivery of human services within the setting. At the agency level, policy documents may include rules and regulations providing insight into institutionally approved behaviors, activities, or procedures. Policy documents can also provide information about the broader human service system. These may be complemented by annual reports containing details of the structure, purposes, operations, and resources of a human service agency or organization. Memos, meeting minutes, procedure statements, departmental plans, evaluation reports, press accounts, public relations materials, information statements, and newsletters likewise extend our understanding about the organization and operation of an agency.

In some environments, documentation is prolific. Researchers need to be selective, briefly scanning a range of documents to ascertain the information contained and its relevance to the project's focus. They should keep records of documents reviewed, noting any significant information and its source. In some cases, researchers may be able to obtain photocopies of relevant documents.

In reviewing documents and records, researchers should always keep in mind that they are not finding the "facts" or the "truth." Information is always influenced by the authors or is written in accordance with particular people's motives, agendas, and perspectives. This is just as true at the organizational level as it is at the level of the individual, since people or groups in positions of influence and power are able to inscribe their perspective, values, and biases into official documents and records. Documents and records, therefore, should always be viewed as just information from another source or stakeholder, having no more legitimacy or "truth value" than any other stakeholder.

Records

Confidential records often are not available for public scrutiny, and researchers may need special circumstances and appropriate formal approval to gain access to them. Where research is "in-house," however, a review of records can often provide invaluable information. Individual files detailing client histories, case notes, charts, or district or state records may provide information central to the inquiry. Comparisons with related human service organizations and agencies may reveal interesting information providing much needed perspective to a study. Perceptions that a service organization is poorly funded, or that a particular client group has low access to services, may not be borne out by a review of the records. As with all other information, however, such information needs to be carefully interpreted since much of it is recorded in statistical form that can be quite misleading. In circumstances where statistical information is used, the research team needs to include someone with the relevant expertise to interpret the information acquired.

Client Case Notes

Client case notes serve as a wonderful information resource but are highly sensitive and should not be used without stringent precautions to protect the confidentiality of client and worker. They may, however, enable research participants to review a chronological record of the types of activity in which human service professionals and their clients engage. Information from case notes provides a useful addition to other data, but the notes should be collected parsimoniously since they tend to accumulate with astonishing speed. As with other artifacts, case notes should be selected according to their relevance to the research issue and should be gathered after preliminary analysis of interview data has provided the means to focus selection of this information.

Materials, Equipment, and Facilities

A review of material and equipment (see Figure 4.5) provides useful input to the inquiry since there is a vast array of artifacts that are involved in human service delivery. Agencies, neighborhood centers, and homes may contain a large variety of equipment and facilities, including resources for community groups or special aids for the disabled and frail aged. Researcher participants should carefully review materials, equipment, and facilities as part of their observations. As with other observations, the focus and direction of reviews will be determined by information acquired in interviews.

Case notes	Research reports
Intervention protocols	Demographics
Training programs	Statistics
Case reports	Databases
Client histories	
Client charts	Legislation
	Rules and regulations
Posters	Policies and procedures
Manuals	Annual reports
Research papers	Budgets
Reference lists	Archives
Bibliographies	
	Constitutions
Work portfolios	Meeting minutes and agendas
Performance appraisals	Rosters
Attendance records	Correspondence
Case records	E-mails
	Memos
Diaries	Reports
Calendars	
Phone logs	Circulars
Car logs	Notice boards
Schedules	Pamphlets and brochures
Appointment books	Educational materials
Mileage records	

Figure 4.4
Documents and Records

Newspapers	Furniture
Journal articles	Computers
Magazines	Televisions
Television reports and documentaries	Projectors
Radio programs	
Films	Rooms
Photos	Space arrangements
Maps	Lighting
Posters	Ventilation
	Air conditioning
	Heating
	Storage facilities

Figure 4.5
Materials, Equipment, and Facilities

Research facilitators should be wary of focusing on details that participants interpret as having little significance to the issue being investigated. This should not be seen as a fixed rule, however, since an outside observer may focus on features that are so commonplace that other participants don't think them worthy of comment. It is possible, for instance, for people to take for granted equipment that is dilapidated or in poor repair that significantly affects their activities. Research facilitators may record this information but judge its significance only in conjunction with other stakeholders.

> **Ernie:** A community support agency I visited was located in an old warehouse in the inner city. The downstairs waiting room and consulting rooms had no windows on the outside world. Related services for aged care clients were provided in a building across the street, and the drug and alcohol unit that provided community outreach services was located in yet another building further down the block. Unsurprisingly, the physical layout of the building had extremely negative effects on staff communication and client access.

Recording Information

As researchers review artifacts, they should take careful note of information they consider relevant to the inquiry. They should list information they have reviewed, together with a summary description of the nature of the material. In the process, they should record which information may be made public and which must be kept confidential. The intent of the summaries is to provide research participants with information about materials that might enhance their inquiry. If, for instance, participants have a perception that child abuse cases are declining, then access to appropriate records will enable them to check whether or not this is so. This information will allow participants to extend, clarify, or enhance existing issues and perspectives as they emerge.

Surveys

A survey is another means of providing input into an action research process. Unlike "quasi-experiments" that use statistical analysis to test a hypothesis, surveys are sometimes used in action research to acquire information from larger groups of participants. A survey may be used, for instance, to acquire information from a particular client group. The major advantage of surveys is that they provide a comparatively inexpensive means to acquire information from a large number of people within a limited time frame. Their disadvantages are that it is frequently difficult to obtain responses from those surveyed and that the information that can be obtained through surveys is fixed and limited.

Creswell (2002) describes the different ways surveys can be administered—self-administered questionnaires, telephone interviews, face-to-face interviews, computer-assisted interviews, and website and Internet surveys. He suggests there are two basic survey designs: a cross-sectional design that collects information from people at one point in time and a longitudinal design that studies changes in a group or population over time. Surveys always obtain information about people's perspectives on an issue, rather than their actual behaviors. A survey of client perspectives on services provided by an agency, for instance, may focus on client attitudes, beliefs, and opinions or may elicit information about clients' perceptions, feelings, priorities, concerns, and experiences. The latter is more appropriate for action research, which focuses largely on the perspective and experience of participants.

Researchers may increase the validity of a survey by ensuring it is grounded in concepts and ideas that more closely fit the experiences and perspectives of those surveyed; they can accomplish this by doing face-to-face interviews with a small sample of participants (see "Interviewing," pp. 57–64). They may then use that information to formulate questions for the survey instrument. Surveys can be conducted through face-to-face interviews or through paper-and-pen questionnaires, and each may be administered to individuals or groups. Paper-and-pen questionnaires are useful when researchers require specific information about a limited number of items or when sensitive issues are explored.

Questions in action research surveys may be comparatively unstructured and open-ended to maximize opportunities for respondents to answer questions in their own terms, or the questions may be highly structured to acquire specific information related to issues of concern.

Conducting a Survey

- **Determine the purpose, focus, and participants.**   Prior to constructing the survey instrument (questionnaire), carefully define:
  - The issues to be included
  - The type of information to be obtained
  - The people from whom it will be acquired
- **Formulate questions.**   Ensure that questions:
  - Cover all issues and all types of information identified
  - Are clear and unambiguous
  - Do not include two issues in one question—e.g., Are agency hours adequate, and at suitable times?
  - Are framed in positive terms, rather than negative
  - Do not contain jargon likely to be unfamiliar to respondents
  - Are short and to the point
- **Provide appropriate response formats.**   Formats should allow sufficient space for responses to open-ended or semistructured questions. Questions may take the following forms:
  - **Open response:**   E.g., How many minutes should be allocated for a consultation? _____ minutes
  - **Fixed response:**   E.g., How frequently should you visit the social worker? Daily _____, every two days _____, every three days _____, weekly _____, other _____
  - **Dual response:**   Responses choosing between two alternatives, e.g., yes/no, agree/disagree, male/female

- **Rating response:** E.g., Using the following scale, circle the most correct response: 1 (strongly disagree), 2 (disagree), 3 (neutral), 4 (agree), 5 (strongly agree)
- **Provide framing information.** Inform potential respondents of the purpose and nature of the survey. Include information about the likely duration of the interview or session and the types of response required (e.g., extended responses or precise responses).
- **Test the adequacy of the questions:** Have preliminary interviews or questionnaire-completing sessions with a small number of people. Modify questions that prove to be inappropriate or ambiguous.
- **Administer the questionnaire or conduct the survey.**
- **Thank people for their participation.**
- **Analyze the data.**

When more complex, extended, or analytic surveys are contemplated, researchers should use appropriate sources to ensure effective valid designs (e.g., see Bell, 1993; Cook & Campbell, 1979; Creswell, 2002; Fink, 1995; Oppenheim, 1966; Youngman, 1982).

Statistical and Numerical Data

Human service agencies and organizations generate large amounts of numerical data related to client well-being, including case notes, test results, and information concerning organizational inputs and outputs, inventories, and financial statements. Other sources of quantitative data that may enhance an action research process include information in official reports and records, as well as that available in research studies and reports.

Unlike experimental research, where statistical data are used to test hypotheses, action research uses numerical and statistical data as another form of information to extend or clarify participant understandings of an issue or problem. Surveys also provide numerical information that can be used to test the applicability of specific concepts and ideas to broader populations. Numerical and statistical data are particularly useful when there is lack of clarity about the occurrence of particular phenomena. Depending on the nature of the study, statistical information may provide descriptive information related to:

- *Occurrences* of a phenomenon, e.g., the number of clients who utilize an agency or the number of families experiencing crisis
- *Comparisons* of different occurrences, e.g., differences in the occurrence of a condition in men and women
- *Trends, or history* of occurrences over time, e.g., whether the number of teen pregnancies in a population or sample is decreasing over time
- *Central tendencies,* e.g., measures of the mean period of unemployment for a particular youth group
- *Distribution of scores,* e.g., the spread of scores of the incidence of STDs among different age groups

- *Correlations* that measure the degree of relationship between any two phenomena, e.g., the extent to which participation in unlawful activity is related to the quality of youth leisure facilities

Inferential or analytic statistics, including such techniques as analysis of variance, multiple regression analysis, and factor analysis, assist researchers to determine the effect of different factors on a phenomenon of interest, e.g., the extent to which the prevalence of a sexually transmitted disease may be attributed to or affected by age, gender, social class, education, and so on. A wide range of research studies reported in professional and academic journals provides a rich body of information with the potential to inform research participants about particular social and human service issues.

Rarely, however, do statistical data provide "the answer" to an issue or problem since the information must first be interpreted to understand precisely what the data are saying and to judge the relevance of the data to the people and the setting of any study. Part of the job of qualitative interpretation, therefore, is to find out what the numbers are saying, to ensure that people understand the significance of the information, to clarify what the information means in terms of the issue being investigated, and to assess its relevance to the current context. Statistical information, however, can be useful in assisting people in their deliberations. Where there is disagreement about the efficacy of particular interventions, for instance, numerical data can clarify the situation and enable research participants to move forward in their inquiries. It is important, however, that people ensure that "all the evidence is in," since it is easy to extract the results of a single study or to focus on one part of a table of statistics and interpret the information out of context. As with all other information, quantitative information needs to be carefully interpreted to ensure it assists in clarifying and extending understandings emerging in the study.

Reviewing the Literature

As indicated in Chapter 3, reviewing the literature is an ongoing facet of stakeholder processes of inquiry. As issues and perspectives emerge, the literature review becomes more focused, enriching the information base of an inquiry. In action research, "the literature" is positioned quite differently from that in traditional academic research, being viewed as the source of other views or perspectives, rather than as the source of "truths" or "facts." Facts, according to Smith (Denzin, quoted in Frus, 1994), are social constructions, as much in need of investigation and exploration as other features of the context. Literature reviews also should be quite thorough to ensure that limited perspectives are not used as ammunition to force particular types of action.

In an action research process, therefore, the literature might best be seen as another set of perspectives, providing useful information to be incorporated into the perspectives and accounts emerging in the research process. In Figure 4.6, worker

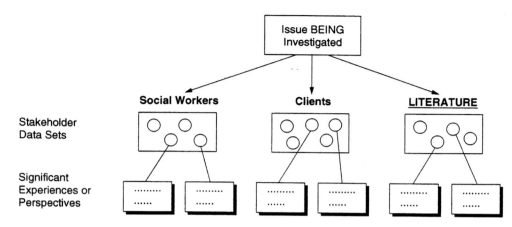

Figure 4.6
Including Information from the Literature

and client perspectives are obtained through interviews, analyses of which provide understanding of stakeholder experiences and perspectives on an issue. A review of literature may reveal perspectives, interpretations, or analyses emerging from other studies of that issue. Or a literature review may turn up discrete information related to a particular condition or treatment, providing research participants with information that can enhance, complement, or challenge the constructions arising from their study.

Processes for Reviewing and Deconstructing the Literature

A variety of sources may contain useful literature that speaks to the issue being investigated, including academic texts and journals, professional journals and publications, and institutional or departmental publications and reports. These may contain accounts of successful practices, projects, or learning processes; demographic information pertinent to the location or group studied; or indications of factors likely to have an impact on the study. They also may provide information about previous research on the issue, existing programs and services, or accounts of similar projects. Care needs to be taken in applying generalized information to the specific site of the study, however, since it is possible that the conditions in the setting, or the nature of particular groups, differ significantly from those from which other studies are drawn. Although they may provide generalized analyses of an issue, the results of other studies may not provide the basis for action in any particular local setting.

The literature is not a body of "truth," however, since studies may comprise a range of different theories, diverse ways of conceptualizing an issue, and different assumptions, values, and ideologies embedded in the research texts. These often unrecognized assumptions and sets of ideas sometimes either are inappropriate to the research in which participants are engaged or unconsciously impose a way of conceptualizing a situation or an issue that fails to take into account the concrete realities facing people in their specific situations. Part of the researcher's task, therefore, is to deconstruct the literature, revealing the inherent concepts, ideas, theories, values, and ideological assumptions embedded in the texts of their writing.[1]

Reviewing and deconstructing the literature require research participants to:

- Identify sources containing information relevant to their inquiry
- Distill the main features of lengthy articles or reports
- Identify information, concepts, or ideas that illuminate or resolve emerging issues
- Deconstruct concepts and ideas, revealing unintended preconceptions, assumptions, or biases
- Include distilled information in ongoing processes of reflection and analysis

A review of the literature may incorporate materials from libraries, community organizations, government agencies, or websites. Often material may be accessed through computerized search processes and databases. Research participants may use a web search engine to locate resources or may gain assistance from the help desk at their local or university library. They should be wary of using abstracts, however, since they often contain distorted or poorly formulated information. If a piece of literature seems pertinent, then it should be read in full-text form.

Using the Literature Review

As material from the literature enters the research cycle, participants can make decisions about its worth or relevance. It may provide information that enhances or confirms the perspectives already reported or that challenges the views and experience of stakeholder participants. The literature may also contain information suggesting actions to be taken or provide examples of actions taken in similar contexts. For formal reporting procedures, an extended review of the literature also provides evidence that participants have thoroughly investigated a variety of sources of information and taken the information into account in their investigations.

Information emerging from the literature review, therefore, may be used:

- As part of the ongoing processes of reflection and analysis
- As information to be included in emergent understandings
- As material to be included in reports

---

[1] The emphasis on deconstruction is another facet of qualitative research. Quantitative research assumes value-free or value-neutral research generalizable to all contexts. Qualitative research highlights the cultural and context-specific nature of knowledge and the importance of understanding an author's perspective, since authors often infer truths about an issue on the basis of their own experience and perspective and fail to take into account the often different experiences and perspectives of those about whom they write.

Emerging Accounts

As participants accumulate information from a variety of sources, they acquire the materials from which new understandings emerge, enabling them to formulate action to remediate the issue or problem on which the study has focused. As indicated in Figure 4.7, participant accounts derived from interviews provide primary material for constructing accounts that resonate with the experience and perceptions of research participants. These preliminary accounts, however, are modified, clarified, enriched, or enhanced by information from other sources. Information from observation, together with material derived from reviewing documents, records, and other artifacts, may extend and enrich accounts derived from participant perceptions. Insightful or useful information may also be obtained from the literature reviewed during the processes of inquiry.

The accounts and understandings emerging from these processes of data gathering and analysis are not static, however, and continue to be enriched, enhanced, and clarified as researchers enter continuing cycles of the process, adding further information from the same or other sources. The continuing Look-Think-Act cycle may incorporate information from the diverse sources identified in previous sections of this chapter.

Figure 4.7 typifies the process of data collection, though the reality is messier since information and analysis converge in the research arena from a variety of sources, sometimes serendipitously, and at odd moments in the research process. The art and craft of research is in the skillful management of this diverse body of information, distilling and organizing data into a coherent and clear framework of concepts and ideas that people can use for practical purposes.

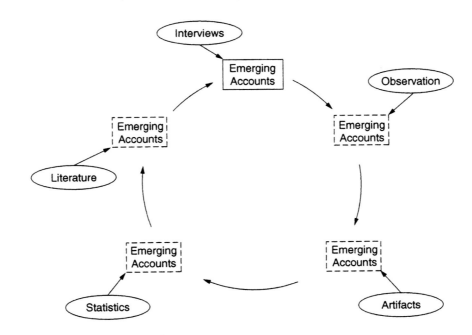

Figure 4.7
Building the Picture:
Emerging Accounts

SUMMARY

The major purpose of this part of the research process is to gather information from a variety of sources.

Participants need to develop *trusting relationships* enabling the easy interchange of information.

The *interview* is the primary tool of data gathering, providing extended opportunities for stakeholders to reflect on their experience. Key features of the interview process include:

- *Initiating* interviews
- *Interview techniques*, including grand tour, mini-tour, and prompt questions to obtain participant perspectives
- Obtaining information collaboratively through *focus groups*

Information is also acquired through *observing* settings and events.

A review of *artifacts* provides a rich additional source of information. These may include:

- *Documents*
- *Records*
- *Case notes*
- *Materials, equipment, and facilities*

Other useful information may be acquired from *numerical and statistical* information from these sources or by use of a *survey*.

Academic, professional, and organizational *literature* also may provide useful information for research participants.

Giving Voice: Interpretive and Qualitative Data Analysis

5

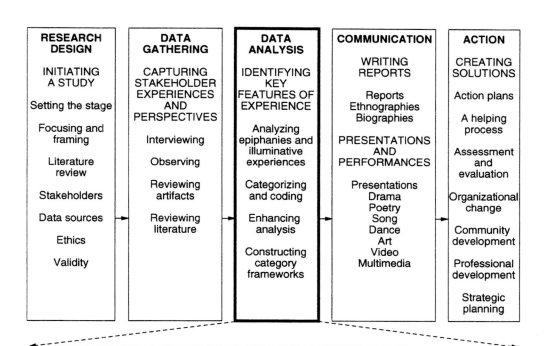

RESEARCH DESIGN	DATA GATHERING	DATA ANALYSIS	COMMUNICATION	ACTION
INITIATING A STUDY	CAPTURING STAKEHOLDER EXPERIENCES AND PERSPECTIVES	IDENTIFYING KEY FEATURES OF EXPERIENCE	WRITING REPORTS	CREATING SOLUTIONS
Setting the stage			Reports Ethnographies Biographies	Action plans
Focusing and framing	Interviewing	Analyzing epiphanies and illuminative experiences	PRESENTATIONS AND PERFORMANCES	A helping process
Literature review	Observing			Assessment and evaluation
Stakeholders	Reviewing artifacts	Categorizing and coding	Presentations Drama Poetry	Organizational change
Data sources	Reviewing literature	Enhancing analysis	Song Dance Art	Community development
Ethics		Constructing category frameworks	Video Multimedia	Professional development
Validity				Strategic planning

Contents of This Chapter

This chapter describes ways of distilling the large body of information (data) collected in the previous chapter. Two alternative approaches to data analysis are presented. The chapter:

- Explains the *purpose* of data analysis in naturalistic inquiry and qualitative research—distilling the data.
- Presents procedures for two alternative approaches to data analysis:
    1. *Analyzing epiphanies* by *deconstructing*, or "unpacking," significant experiences to reveal their key features.
    2. *Categorizing and coding* procedures for analyzing data. Researchers "unitize" the data and select and sort the data into a system of categories.

- Presents procedures for *enhancing data analysis* by including data from diverse sources.

The Purposes of Data Analysis

The framework depicted in Figure 5.1 signals the move from data gathering to data analysis. The Think component of the Look-Think-Act process indicates the need for research participants to reflect on information they have gathered and identify its most important features and elements. The purpose of this reflection is to transform a sometimes large and unwieldy body of information into a relatively compact system of ideas and concepts that provides clarity and understanding to research participants' inquiries.

While data analysis in action research has much in common with the general methodologies of naturalistic inquiry and qualitative research, its purposes are distinctively different. Traditionally, research has sought to establish theories or conceptual schemes to explain how and why people act as they do. Action research, however, uses this type of explanatory theory as background information, choosing to focus instead on the ways people purposefully construct and make meaning of their social worlds. The intent is to understand the ongoing, experienced reality of people's lives rather than seeking to explain events in terms of an existing psychological or social theory. As explained in Chapter 2, the focus is on people's theories in action. Action research employs a mode of inquiry that enables a life-world to become directly accessible to an audience, capturing voices, emotions, and actions within the stories that shape and give meaning to each person's experience.

In this context the *purpose* of data analysis is to reveal the concepts, ideas, meanings, and interpretations through which people make sense of their experience. These are then used to construct a framework of concepts that provide the basis for reports and accounts. Action research employs analytic processes that focus on the concepts and ideas people naturally use to observe, describe, and interpret their experiences (Spradley, 1979a; Spradley & McCurdy, 1972). This represents an approach to research that has the clear intention to learn from and with people, rather than studying them.

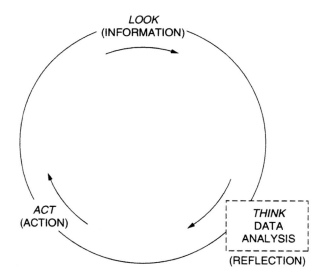

Figure 5.1
Reflection in Action
Research

The *process* of data analysis requires participants to sift through accumulated data to identify the information most pertinent to the problem they are investigating. This process of distillation provides the material for an organized set of concepts and ideas that enable people to achieve greater insight, understanding, or clarity about events of interest. The intent is to accomplish "commonsense" solutions to problems, by finding concepts and ideas that make sense to the different stakeholders involved. One of the essential features of action research is the move to directly engage the experience and perspective of all participants to ensure that the "sense" made of the data is "common" to all.

This differs from usual research practice, in which researchers analyze data in isolation from the research context and subjects, formulating categories and schema that appeared to make sense when applied to a particular theory. In much research, theoretical formulations often dominate proceedings, inscribing academic perspectives into the process and silencing the voices and perspectives of participants. Though there is still a need for objective research that engages these types of practices, action research tends to focus on a more phenomenological approach to analysis.

This chapter presents two alternative approaches to data analysis. The first, epiphanic analysis, seeks to preserve participant perspectives by using "epiphanic moments" (Denzin, 1989b)—illuminative or significant experiences—as primary units of analysis. The ultimate intent is to give voice to the participants, revealing key meanings in their language and providing a body of ideas and concepts that clearly mesh with important elements of their experience. The second approach— categorizing and coding—is a more traditional form of qualitative analysis that refines large amounts of data into a more manageable body of ideas. The purpose of this process is to formulate a system of concepts that reveals patterns and themes within the data.

Ernie: Human service workers rarely have time to stand back and reflect on their professional practices due to tight schedules and multiple commitments of their work. When they have opportunities to talk about and reflect on their experiences, however, they often gain significant insights into their professional life. I've frequently seen professional workers' eyes light up in the course of interviews or focus group dialogues as they "see" themselves or aspects of their work in new ways. Merely having time to focus their attention in a systematic way is illuminative.

I once facilitated a review session with a group of social workers from different agencies within a small city. As they shared their stories and built trust in each other, they gained deep insights as they identified key features of their work. They discovered, for instance, that many of them were dealing with very similar cases on a one-to-one basis in isolation, in some cases working independently with the same families. They also realized that many aspects of their work ran across cases and agencies, and they became conscious of the benefits that would arise from working collaboratively. The process of analyzing their experience enabled participants to extend their understanding of their work in

that city, and provided concepts and ideas they could use to devise effective actions to resolve some of their deep-seated problems. In these ways "data analysis" became not just a technical research routine, but also the means to
understand more clearly the nature of their professional work.

Data Analysis (1): Analyzing Epiphanies

The focus of interpretive research on meanings people give to themselves and their
life experiences requires researchers to capture the voices, emotions, and actions of
those studied in order to acquire "empathetic understanding" of another's life experience (Denzin, 1989b). The following analytic procedures enable research participants to enter each others' worlds and to understand the events, actions, activities,
behavior, and deep emotions that emerge from the ongoing reality of human experience (Denzin, 1997). It is as important for clients to understand how human service
workers interpret events as it is for human service workers to understand how their
clients make meaning of their experience.

The intent of these procedures is to enable researchers to accurately and authentically represent people's lives in nonauthoritative and nonexploitive ways. The
procedures employ methods that not only utilize participant voices, but also capture
the concepts, meanings, emotions, and agendas that provide the basis for solutions
to problems affecting their personal, institutional, and professional lives. They enable
the voices of the participants, their structures of meaning, their interpretive
processes, and their conceptual frameworks to structure and guide data analysis
(Genat, 2002; Young, 1999). The procedures are based on a methodology of interpretive analysis suggested by Denzin (1989b), and they focus on *epiphanies*—illuminative moments that mark people's lives.

Epiphanies and Illuminative Experiences

Epiphanic experiences are illuminative moments of crisis or transformational, turning-
point experiences, resulting in significant changes to people's perceptions of their
lives (Denzin, 1989b). Epiphanies take a variety of forms, from the devastating experience that affects a person's life only once, through cumulative epiphanies that
emerge over time, to minor epiphanies that are significant but not highly momentous.
Epiphanies can be either positive or negative. They may include the experience of
exhilaration or despair related to achievement or failure, the sense of wonderment
(or frustration) emerging from a particularly difficult change process, or a sense of
injustice resulting from an unfair or particularly distressing comment from a colleague or administrator.

Epiphanies may vary in intensity, from the life-shattering experience of complete
failure or triumphant success to less calamitous events that have significant, but not
dire, effects on people's lives. They emerge as moments of human warmth or hurt, or
as moments of clarity that add new dimensions to people's life experience, investing
them with new ways of interpreting or understanding their lives. An epiphany may

occur instantaneously—the "ah-ha" experience, the "lightbulb" that enables a person to say, "So that's what is going on." Or an epiphany may evolve gradually, through a cumulative sense of awareness that emerges through an ongoing process of experience and reflection.

Rhonda Petty reveals how she came to understand the concept of epiphany. She writes:

> When I first read Denzin's (1989) definition and description of epiphanies I associated them with psychotic behavior or life-threatening diseases. My interpretation was too narrow. As Denzin wrote, epiphanies are turning-point experiences, interactional moments that mark people's lives and can be tranformational. My own experience demonstrates, however, that epiphanies can stem from the unlikeliest of sources—a book, a conversation, or the click of a telephone. (Petty, 1997 p. 76.)

Epiphanies can arise from seemingly minor events, and may be best thought of as significant experiences that are set aside from the humdrum, routine events that have little apparent impact on events. They are experiences that are in some ways distinct and are cause for particular comment or response from those involved. They are "moments of truth" that change or add meaning to people's lives and therefore provide a means to capture people's lived experience and more clearly represent their life-world. When shared with others as stories or narratives, they provide key meanings central to the narrator's experience and allow significant insight into the key elements participants use to construct and give meaning to their ongoing lives.

Interpreting Epiphanies and Illuminative Experiences

Interpretive data analysis first identifies epiphanic or illuminative experiences in the lives of research participants and then deconstructs, or "unpacks," descriptions of those events to reveal the elements of experience on which those events are built. As researchers we deconstruct those events to reveal the terminology, concepts, and structures of meaning embedded in participant accounts. By starting with the experience and perspective of primary stakeholders and by building understanding of events in their terms, we give voice to these participants and develop understandings that resonate and are consistent with the world as they know and understand it. We seek emic (insider) constructions that are true to their worlds and their purposes.

We do not formulate only individual accounts, however, but descriptions of the experience of *groups,* individuals often interpreting events according to their membership in a particular group. Social workers, clients, and family members, for instance, are likely to see an issue from quite different viewpoints. We therefore formulate *joint accounts,* providing insight into the perspective and experience of each stakeholding group.

Figure 5.2 shows how data related to the perspectives of social workers, clients, and family members are analyzed and used as the basis of a report on a human service issue.

Steps in analyzing epiphanies include:

- *Review field notes* of stakeholders' interviews and focus groups.
- *Select* individual participants (*key people*) who have experiences that are either particularly significant or typical of members of their group.

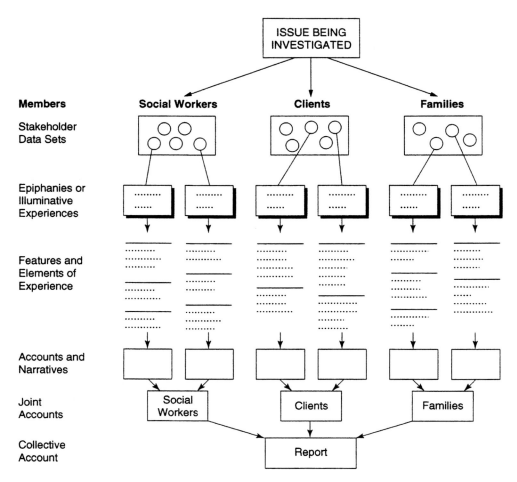

Figure 5.2
Analyzing Epiphanies

- Identify *epiphanies or illuminative (significant) moments* within the experiences of those individuals.
- Deconstruct descriptions of those experiences to reveal the *features and elements* of which they are constructed.
- Use those features and elements to construct *individual accounts* describing how each person experiences and interprets the issue being investigated.
- Review individual accounts to *identify common and divergent features* and elements of the experiences.
- Use this material to construct *joint accounts* that reveal the significant perspectives and experiences of each stakeholding group.
- Review joint accounts to identify common and divergent features and elements of the experiences *across or between groups*.

- Use across-group material to construct a *collective* account. The collective account provides an overall version chronicling events by comparing and contrasting the perspectives of the different stakeholding groups within the setting. It identifies points of commonality of perspective and experience and points of discrepancy, diversity, or conflict.

Points of commonality emerging from this analysis provide the basis for concerted action, while discrepant perspectives, viewpoints, or experiences signal the need to negotiate agendas and actions around unresolved issues.

Selecting Key People

The previous processes assume that it is not possible to focus on every perspective because of constraints of time or resources. As in other forms of research, it is necessary to select a sample of people who will become the focus of research activity (see Chapter 3). In the process of data analysis, it is likewise sometimes beneficial to focus attention on a smaller number of people to explore their experience in depth and to reveal with clarity the elements and features of experience that have significant impact on events. The purpose of selecting key people, therefore, is to identify those individuals whose experiences or perspectives either seem *typical* of other people within the setting or appear particularly illuminating or significant (Creswell, 2002).

Sometimes persons may be chosen because other people in their group hold them in high esteem or because their contribution to the life and work of the group is seen as particularly significant. "Significance" is a flexible term since it may connote negative as well as positive events and behaviors. A client in an agency whose behavior is disruptive, or a social worker who constantly complains about the organization of the agency, may have a significant impact on ongoing events in a human service. Either of these person's perspective may be as illuminative to a research process as that of the director of the human service agency or a highly qualified human service professional.

Key people may be thought of as those likely to provide important information or to have a significant impact on events within the organization. In commencing interpretive analysis of data, research participants will select a number of persons from each stakeholding group, ensuring that they choose people who:

- Represent diverse perspectives from within the group
- Are likely to have a significant impact on the group
- Have seemingly typical experiences and perspectives
- Have particularly unusual or significant experiences or perspectives

Participatory processes assist researchers to select people whose experiences and perspectives are likely to illuminate the complex and diverse nature of people, events, and other relevant phenomena. Even in nonparticipatory processes, however, participants may assist in identifying key people, as researchers ask questions like "Who do you think might provide useful perspectives on this issue?" Or "Who in your group would give me a quite different perspective?"

The first step in interpretive data analysis, therefore, is to identify those people from within each stakeholding group whose combined experiences and perspectives will provide the material from which an understanding of that group will be drawn. The following steps of analysis describe the procedures through which these accounts are drawn, the experiences of those selected being subject to further analysis.

Identifying Epiphanic or Illuminative Experiences

The next step—identifying epiphanic or illuminative experiences—has no magical recipe for revealing "true" or "real" epiphanies. Rather, data analysis starts with a process of selecting those events or features of a person's experience that are especially *significant*, in relation to the issue being investigated. Sometimes they are most evident when strikingly significant events emerge within the research process itself or are revealed in accounts presented in interviews. At other times, however, judgments are made on the basis of an intimate knowledge of the person, the events, and the context that comes from extended engagement. Significant or epiphanic events are identified according to the expression of the participant.

The first "reading" of the data by a researcher, therefore, requires an empathetic, interpretive analysis responding to the internal question, "What are the most significant experiences for this person (in relation to the issue investigated)?" The participant's descriptions of events provide clues, but the complex nuances of emotion and nonverbal cues displayed in interviews also provide information suggesting those events that might usefully be singled out for further analysis. Sometimes significant events or features of experience are self-evident, the participant providing animated, agitated, or emotional descriptions of events and experiences that touch their lives in dramatic and consequential ways. At other times, a more focused and subtle reading is required to identify those features of experience that have a significant impact on the lives of the persons involved. Sometimes it is evident in the extent to which people focus on a particular event or experience, or perhaps in their tone of voice, their language and terminology, their countenance, their body language, or the emphases given to certain events.

We often use analysis of epiphanic or illuminative moments in the course of our teaching and research work. These provide a basis for understanding those aspects of people's experience which are particularly significant and assist us to understand more clearly the issues and events which most concern the people with whom we work. In a study with human service professionals within an urban human service agency, epiphanies emerged in focus group discussions, in one-to-one interviews, and in everyday conversations with individuals. Nevertheless, it was within focus group discussions, where the human service professionals shared the experiences of working within the organization and servicing a similar cohort of clients, that some rich, illuminative moments of realization emerged. As each individual shared his or her experience, others would reflect on their experience of similar situations and their own unique responses. For instance, as the workers discussed the particular kinds of situations they encountered when visiting clients in the community, one exclaimed:

"I think we create dependency . . . I'm not a lawyer, and I've been spending all week at court—I'm not a lawyer—I'm a [human service worker]—and I feel like everything that I've learnt, like all the professional stuff—that's not important!—it's all the social stuff—I feel like the social takes over—more than the psychological or anything to do with case management . . . like I can see the point of someone going with them [to court]—it's just that it seems, it is always the [human service worker]—and it should be the family, or even agency's job . . . [human service workers]—see this is what I mean—it's like the jack-of-all-trades . . . when you are doing all these other things . . . there's not enough of a person to go around."

This outburst of frustration reveals crucial elements of this community worker's experience: She felt besieged and pulled in competing directions by the multiple demands; she believed that a human service worker should provide predominantly social or community services rather than psychological services; she feared she was fostering emotional dependency amongst her clients; and she felt subject to directives from psychologists, lawyers, and administrators. Initially, these emerged as key features of one community worker's experience. Subsequently, the data revealed them as also important features of her colleagues' experiences.

The same study revealed an epiphanic event within the worklife of one of the participants. Though other human service workers were not involved in that specific event, analysis of her experience revealed features and elements that were characteristic of other workers' experiences. The information acquired by exploring one person's experience provided the basis for a richly textured description relevant to others.

Epiphanies and significant events, therefore, take on a range of complexions, in terms of both their intensity and their meaningfulness to participants. Sometimes a relatively trivial event can create great emotion, while at other times what appear as momentous events create little response. Examples of interview data signaling epiphanic or significant events include:

"If he does that one more time I'll scream!"

"Goddamnit! Is she just dumb? I've explained it to her six different ways and she just doesn't get it. She's going to blow her parole!"

"Oh, Jane. That is just wonderful. Your tests are clear. I knew you had it in you."

"It was so important that we did this ourselves. If others had done it for us we wouldn't have learned anything!"

The deconstruction of these moments provides the material from which to construct epiphanic descriptions or accounts. By analyzing the events and meanings surrounding these descriptions, we can construct an understanding of their significance. Epiphanic moments enable us to focus on those features and elements of experience that make a difference in the lives of participants.

Sometimes the meanings of the words are self-evident, but more often it is necessary to provide information about the ways in which the words were delivered, as well as other nonverbal information. It is not unusual for people to come to tears as they speak of events with sometimes barely contained emotion. In the previous examples, the meanings are reasonably clear, but people engaged in data analysis need to take into account the levels of excitement, frustration, anger, and voice tone—they need to factor in the shining eyes and the excited tones of the research participant—in order to understand the significance of the words spoken. The *expression* of the words is at least as important as the words themselves.

> ***Ernie:*** Sometimes epiphanies are revealed unexpectedly. Many times as I've interviewed people I've been struck by the emotive force of their description of particular events. I was recently surprised, however, to find my eyes "leaking" as I was being interviewed about an event in a cross-cultural training program in which I had been involved. Though I thought I was recounting events in a fairly objective way, I had not realized the extent to which they had affected my work. The interviewer informed me that it was not unusual for people to be moved to tears as they described events within this program. I coined the phrase "ethnographic tears" as a way of indicating the possibility of engaging people's deeply felt experience within an interview.
>
> Recently I spoke with a colleague who revealed, in the course of a very ordinary discussion, that she had been undergoing blood tests. As she spoke of her disappointment and fears, tears welled up in her eyes. She described the effect those results were likely to have on her family and worklife and, in the process, revealed much about her family life, her approach to her work, and her relationship with her family members and work colleagues. In this case, the "real" life that existed beneath the surface of her apparently ordinary professional life provided much broader insight into her life-world.

Eventually, however, the choice of epiphanies or significant events requires direct use of member checking with the person concerned, as well as triangulation with the others, since it is easy to misinterpret or wrongly choose events in other people's lives. Ideally, when data are member-checked, i.e., when the participants read the information they have provided, the participants should be asked which events were most significant. This is accomplished by asking a grand tour question (Spradley, 1979a) framed something like, "What, in all this, is most significant for you?" This provides opportunities for participants themselves to identify those events with the most impact on their lives. You might further ask, "Is there anything in your work that really moves, excites, or concerns you?" When asking this, though, there is a need for care since participants may not have moving, exciting, or problematic experiences, but nevertheless have features of experience that affect their lives or work. One step back from this is a procedure in which the researcher identifies significant events and checks their importance with participants.

Although I focus on "events," sometimes significance resides in no particular event, but is found in people's actions and responses or in the impact of features of the environment—physical space, dress, and so on. Significance is revealed in body language—the nonverbal communication that gives us clues about the impact of events. A frown, a smile, a look of pain or anger, or forceful language suggests the need to focus on what is said:

> "She's such a *bitch*—dressing like that and talking like that. I just can't stand being around her."

> "I won't work there much longer. The office is so small I can't even *think*, let alone do my work."

> "When I saw the work that kid had done I almost cried. It was fabulous."

As researchers we explore participant descriptions of events, we review interview accounts to identify illuminative moments or significant experiences. We then deconstruct those elements to extend our understanding of the features and elements that compose it. In a recent study a participant commented, "I suddenly realized what was bugging me. The office is so small I can't even think," and the facilitator was able to assist her to explore related features of that experience. Comments on the size of an office, in this instance, were related to the number and complexity of the person's work activities and to the space she felt she needed to store materials and do the work required of her. As became evident in reviewing the data, the work itself was the significant feature of the experience, even though the size of the office had been the straw that broke the camel's back and had become the immediate focus of agitated comment. Identifying epiphanies and significant experiences, therefore, requires a researcher to search for significant events in people's lives, but also to make connections between related phenomena.

Epiphanies do not need to be associated with momentous events. Minor epiphanies occur quite regularly as people reflect on their experience, sometimes commenting on the "little lightbulb that went on in my head" as they realize the significance of something they have described. These might be more appropriately called illuminative moments since they reflect processes of understanding and clarity that sometimes emerge as people think about their own experience or hear other people's stories.

Deconstructing Epiphanies: Features and Elements of Experience

A central purpose of action research is to evoke an understanding of the way people experience events and phenomena in their lives. Participants start by identifying those experiences that seem to be particularly significant—epiphanic or illuminative moments. The next step in this process is to deconstruct the epiphanies, ascertaining those features and elements that enable an audience to understand the nature of the experience. We need to ask, "How is this event significant for the persons themselves?

What are the features that make up this event?" We are, in effect, unpacking, or "interrogating," the epiphany, seeking to reveal the web and warp of the tapestry of people's lives. In doing so we utilize information drawn from the data, using the concepts, terms, and language employed by the people to describe events—applying the verbatim principle described previously (see Chapter 4).

Figure 5.3 provides an example of this process. The participant, reflecting on her experience, focused on how the work had been "really difficult to start with." Major features of "difficulty," recorded in interview field notes and member-checked with the participant, included "getting to know the people," "getting their trust," "doing a sort of Band-Aid treatment," and "there doesn't seem to be any point in it." Further analysis of field notes indicates the elements of experience associated with each of these. "Doing a sort of Band-Aid treatment," for instance, was associated with "doing the same things day in and day out," "no improvement—nothing is happening," "telling everyone what to do," "[telling everyone] if you do this it's going to get better," and "it doesn't seem to get better."

In a recent study, a powerful epiphany was identified within a one-to-one interview with a community health worker. She finds the work with a marginalized group of clients almost overwhelming:

"When I was going out in the field I found it really difficult to start with. It was just sort of getting to know the people and getting their trust. You sort of feel like you are just doing a sort of Band-Aid treatment out there. You're just going out there and doing the same things day in and day out with no improvement. Nothing is happening . . . you're going out there telling everyone what to do—that it's going to get better—if you do this it's going to get better—but it doesn't seem to get better . . . sometimes you feel what's the point—there doesn't seem to be any point in it . . . why am I doing it? The main hassle is the fact that it is the same problems—they don't go away."

Epiphany	I found it really difficult to start with
Major Features	getting to know the people
	getting their trust
	doing a sort of Band-Aid treatment
	there doesn't seem to be any point in it
Key Elements	(of "doing a sort of Band-Aid treatment")
	doing the same things day in and day out
	no improvement—nothing is happening
	telling everyone what to do
	[telling everyone] if they do this it's going to get better
	it doesn't seem to get better

Figure 5.3
Deconstructing an Epiphany

Elements of "getting to know the people," "getting their trust," and "there doesn't seem to be any point in it" would likewise emerge from further exploration of the data. Having identified an epiphany, therefore, researchers should ask:

- What are the major features of this epiphany?
- What elements (details) make up each of those features?

Researchers should deconstruct each epiphany to reveal the different features of experience inherent in the event. Sometimes a single epiphany is sufficiently powerful to provide the basis for a detailed analysis of a person's experience, while other accounts may require ongoing analysis of a number of minor epiphanies, illuminative moments, or significant events.

As research participants identify a particular significant experience (or epiphanic event, or illuminative moment), they may use a framework of concepts that assists them to identify the features and elements of that experience. For example, they may ask themselves questions drawn from a framework suggested by Spradley (1979b) that includes *acts, activities, events, actors, times, places, purposes,* and *emotions.*

- **Acts, Activities, and Events:** What did people do? What *acts* (or *activities*) were associated with that event or experience?
- **Actors:** *Who* was involved?
- **Times:** *When* did these things happen? What was the *duration* of each significant act, activity, or event? How long did it go on?
- **Places:** *Where* did these things happen?
- **Purposes:** *What* were people trying to do? What was their *intent* or *purpose?*
- **Emotions:** *How* did the different people *feel* about what was occurring?

A useful framework—*what, who, how, where, when,* and *why*—provides a similar way of identifying useful or relevant detail.

We are not attempting to include *all* possible details since the possibilities are infinite. We do not need an extended description of the more mundane, taken-for-granted details of everyday life. Instead, we need to identify the significant features of people's experiences or perspectives. It's important that we don't let the framework drive the data analysis process, starting with "acts" and working down through "activities," "events," "actors," and so on. The trigger for selecting features and elements are those aspects that are seen or felt by participants to be an important feature of their experience. Framework concepts merely serve as reminders of the type of phenomena that might be included.

In all this, researchers need to focus their analysis by ensuring that the information revealed is associated with the issue or question that provides the focus for the study. Ask, "How does this event illuminate or extend our understanding about the issue we are investigating? Does it provide answers to the questions that assisted us to frame our study?" In some cases, the analysis will reveal information indicating the need to extend the boundaries of the study or to focus on issues that were not part of the original plan. The iterative or cyclical nature of the research process enables us to build understanding and extend our study accordingly.

Epiphanies in Observations

Sometimes epiphanic moments occur in the course of observing events and activities within a research setting. Any agency or organization is likely, over a period of time, to experience disruptive events that disturb their relatively orderly routines and procedures. A client outburst, a conflict between a human service professional and a client, or an altercation between staff members signals an epiphanic event that may provide worthwhile focus for further exploration. The event itself tells part of the story, but description and analysis by participants reveal the meanings and experiences associated with the event that have the potential to greatly increase understanding about the issue investigated. Significant events, therefore, provide the focus for follow-up interviews to enable participants to examine and deconstruct events and explore the meanings embedded in singular events. A single event sometimes provides deep insight into the underlying structures of behavior or into the ways everyday events are experienced or interpreted by the people involved.

Epiphanies may appear as representations rather than actual behaviors. They may be depicted in artwork that enables people to explore or represent their experience of a particular issue, or they may be found in less formal, "street-wise" representations, like the graffiti that often appear on agency buildings in the form of pictures or slogans—"Mrs. Jones is a . . . ," "Eveready Agency sucks," and so on. While all graffiti are not significant, they may give insight into a person's orientations or be associated with particular events that signal unresolved issues in the life of an organization. They may provide a focus or a context for further exploration revealing key features of client or agency life.

Constructing Conceptual Frameworks

Once epiphanies have been deconstructed, revealing the key features and elements inherent in participant experiences, the analyzed information is organized into a carefully structured system of concepts that assists people to clearly understand the import of what has been revealed. This structured system of concepts not only provides a summary of important information, but also supplies the basis for writing reports and planning actions.

The following example shows how a deconstructed epiphany—the analysis of significant events within an action research project—provided the framework for a written report.

Deconstructing an Epiphany: Case Example

The following excerpt, taken from a study of human service workers (Genat, 2002), demonstrates the way unpacking a description of an epiphanic event provides the framework for a report on human service worker roles:

> In the course of a study of an agency, a community worker—Ruby—shared her concerns about the scope of her work. There is a defining moment when her acute exasperation leads her to question the mandate of community workers to provide the appropriate, and indeed extraordinary, services.

Following a particularly frustrating staff meeting, she sits with her colleague, Merle, at the kitchen table in the staff room. Slumped to one side, gloomily resting her cheek in her cupped hand, she broods pessimistically on the potential of community workers to have any effect on the situation in which they are working.

"They wanted all us [community] workers 'cause we were going to change everything but we're so strictly dictated to it's changed nothing— some of us have great ideas and we could do it all but we just can't do it—instead of like—handing things to us—we're always dictated to . . . we don't get enough say in the program. . . I thought yes we've got a power, we're united, but then last week it just killed it . . . we say we want to have our own voice!—you should'a been there—there was all these powerful community workers that just agreed to everything [the social worker] said . . . people are still dying—Daisy died . . . people are just dying of things that could have been changed; I mean they may just as well employ social workers."

This epiphanic event provided the basis for an ongoing analysis of community worker roles. The following framework of headings indicates the end result of the analysis. Underlying headings comprise the major features of experience emerging from an analysis of this and other epiphanies, while elements beneath comprise the detail of each feature.

The Situation of Community Workers in the Agency

Lacking Professional Identity, Voice, and Status: "We don't get enough say"
Dominating Doctors: "We're always dictated to"
Unrecognized, Disbelieved, and Dismissed: The case of Daisy
Marginal in the Planning Process: "We have great ideas"

Interaction, Participation, and Status

Vulnerable to exploitation and abuse
Status and participation in workplace forums

Claiming a Professional Domain

Articulating Practice Approaches: The "bottom-up" and the "top-down."
Recognition and Status: Structural barriers
Collective Action: A community worker coalition

This framework of ideas and concepts was used as the basis for a narrative report that powerfully represents the experience of this community worker. Ruby's narrative reveals her anguish at the recognition that neither she nor her colleagues had sufficient authority to make a significant impact. Despite claims about the central role of community workers, the report reveals that they are unable to effect any notable changes because other professionals control their work. At the same time, Ruby's narrative reveals how people are needlessly suffering and dying. She observes not only that community workers have few opportunities to make change individually, but also that they have limited collective power. Laboring under the "dictates" of other professionals, the report suggests that community workers are unable to provide a service distinct from the service provided by social workers. Consequently, it concludes that community workers lack any discernible "professional identity."

Using People's Terms and Concepts: The Verbatim Principle

As researchers engage in data analysis, it is particularly important to use the terms and concepts from the research participant's own talk to label concepts and categories. It is essential to resist the temptation to characterize people's experience in terms that seem to make more sense to the researcher, or to clarify the issue from the researcher's perspective, or to translate the issue into language fitted to theoretical or professional discourses. Later, when the need for joint accounts incorporating diverse terms, concepts, or ideas emerges, terminology may be necessary that allows us to collectively describe similar elements or features with one term or phrase. "I was angry," "She made me feel bad," "I nearly cried when he did that," and "I'm just scared what he'll do next" may be elements of a feature described as "The Emotional Impact of . . . " Generally, however, we should seek terms from within the speech of the participants themselves, adding additional words only to clarify meaning or extend understanding when the original words themselves are insufficient for the purpose.

Maria Hines, a member of a city neighborhood collective, is most explicit about her experience of analyzing data in a project in which she participated. With a slight frown she describes how "I never knew how difficult is was *not* to put my own words and meanings in. We had to really concentrate to make sure we used what people had actually said and not put in our own words. It was *hard.*"

These words remind us to focus clearly on one of the central features of action research, consciously seeking to understand the perspective of others and to use those perspectives to formulate actions. This is very important in data analysis, where the possibility of reinterpreting or misinterpreting people's words, concepts, and ideas—taking them and using them for our own purposes—is ever present.

Data Analysis (2): Categorizing and Coding

The previous sections presented processes for interpretive data analysis designed to more effectively represent individual perspectives and experiences. Another process of data analysis, used commonly in qualitative research, is based on procedures for unitizing data and sorting units into categories, each of which is denoted by a label—a conceptual "code." The process is very useful for analyzing large bodies of qualitative data, and it is especially amenable to electronic data analysis software now available. It runs the risk, however, of losing participant perspectives in conglomerating data from a wide diversity of sources and of revealing conceptual structures meaningful mainly to those responsible for data analysis. Using participatory processes of data analysis can minimize both of these weaknesses.

Purposes and Processes in Categorizing[1]

The purpose of analysis in action research is not to identify the "facts" or "what is really happening," but to distill or crystallize the data in ways enabling research participants to interpret, understand, and make meaning out of the collected materials. Initially this involves working with data and organizing them to make connections between events or ideas and to identify commonalities, regularities, or patterns. These new ways of seeing or interpreting the information gathered shed light on events, transforming people's understanding and providing the means to take therapeutic action on the problem at hand.

The process begins by reviewing interview and focus group data, dividing the data into "units of meaning"—unitizing the data—and then using them to construct an organized system of categories and themes (see Figure 5.4). This system of categories provides the basis for research reports and accounts, and for action agendas that guide the ongoing activities of action researchers. Ongoing analysis incorporates data gathered through observation, from a review of artifacts, or through a search of relevant literature, complementing or challenging information acquired directly from research participants.

Reviewing the Research Questions

When it is time to begin the formal analysis, research participants have two primary sources to draw from in order to focus and organize the analysis:

- Research questions generated during the planning and design phase of the project
- Analytic insights and interpretations that emerged during data collection

---

[1] Harry Wolcott (1994) suggests description, analysis, and interpretation as the three purposes of data analysis, the latter being generalized theorizing not specifically relevant to the context at hand. The type of analysis presented herein makes no distinction between analysis and interpretation, as Harry depicts them. The purposes of action research require "theorizing" or "interpretation" that makes sense from the perspective of participants. Generalized theory, more relevant to theory building in the academic disciplines, has less relevance to our current purposes, though they often assist in framing the study. Shirley Bryce Heath (1983), for instance, used ethnographic methods for studying children's language use in different communities. Both data gathering and analysis were affected by understandings about the types of things associated with or affecting children's language, resulting in descriptions of the communities from the people. The "interpretive lens" filtering information was that provided by sociolinguistics.

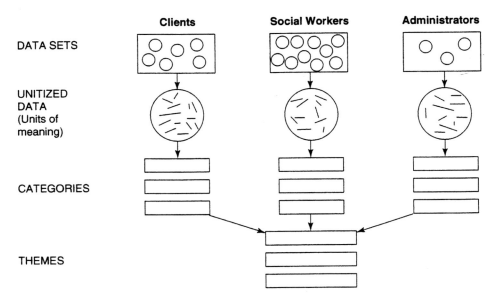

Figure 5.4
Categorizing and Coding

Early negotiations around the purpose of the study usually reveal important nuances of meaning, and so it is appropriate to review the purpose of the research questions with key stakeholders as the formal analysis begins (Patton, 1990). Reviewing the research questions ensures that participants focus their analysis in ways relevant to the purpose of the study and that they maximize the potential for tangible and productive outcomes.

Reviewing Data Sets

Different groups of stakeholders in a research project usually enact different roles within the context and, in consequence, experience events in different ways. In human service settings, for instance, clients often experience and interpret events quite differently from service providers or administrators. Male clients often have different experiences and perspectives than female clients, and social workers have quite different perspectives than psychologists. Client experiences and perspectives are likewise likely to differ according to age, family background, religion, race, ethnicity, and so on.

Often these differences in experience or perspective will become apparent in the course of the study, but an important feature of research is not to assume differences, allowing them to emerge in the course of data analysis. Generally, however, we formulate data sets to acknowledge the important distinctions existing among stakeholders in a setting. This allows us to take account of the differences in perspective and experience of the types of people inhabiting the context of the study. In Figure 5.4, for instance, data from clients, social workers, and administrators are analyzed separately, revealing points of commonality and difference in their perspective of services, the agency, events, issues, and so on.

The purpose of reviewing the data sets is to familiarize researchers with the data, enabling them to take an overall view of the information so that links between items and elements begin to emerge. Those responsible for data analysis should therefore start by reading through all the data.

Unitizing the Data

The next step in the process is to isolate features and elements of experience and perspective, to focus on the specific details emerging from people's talk about events and experiences. Data recorded in interviews and focus groups sessions are first printed and are then divided into *units of meaning*. A unit of meaning might be a word, a phrase, a part of a sentence, or a whole sentence. The sentence "I don't really like the way I organized this project because it's too one-dimensional and I prefer to work more holistically" has a number of distinct units of meaning. These include {I don't really like the way I organized this project}, {the project is too one-dimensional}, and {I prefer to work more holistically}. As indicated here, it is sometimes necessary to add words to a unit so it makes sense when it stands alone.

A variety of methods are used for this purpose. Some researchers isolate units of meaning by physically cutting sheets of interview data with scissors, while others use highlighters to isolate units of meaning related to emerging categories. Sometimes people work with the raw data, but typically the data are typed onto paper and the unitized data are glued to cards, which are then sorted into categories. Computer programs such as NUD*IST, Ethnograph, Nvivo, WinMAX, and Hypersearch are also used to engage in this process electronically.[2] Computer-assisted programs, however, provide only a data storage, managing, and searching tool. They cannot engage in analytic processes such as identifying units of meaning or formulating categories.

The process of unitizing the data results in a large "pile" of discrete pieces of information. From these building blocks researchers sort, select, and organize information into a system of categories that enables participants to make sense of the issues they investigate. The next phase of the process of analysis, therefore, is to categorize and code the units of data.

Categorizing and Coding

Spradley's (1979a) schema for *componential* analysis, similar in concept to analysis of units of meaning, provides a useful conceptualization of the process of categorization. Spradley's approach to analysis is based on the idea that people's everyday cultural knowledge is organized according to systems of meaning they give to phenomena in their lives. These systems of meaning, he proposes, are organized taxonomically, using an hierarchical structure to distinguish the different types of phenomena that constitute everyday life. Category systems divide and define our cultural worlds systematically, allowing us to impose a sense of order on the multiple and complex phenomena we deal with daily.

A simple set of common categories is shown in Figure 5.5. Ingestibles—substances that can be swallowed and ingested—consist of food, drink, and medication.

---

[2] Reviews of these programs may be found on *http://www.sagepub.com.*

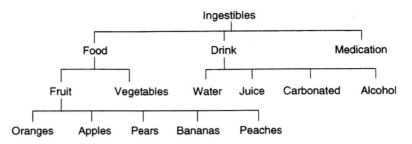

Figure 5.5
Category System for Ingestibles

Each of these includes a number of different items that constitute the category. The category "food," for instance, is made up of fruit and vegetables. The category system is incomplete, but it provides an illustration of the way people organize phenomenon in order to assist them to define and communicate their experience.

Systems of meaning are inherent in every culture, and one of the early tasks in the life of a baby is to learn to understand the different types of people with whom he or she comes into contact, distinguishing "mother" from "father," "brother," "sister," and so on. The research act requires participants to uncover the systems of meaning inherent in people's experience, organizing their experience in ways that promote clarity and understanding.

Having identified units of meaning inherent in the interview data, researchers will then identify those that are associated with each other and that might therefore be included in the same category. The example in Figure 5.6 provides a way of categorizing the different types of staff in a human service agency.

In the taxonomy shown in Figure 5.6, two major types of workers are identified from the data—*professional staff* and *support staff*. Different types of professional staff include *social workers, psychologists,* and *legal.* Participants make important distinctions between social workers according to whether they are classified as *child protection, community,* or *family support* workers. As the system of categories is organized, decisions must be made about the placement of each item into a particular category or subcategory. There may be a need to decide whether a social worker who has major *administrative* responsibilities is classified as support staff or professional staff. Items are placed within particular categories or subcategories according to a system of *inclusion,* based on the *attributes* of each element. The categories "child protection" and "community" worker, for instance, may be identified by asking *structural questions* to determine who should be placed in each category—e.g., "Can you name all the child protection workers here?" "Who are the community workers?"

We extend our understanding of why people should be placed into particular categories by asking *attribute questions* that identify the reason for placing a person in a particular category—e.g., "What is a child protection worker?" Answers to these questions would provide the criteria employed for making a decision to define a social worker as a "child protection" worker as opposed to a "community" or "family

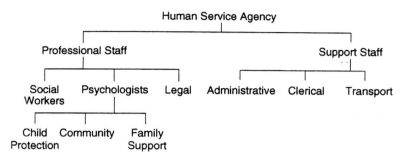

Figure 5.6
Taxonomy of an Agency

support" worker. A child protection worker might be identified, according to the system of meanings used in this agency, as one who:

- Works for the agency
- Works mainly on child protection cases
- Has social work credentials
- Is supervised by the director of professional services
- Works in conjunction with community and family support workers

These *attributes* define a "child protection" worker and allow researchers to make decisions about which workers may be included in that category.

When we place phenomena into a category, one of the principal tasks is to name that category to identify the type of phenomena it contains. Apples, pears, and oranges might be identified as "fruit," for instance. This process is called *coding,* and thus the term used to name the category is called, by some researchers, the *code* for the category. Spradley uses the words "cover term," rather than "code," to refer to the category name.

Researchers should first determine whether an existing term occurs naturally in the language or terminology of the people from whom the information has been acquired. If not, the researchers should provide a label for the category that clearly identifies the nature of the category. "Fearful," "mistrustful," "resistant," "apathetic," and "compliant," for instance, might be identified by the code or cover term "client responses."

As information is placed in categories, we become aware of the need to define more clearly the meanings intended by research participants in order to understand how the word or phrase is being used and whether it should be included in one category or another. The codes or cover terms will eventually provide a structured set of categories that assists us to organize and make meaning of the experiences of diverse groups of people. The system of categories also provides a framework of events, activities, behaviors, and materials that assist in understanding events and formulating actions to deal with those events.

Categorizing and coding, therefore, requires researchers to:

- Unitize the data
- Sort units into categories

- Divide categories into subcategories, where appropriate
- Code each category using a cover term expressing the type or nature of information in the category or subcategory
- Identify the attributes defining each category or subcategory

Other formats for coding and categorizing data may be found in Arhar, Holly, and Kasten (2000), Bogdan and Biklen (1992), and Creswell (2002). These resources provide detailed instructions for developing descriptions and representing findings.

Organizing a Category System

As researchers formulate categories, they first place them in an organized system that identifies features and elements of experience in ways that clarify the relationship between them. Categories do not fall automatically into a structure or system, and decisions must be made about which categories are given priority and where they are placed in relation to each other. In the community worker project featured in Figure 5.7, major categories identified by participants included "clients," "social workers," and "community workers," each containing subcategories revealing the different perspectives associated with each category. "Social workers," for instance, included the subcategories "professional competence," "continuity of care," "professional oversight," and "professional training." Details within those subcategories were composed of units of meaning revealing people's experiences or perspectives

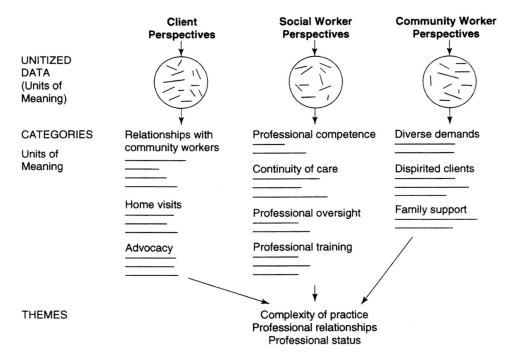

Figure 5.7
A Category System for a Community Work Study

related to the issue studied. Note that there is no right way of organizing the data. It might as easily have been organized with "professional competence" as a major category, and client, social worker, and community worker perspectives presented as subcategories. The general process is depicted in Figure 5.7.

In Figure 5.7, different categories of experience and perception have emerged for clients, social workers, and community workers. The first cluster of units of meaning is labeled "relationships with community workers," the next is called "home visits," and the final category emerges as "advocacy." Community worker categories (i.e., labels chosen to characterize the clustered units of meaning) include "diverse demands," "dispirited clients," and "family support." Categories of experience and perception associated with social workers include "professional competence," "continuity of care," "professional oversight," and "professional training." Although category labels provide no common elements across stakeholding groups, it is clear that some issues are related, and these have been identified as "themes," each designated by a code. The category "relationships with community workers" has been associated with "family support" and "advocacy," which, together, are identified as a theme coded "professional relationships." The categories "diverse demands," "dispirited clients," and "continuity of care" have been linked as a theme having the code "complexity of practice." The categories "professional training," "professional competence," and "professional oversight" have been linked under the code "professional status."

This system of categories provides useful information about the types of people whose perspectives are presented, the issues concerning them, and the relationship between some of those issues. The way of organizing these categories into a framework assists to clarify the significant features of experience emerging in the process of investigation. At a later stage, they also provide the agenda for planning actions related to those issues.

Researchers therefore construct a system of categories and subcategories, organizing the emerging information in ways that make sense to the participants. The researchers do so by using terms, or codes, they recognize as representing or encompassing their experience and perspectives, but providing new, interesting, and clarifying ways of organizing data.

Enhancing Analysis: Incorporating Diverse Sources of Data

Data analysis for both epiphanic analysis and categorizing and coding has so far been based on information derived from interviews. A variety of other data have the potential to enhance the data analysis. Information acquired through *observations, artifact reviews* (documents, records, materials, and equipment), and *literature reviews* might be used to complement, augment, or challenge features of the preliminary analysis of data. In the example in Figure 5.7, for instance, interview information related to "professional status" might be enhanced, extended, or brought into question by data from organizational records or reports. Likewise, perceptions about "complexity of practice" might be given more credence or might be challenged by information from client files or from comparison with reports on community work practice in other settings. Once interview data have been analyzed, researchers should review other available information, focusing especially on information pertinent to the identified issues, features, or elements.

Other data also include information gathered from the literature review (see Chapter 4). Although action research is driven by participant perspectives, authors of papers and reports might be viewed as secondary stakeholders since their writings have the potential to influence the research process. In this respect, viewpoints within the literature are treated as another set of perspectives, having the same status and validity as those of other "stakeholders."

Research participants may find it fruitful to review information within the professional, bureaucratic, or academic literature that might throw light on issues and elements emerging from data analysis. There is a broad range of research that challenges many of the commonly held assumptions circulating in agency and community contexts, or that reveals the uncertain nature of many of the so-called spray-on solutions that arise from time to time. A thorough review of the research literature on any topic often provides a unique resource assisting people to refine their analysis of the problem investigated. Pertinent information is identified and included in the process of analyzing, enhancing, clarifying, or extending participant perspectives.

Noninterview data are especially important when working with young children who frequently have a limited ability to talk of their experience in abstract terms. As human service professionals engage in child protection, family support, and other types of activities, they will necessarily have to acquire information from children. As already indicated, interviews with children are somewhat problematic, but there are many other ways in which children make meaning of their experience and communicate with others. When working with children, researchers may carefully observe the ways the children behave, interact, and talk to others. Equally important to note are the meanings inherent in children's drawings, songs, stories, and poems; their descriptions of events, and their responses to events and activities. These "artifacts" assist us in understanding how a child makes meaning of events in his or her life, helping us to construct accounts clearly representing the child's perspective. If we can fathom ways of making events meaningful from the perspective of the children, then our work becomes easier and more rewarding.

Bill Genat's (2002) study provided a clear description of the experience of Indigenous health workers with whom he worked. His compelling account of their work in family, agency, and community settings provides keen insight into their daily encounters with their clients and colleagues. The review of the literature that follows their accounts provides an interesting complement to their perspectives. There is obviously much they share with Indigenous human service workers in other parts of the world. In some instances, however, the literature points to contexts where Indigenous workers have quite different experiences, pointing to the need to be wary of generalizing across settings. Perspectives in the literature provide a point of reference enabling a richer understanding of human service worker roles.

Reviewing information related to children's events and activities provides richly rewarding information that assists researchers, including the children themselves, to make sense of the issue at hand. Analysis of these types of data requires interactive processes that first identify significant features or elements of experience and then check the ways children make meaning of or interpret those features of experience. Researchers should review data related to:

- Observations of children's activities or their participation in events
- Aural or visual recordings of their activities, including verbal interactions
- Drawings and other artwork
- Letters
- Stories, verbal and written
- Play
- Drama

Researchers should work with children to identify significant features and elements of these types of information, constructing understandings on the basis of the way the children interpret the information reviewed.

Noninterview data provide a variety of rich resources having the potential to enhance and clarify understandings emerging in the inquiry. The process of incorporating noninterview data is described schematically in Figure 5.8, though the cyclical nature of action research will mean that the revised analysis may be subject to further exploration using participant interviews or focus groups. A similar process is depicted in the data collection procedures shown in Figure 4.7. Incorporating noninterview data may enable participants to extend their understanding or reinterpret their experience, leading to stronger analysis that provides the basis for more effective action.

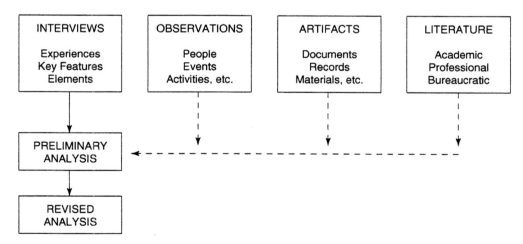

Figure 5.8
Incorporating Diverse Data

Using Category Systems: Frameworks for Reports and Accounts

Systems of categories emerging from both approaches to data analysis provide frameworks of concepts that supply a structure for reporting. A community worker study, for instance, used the following system of categories as a framework for structuring a report:

I. Introduction
II. Community Worker Perspectives: Confronted by Complexity
   Diverse Demands, Multiple Dilemmas: "A Jack of All Trades."
   Engaging a Dispirited Response: "You feel what's the point."
   A Breakdown in Family Caring: "They don't care."
III. Client and Colleague Perceptions
   Client Perceptions of Services: "Talking to your own people."
   Psychologist's Perceptions: "They don't understand behavioral indicators."
   Administrator Perceptions: "Community workers could do more."
   Social Workers Perceptions: A Professional Perspective on Status
IV. Situating Community Workers in the Agency
   Lacking Professional Identity, Voice, and Status
   Interaction, Participation, and Status
   Claiming a Professional Domain
V. Marginality Amidst Complexity: Community Work Practice
   Key Experiences of Community Workers
   Comparative Accounts from the Literature
   Implications

Details within the report derive from the units of meaning which provided the basis for each category or subcategory. Thus the report included a heading "Community Worker Perspectives" and a subheading—"Diverse Demands"—commences with the following text: "There's a lot of welfare stuff—and I reckon we deal more with the social welfare stuff than actually going out doing accommodation checks, checking drug tests, and that sort of thing—in my experience. I think we do a lot of welfare stuff—things like getting housing, getting food for the families." The text continues to present details of how community workers are experiencing and interpreting the diverse demands within their communities, including the full range of elements drawn from the unitized data within the "Diverse Demands" category.

Analyzing Data Collaboratively

Data gathering and analysis in action research is much more effective when it is accomplished as an interactive process between stakeholders. Although it is important for people to have opportunities to explore issues individually in the earliest stages of an inquiry process, continued explorations increase in power as people participate in processes of collaborative inquiry. Focus groups provide a context in which individual information can be shared and further exploration engaged. Sharing may take place initially within each group of stakeholders, though eventually diverse stakeholding groups should be brought together to share their perspectives, to identify common issues or agendas, and to explore ways of dealing with issues on which they fail to concur.

Data gathering becomes an ongoing part of the Look-Think-Act process. As information is gathered, analyzed, and actions emerge, the process often leads to the need for further exploration, or the acquisition of more information, an ever increasing circle of investigation extending participants' understandings and providing the basis for strong and effective action.

Figure 5.9 represents this process. Participants share accounts emerging from individual interviews, formulate a joint account, then return to the interview phase to reflect on and extend their own accounts. There may be a number of iterations of this process during an extended study of a complex issue.

A similar process is envisaged in Figure 5.10, where initial focus group exploration provides the material to develop an initial account. This account provides a framework of concepts and themes that are used for further exploration of people's experience and perspectives of the issue. Again, the process is designed to assist groups to achieve deeper understanding and greater clarity, providing the basis for actions that resolve the issue(s) explored.

Analyzing data in focus groups enables stakeholders to come together to share information deriving from their own perspectives and experiences. This not only extends

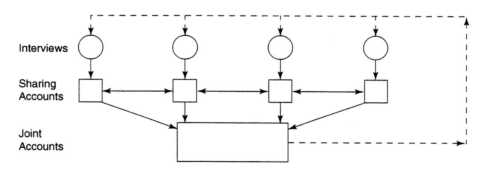

Figure 5.9
Developing Collaborative Accounts

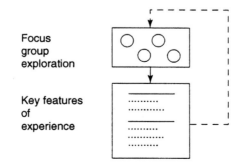

Figure 5.10
Focus Group Analysis

understanding between the diverse individuals and groups, but also corporately enables them to construct a framework of ideas for ongoing collaborative action. As these procedures progress, they trigger new ideas or memories in participants, leading to a productive extension of the research process. It enables participants to identify perspectives and experiences they have in common and assists in identifying areas in need of further negotiation or study.

> **Ernie:** Over the years I have been impressed by the amount of energy and goodwill emerging from well-prepared focus groups. Positive and productive outcomes are never certain, since a history of antagonisms or the presence of authoritarian figures may inhibit group discussions or interaction. I have experienced, however, a high degree of success in this type of activity. A recent half-day workshop with faculty within a university college illustrates the types of outcomes possible. Faculty explored the use of technology in their work, sharing ways they currently used computers to enhance their teaching and research, and identifying future uses. The level of animation in their discussions and the extensive lists of useful information emerging from their discussions were testament to their enthusiasm and the extent to which they appreciated opportunities to learn from each other. It also provided clear direction for the project team who had set up the workshop, indicating directions to take in resourcing faculty to extend their use of technology to enhance their work.
>
> The productive buzz that continued through this workshop was not the result of idle gossip or general conversation. As I walked around the room listening to group conversations to monitor the progress of their discussion, I was taken by the intensity of their focus. In professional contexts, opportunities for practitioners to get together to discuss the broader dimensions of their work are infrequent. Group discussions focused clearly on issues of interest or concern provide a wonderful context for reaffirming the broader contexts of professional work, taking people out of the sometimes humdrum organizational trivia of everyday institutional life and reminding them of the underlying nature of the work they do together.

Conclusion

Data analysis is the process of distilling the large quantities of information to reveal the central features of the issue investigated. The process of crystallizing information into a category system provides the basis for increased understanding of the complex events and interactions comprising everyday events in agencies, organizations, homes, and community settings. The process is not merely a technical routine, however. Its purpose is not to delineate a relatively small number of variables affecting the focus of study. Its major purpose is to provide the basis for richly evocative accounts and reports providing stakeholders with information and understanding upon which to make informed decisions about policies, programs, and practices for which they are responsible. It also provides the building blocks for therapeutic action within the research process, clearly delineating issues and agendas requiring attention. When engaged collaboratively, it also provides a rich field of interaction enabling stakeholders to develop productive relationships that are a central feature of a successful action research process.

SUMMARY

Giving Voice: Interpretive and Qualitative Data Analysis

The *purposes* of data analysis

- **To reduce, distil, or crystallize large quantities of data**
- **To provide clarity and enhance stakeholder understandings of issues and events.**

Two approaches for analyzing data are presented:

1. **Analyzing Epiphanies**
   - **Select key people from within each stakeholder group**
   - **Review the data for each selected person**
   - **For each, identify epiphanies or significant experiences**
   - **Identify major features of those events or experiences**
   - **Identify the elements of experience associated with each feature**
   - **Use identified features and elements to formulate a framework of concepts and ideas that represent each person's experience of the issue investigated**
   - ***Make connections:* Identify similarities and differences between features or elements in stakeholder experiences**
   - **Use frameworks to construct accounts and/or reports**
2. **Categorizing and Coding**
   - **Review the interview data for each stakeholding group**
   - ***Unitize the data:* Divide into units of meaning**
   - **Formulate *categories, subcategories* and *themes* identifying patterns, connections, commonalities, or regularities within the data**
   - **Organize these into a category system**
   - **Incorporate information from noninterview data**
   - **Use the category system to provide a framework for accounts and reports**

Collaborative Data Analysis

Focus groups may be used to analyze data and share information collaboratively

---

Representation: Communicating Research Processes and Outcomes

6

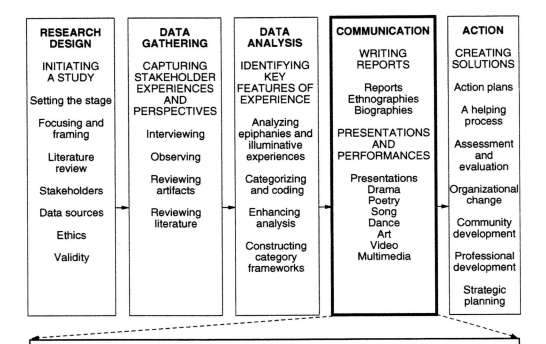

RESEARCH DESIGN	DATA GATHERING	DATA ANALYSIS	COMMUNICATION	ACTION
INITIATING A STUDY	CAPTURING STAKEHOLDER EXPERIENCES AND PERSPECTIVES	IDENTIFYING KEY FEATURES OF EXPERIENCE	WRITING REPORTS	CREATING SOLUTIONS
Setting the stage	Interviewing	Analyzing epiphanies and illuminative experiences	Reports Ethnographies Biographies	Action plans
Focusing and framing				A helping process
Literature review	Observing	Categorizing and coding	PRESENTATIONS AND PERFORMANCES	Assessment and evaluation
Stakeholders	Reviewing artifacts	Enhancing analysis	Presentations Drama Poetry Song Dance Art Video Multimedia	Organizational change
Data sources	Reviewing literature			Community development
Ethics		Constructing category frameworks		Professional development
Validity				Strategic planning

Contents of This Chapter

This chapter describes ways that research participants can inform each other and key stakeholders about research processes, findings, and outcomes.

This chapter focuses on:

- The *purposes* for reporting research processes and results
- The different means used to *communicate* this information, including written reports, presentations, and performance
- Procedures for developing *written reports*
- Procedures for preparing and staging *presentations*
- Procedures for preparing and producing *performances*

Introduction

As research participants work through iterations of the Look-Think-Act framework, an important "act" is to inform each other and key stakeholding audiences of the outcomes of their activities (see Figure 6.1). Regular communication ensures that all participants and stakeholders acquire a body of shared meanings that enable them to devise effective solutions to research issues or problems. Participants need to *represent* the information in ways that increase clarity and understanding for all participants and stakeholders.

This chapter presents a variety of approaches to communication, each intended to ensure that participants and audiences of a project acquire clear understandings of both the processes and outcomes of research. According to the desired purposes, therefore, research participants may construct narrative, ethnographic, or biographic accounts that inform various audiences and stakeholders. They may also formulate presentations or performances as alternative effective means of communication.

Communication in Action Research

As the study continues, it is essential for all participants and stakeholders to be informed of the progress of the study in order to do their part in bringing the project to fruition. If research reveals the need for significant changes in the way their agency operates, or in the way intervention or care is provided, for instance, they may need to inform agency administrators and/or their clients' family members in order to accomplish their goals. In larger studies, such as the evaluation of a project, the development of a new service, or the institution of a new program, the research will require ongoing communication among diverse stakeholding groups. In all these

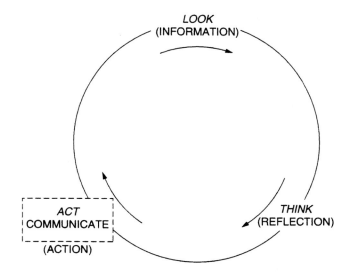

Figure 6.1
Communicating in Action
Research

circumstances participants need to communicate significant features of the investigation using reporting processes that enable all parties to be fully informed.

There are two major strands of communication. One strand requires an ongoing written record of the project, so that people can review their progress systematically and resolve disputes that arise. The other strand is to provide reports and accounts for participants to share their experiences and perspectives, providing the means by which larger audiences can extend their understanding or gain a better picture of "what's going on."

Purposeful communication provides the means for all parties—clients, human service practitioners, administrators, and families—to understand the forces that operate in each others' lives, affecting their behaviors, performances, and practices. As participants become increasingly aware of the influences at work, they can take into consideration diverse agendas and imperatives and work toward mutually meaningful solutions to problems. Effective communication enables understanding.

Research participants may report to each other for the following purposes:

- To share information, keeping people informed of the processes and outcomes of the investigation
- To enable stakeholders and other audiences to understand each others' perspectives and experiences
- To check the accuracy and appropriateness of information emerging from the investigation
- To provide an ongoing record of the project

A youth worker was asked to investigate why a rural town was experiencing substantially increased levels of juvenile crime. He discovered that high levels of unemployment and lack of leisure facilities were important contributing factors to the situation. As he talked with people around town, he discovered that many people were aware of the situation, but efforts to deal with the situation were fragmented and ineffective. The youth worker organized a meeting attended by representatives from local organizations and agencies, the school, and police to review the situation. As people spoke, they discovered a wealth of resources in the community and could cooperatively develop employment, training, and after-school and leisure programs for local youth. Within a very short time frame youth crime levels in the town decreased dramatically. By establishing communication between groups the youth worker had effectively provided conditions to resolve a significant community problem.

Different Strokes for Different Folks: Forms of Communication

The way information is shared is critical since it is imperative not only that people acquire relevant information, but also that they understand the dynamic ways in which features of the situation impact on the lives of the people involved. The "objective" formal reports so common in institutions often are inadequate vehicles for these purposes, frequently being framed in formalized language focusing on institutional structures and agendas.

Reporting procedures and formats, therefore, need to clearly differentiate among the different research audiences and purposes—academic, public, professional and organizational:

- **Academic:** University research focuses principally on the development of a *body of knowledge,* shared with a community of scholars. The outcomes of research are reported in journals and books stored in university library collections. The knowledge is also passed on to students in order to *inform and educate future professionals.*

- **Public:** Research may be used to *inform and educate clients and public groups* about significant issues. Findings from localized investigations for community groups or from research sponsored by government bodies, public interest groups, or community groups may be reported at meetings or in the media. These results are sometimes incorporated into television documentaries or are presented on stage or in public as street theater. Thus the outcomes of research on levels of domestic violence, homelessness, environmental issues, staffing levels, and so on, are increasingly released directly into the public domain.

- **Professional and Organizational:** Research is increasingly used for direct professional and organizational purposes *to improve or strengthen programs, services, and practices.* Research outcomes can be applied directly to the development of new programs and services, or outcomes can be used to formulate solutions to significant problems in institutions, organizations, and community contexts. Human service practitioners engage in research to better inform their casework or preventive practices or to seek solutions to problems in their work with clients. Human service agencies and departments engage in research to assist in the formulation of new programs or to solve deep-seated social problems, such as teen pregnancy, drug abuse, and child neglect.

The diverse audiences and purposes of action research require researchers to think clearly about the types of reporting that will enable them to communicate effectively with particular audiences. Examples of a range of different report formats are provided in Chapter 8. These do not include a full range of possibilities, as will become evident in the latter sections of this chapter. Depending on the stakeholders, the purpose, and the context, reporting may take the form of written reports, presentations, or performances.

Written reports provide an easy means to communicate information. They may take the form of short, informal reports that present specific information, or they may be more complex formal reports that give detailed information about all facets of a project. Written reports are the most common medium for maintaining a record of progress or recording the outcomes of a research process. They have great utility at all stages of research.

Verbal and visual *presentations* provide richer possibilities for engaging people in processes of communication. They provide more diverse and creative means of enabling people to share focused, richly textured understandings of their research activities. Verbal and visual presentations are especially effective means for nonprofessionals or cultural and ethnic minorities to exchange information and share experiences. For these groups, visual, poetic, musical or dramatic *performances* also provide effective ways to communicate visceral understandings of their experiences and perspectives.

Reports, presentations, and performances, therefore, provide diverse means for participating human service practitioners, clients, families, community groups, administrators, and others to convey the processes and outcomes of their research. They provide multiple methods for presenting new understandings with clarity, precision, and authenticity, enabling people to contribute effectively to the ongoing development of actions and events designed to improve their situation.

Reports and Accounts: Writing People's Lives

Written reports are derived from the products of data analysis (see Chapter 5). Key features and elements identified in these processes serve as the basis for accounts reflecting the perspectives, perceptions, and experiences of individuals and groups participating in the process. They may take the form of:

- Individual reports
- Group reports
- Progress reports
- Evaluation reports
- Final reports

As Denzin (1997) suggests, reports are not meant to be definitive or objective accounts, but evocative accounts that lead readers to an empathetic understanding of people's lived experience. Accounts or narratives thereby provide insight into people's lives, recording the impact of events on their day-to-day feelings of well-being and their capacity to interact appropriately and productively with the life-world that confronts them. Narratives reveal the rich, densely-layered tapestry of human experience, as well as the complex emotional world that lies beneath the surface of seemingly innocuous events and emerges in those special moments of triumph, success, love, struggle, loss, or discord that have such a dramatic effect on people's lives.

In action research we seek to produce evocative accounts conveying accurate insights into and understandings of the impact of events on people's lives. Writing evocative accounts entails more than the bland reporting of events. It requires report writers to find the textual means to elicit those forms of understanding. A government report that referred to the "inadequate sewage" in a community failed to evoke an understanding of the stench of excreta and the people's ongoing fear for their children's well-being. Objective reports are sometimes dangerously uninformative. Extended ethnographic accounts composed of full, richly textured narrative provide the possibility of in-depth insight into the community and institutional contexts in which events are played out. They describe the history of the situation and reveal the interactional and emotional features of people's experience. Even shorter reports such as meeting minutes, team reports, progress reports, and so on should capture the essence of people's experience.

Life Stories: Biographies, Autobiographies, and Ethnographies

Written narrative accounts enable people to tell stories that illuminate the often complex and deeply problematic nature of their lived experience. In contrast to psychological case studies that interpret individual behavior from within a framework of disciplinary theory (personality, behaviorism, etc.), biographies and ethnographies provide the means to understand people's lives from their own perspectives.

Research processes provide the means for stakeholders to reflect on and describe their experience and to distil or crystallize salient features that may form the basis for ongoing interpretive action. This material may be used as the basis for biographic or semifictional reports that portray the history of their experience or that bring into sharp focus the significant features of their lives—epiphanic or defining moments—revealing the underlying dynamics of their experience. Often the mere act of "telling their own story" is therapeutic, revealing to the individuals concerned features of their lives that they had inadvertently repressed or that they had taken for granted as a necessary, though damaging, feature of their lives. Conversely, it may uncover hidden positive dimensions of experience, enabling them to see their worlds in a more positive light or to recognize potentials of which they had not been aware.

The process of writing personal accounts of experience as part of an action research project is not intended to reveal the "facts" or the "truth," but to enable participants to look at their lives in different ways—to reinterpret events, experiences, and responses and to come to new ways of understanding their situations. Autobiographic

Rosalie: We have witnessed many situations where people have been greatly enlivened by opportunities to "tell their stories" and listen to the stories of others. In agencies, workshops, program development projects, and many other arenas we have experienced the satisfaction that comes from this process. What we see is not only a *sense of worth* emerging from people who feel, sometimes for the first time in their lives, that someone is really listening to them; that they have something worthwhile to share with others. On more than one occasion a person has burst out in the moment, or quietly said later, "This changed my life!"

Something quite wonderful happens in the process of storytelling. Not only do the storytellers experience the exuberance of being heard and acknowledged, but they may learn something significant about themselves and their experiences. It is illuminating and sometimes revelatory. We have often seen people—storytellers and/or audience—in tears as their stories emerge. The teller does not need to be a practiced orator. Sometimes the straight recounting of events by simply spoken people—moms, old folk, children—has a dramatic impact on an audience, the "presence" of the people themselves speaking volumes. When people tell stories of their lives, it is no small thing.

and ethnographic accounts provide potential useful resources, enabling individuals and groups to reevaluate their place and their interaction with others in the context, to "connect and join biographically meaningful experiences to society-at-hand and to the larger culture- and meaning-making institutions" (Denzin 1989a, p. 25).

While ethnographic accounts largely have been written by external authors, we now recognize the potential of autoethnographies, personal accounts written by individuals and groups working through self-referential processes of exploration. Sometimes the stories are so sensitive, reaching into the intimate details of people's lives, that people have no desire to have them made public. In these situations it is possible to disguise both the people and the places by using fictitious names or by providing generalized accounts that reveal the major features of their experience without providing the means to identify particular people or places.

Joint and Collective Accounts: Connecting Stakeholder Experiences

While individual stakeholder stories sometimes reveal singular experiences relating only to one person, they often share significant experiences or perspectives with other stakeholders. Further, although they may not share the same experience, participants may be affected by the same events in different ways. We need to make connections between stakeholder experiences, therefore, in order to develop an understanding of the dynamic interactions between individuals and groups. Thus when individual stakeholder epiphanies and features of experience have been identified, we search for connections with others:

- Focus on each epiphany or significant experience for each person.
- Review the data for all other selected stakeholders.
- Identify features or elements of experience common to other stakeholders.
- Identify points at which other stakeholders' experience or perspective has been affected by the original epiphany or experience.
- Record those features or elements as a sublist of the original epiphany.
- Take note of the number of times an experience or element is repeated for different stakeholders.

Using this information to formulate accounts and reports (see Figure 6.2) will provide information about the extent to which stakeholders share any experience or perspective. By comparing information within groups and across groups, we can make judgments about the extent that events, experiences, or perspectives are commonly held by those within a group or are shared with other groups. These types of comparisons provide information that also is important at the "action" phase since it identifies those common elements of experience from which productive action might be formulated. It also identifies those singularly important experiences and perspectives that may need to be taken into account in formulating solutions to the problem investigated. The terminology reveals the extent of commonality—"All clients in this study . . . ", "Many clients shared a concern about. . . ", or "While some clients indicated . . . , others were more inclined to . . . "

Joint accounts offer a summary of individual accounts, but focus particularly on commonalities and differences revealed through cross-analysis of major features and

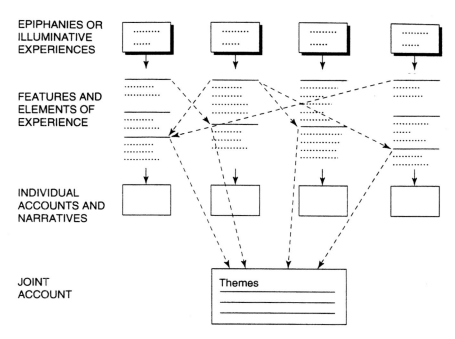

Figure 6.2
Formulating Joint Accounts

key elements. Common or similar features, in this case, may be thought of as "themes." Joint accounts provide ways of presenting the perspective and experience of stakeholding groups in a study—practitioners, clients, administrators, families, and so on.

Collective accounts may present an overview of the main features and elements of experience and perspective for each of the major groups, and thus an organizational report may comprise features and elements drawn from each of the stakeholding groups (see Figure 6.3). Commonalities revealed in these accounts provide the basis for collective action, while points of difference suggest issues requiring negotiation (see Guba & Lincoln, 1989), so that appropriate steps can be taken to defuse or resolve potential conflicts.

Ernie: I was once asked to facilitate a review of a community organization that was failing to provide effective services to groups in the locality, as stipulated by its agreement with its funding agency. I interviewed organization workers, members of client groups, and funding agency representatives, and wrote a report for each of these groups that summarized their perspective on the issue (joint accounts). Each of these groups used their report as the basis for a presentation at the meeting of stakeholders. Discussion on issues arising at the meeting, and following meetings, enabled all stakeholders to develop a plan of action. A final report (collective account) integrated the information

(continued)

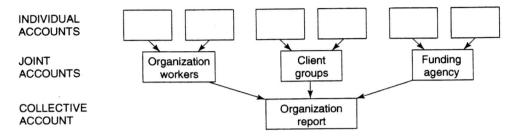

Figure 6.3
Individual, Joint, and Collective Accounts

available and provided the basis for developing a new strategic plan for the organization. Within months, the organization was operating efficiently, providing effective services to community groups in the local area.

Written Reports: Accumulating Knowledge and Experience

Written reports allow human service professionals to accumulate, over time, a store of knowledge and experience that greatly enhances their capacity to deal effectively with problematic features of their worklives. Written reports can provide a historical record of significant events and projects that add to the vitality of the culture of an organization and the community it serves. Written records of activities and projects can form the basis for constructing a strong sense of togetherness and assists the formation of a community. Research reports have the capacity not only to help in developing solutions to particular problems, but also to contribute to the culture of agency and community.

Constructing Reports

Constructing effective and useful reports is an art form in itself. By following some fundamental processes, most people can write a report that is both interesting and informative. The following sections describe procedures for formulating a report. These include:

- Defining the *audience and purpose* of the report
- *Identifying participant perspectives*
- *Reviewing the data*
- Identifying the significant *features and elements of experience*
- Constructing a *report framework*
- *Writing the report*
- *Reviewing and editing* the report
- *Member checking*

Define the Audience and Purpose

Carefully define the audience and purpose of the report. Ask:

- For which particular people (or groups of people) will this report be written—clients, human service professionals, administrators, families? In which locations or particular agencies, organizations, or homes?
- For what purposes will the report be used? To inform people of progress on a project? To assist them to understand features of people's experience? To reveal required actions?

Identify Participant Perspectives

Decide which participant perspectives—those of individuals, those of stakeholding groups—are to be included.

- Note whose experiences or agendas are central to the report.
- Point out which people have important or significant associated experiences or agendas.
- Isolate the data for each of these individuals or groups.

Review the Data

- Read the data relevant to the identified participants to become familiar with the material.
- Note particularly effective quotations illustrating key features of people's experience.
- Note the terminology and language used by participants to describe their experience.

Identify Significant Features and Elements of Experience

- Review the analyzed data to identify relevant material for the report.
- Make a copy of the key features and elements of experience for each individual or group.

Construct the Report Framework

Use the features and elements of experience to construct a framework for the report (see Figures 6.2 and 5.7).

- Make the key features the headings or subheadings
- Use the elements or units of meaning as the content of each heading or subheading.

Write the Report

Refer to the framework as you write the report, incorporating the terminology and language of participants in the body of the narrative. The framework guides the writing process but is not by itself sufficient to adequately capture people's lived experience.

The Couto, Stutts, and Associates study (2000) includes under the heading "The context and origins of broken promises" sections on Individual Stories, Family, Neighborhoods, Schools, and Programs. The text of each focuses on interpretations of young offenders, their voices ringing through the pages of the report.

When asked if Denise should have visited counselors one girl said, "No," because "they ask questions like 'are you crazy?' " Shorty's mom, the boys imagined, took him to church and Bible study, but "he left that when he left school." (p. 45)

Authors of reports and accounts need to encompass in their writing the multiple dimensions of human experience, including emotional, physical, and interactional elements of behavior and perspective, as well as organizational and procedural components. The framework is useful as a checklist for what can be included in a narrative—people, acts, activities, events, purposes, emotions, places, times, and objects. In all this, though, keep in mind that the words and terminology of participants must be central to the report. Not only should the participants' words be used in headings, but their words should make up the body of writing. Some writers string together sections of the unitized data to form the body of the account. Others use quotations prolifically to clearly illustrate the points they are making or the contexts they describe.

The report should include:

- An introduction revealing the purpose and the general contents of the report
- A brief description of the context, drawn from interview and observational data
- Accounts encompassing the key features of stakeholder experiences and perspectives
- Quotations capturing significant features or elements of experience
- A concluding summary highlighting the major features revealed in the report and the implications for action relevant to the issue being investigated

Reports will vary widely in style, detail, and length, according to their purpose or intended audience. In some instances, reports may be no more than a short summary of key points emerging from prior stages of the research, informing participants or other stakeholders of the progress of the project. In other cases, extended reports provide detailed information for the benefit of administration or funding authorities. Formal reports for funding, professional, or academic bodies—annual reports, evaluation reports, theses, or dissertations—often require a meticulous rendering of the research process in highly structured ways.

Review and Edit

Review the report. Check that:

- Its stated purposes have been accomplished: Does the report provide adequate and appropriate information to inform the intended audience?
- All relevant participant perspectives have been included.

In a "Listen to the Families" (Stringer, 2004) project, two forms of a final report were prepared. One, written in English and Spanish on each side of a sheet of paper, presented parents with a one-page summary of the major outcomes of the research process. A longer ten-page report provided more detail for administrators and professional workers and revealed many details of the processes and outcomes of investigation. The former was short and easy to read, enabling parents to see that their "voice had been heard." The latter provided more detailed information that the neighborhood organization was able to present to administrators and professional workers in the associated government organization.

- The language is appropriate for the intended audience.
- The report accurately reflects the perspectives and experiences of participants, rather than that of the author or one stakeholding group.

Ernie: Whenever I'm facilitating report writing, I continually ask the authors the question, "Who is speaking here? Whose perspective is being presented?" It is surprising how often even the most careful report writer will allow his or her own perspective to intrude. When we write accounts, we must take great care to ensure we don't unwittingly present material reflecting our own perceptions and interpretations of the situation. The exceptions are those situations where we overtly include our perspective as a participating stakeholder in a research process.

Member-Check

Give a copy of the draft report to those participants and stakeholders about whom it is written:

- Allow time for them to read and respond.
- Talk with them in person, if possible, or by phone if not.
- Check for accuracy, sufficiency, and appropriateness of information contained in the report.
- Modify or correct according to their input.

Report Formats

Depending on the audience and purpose for which they are produced, research reports differ in length, detail, and reporting style. Reports to groups and individuals communicating progress of activities will tend to be informal and brief, while reports to organizations and institutions are likely to be more formal and detailed. They may be presented in outline or summary form; as a bulleted list; or as a complex, detailed, and/or highly descriptive account. Chapter 8 provides a number of different forms of research reports used for a variety of purposes.

Other reports, however, may take the form of:

- **Case reports**
- **Project plans**
- **Meeting minutes**   informing participants of reports and discussions about project activities and issues
- **Memoranda**   reporting on current activities and issues
- **Formal reports**   for administrative and professional audiences
- **Evaluations**
- **Academic reports**   for publication in research journals
- **Theses and dissertations**

Presentations: Creative Communication

Presentations provide exciting ways to communicate research results to participants and stakeholding audiences. They can captivate audiences by using diverse materials and modes to present participant perspectives and illuminate key features of the research. Presentations provide the means to authentically capture and clearly communicate people's experience. They may range from simple verbal presentations to complex performances incorporating multiple forms of visual and electronic media that effectively communicate with a wide variety of audiences.

Presenters at academic and professional conferences now use a broad range of techniques to engage their audiences. Though direct verbal addresses read from prepared papers are still common, many presentations involve creative and innovative approaches that incorporate charts, overheads, or electronic materials. Other formats include roundtable interactive presentations, poster sessions, and structured dialogues. These forms of communication are efficient and effective in sharing information or reporting on activities.

Such flexible formats are especially relevant in contexts where lengthy written reports may actually inhibit communication with important stakeholding audiences. Some adults and children, especially those from poorer or culturally different contexts, may not have sufficient familiarity with professional or technical language to enable them to read lengthy, formal reports. Further, written reports are often an inadequate vehicle for expressing the full range of participant experiences. They fail to convey the emotional, interactional features of experience, the nature of their social circumstances, or the complexities of their cultural realities. Presentations, where carefully prepared and authentically presented, provide the means for more clearly and effectively communicating the concrete reality of peoples lives and the elements that need to be taken into careful account when taking action. As with written reports, presentations should be thoughtfully and creatively planned so that they suit the particular audience, enable presenters to be clear about the purposes of their presentation, and deliver the desired outcomes.

Richard Couto, Nancy Stutts, and their associates (2000) engaged in a collaborative study of court services and the needs of at-risk children and their families. Working with detained juveniles, juvenile court system officers, detention center staff, police officials, social service agency staff, educators, prosecutors, and defense attorneys, they identified, then reported on recurring systemic problems in the juvenile justice system, gaps in services, and possible effective interventions.

They used a variety of techniques to communicate elements of this study to different audiences. Juvenile detainees assisted in writing stories, film scripts, charts, and drawings of the experience of two youthful offenders—Shorty and Denise.

These wonderfully expressive stories provided the basis for ongoing discussions within the research process, and were incorporated into a formal report. The formal report integrated key elements of the perspectives of key stakeholders and included sections on the juvenile justice needs of children, their family, neighborhood and school contexts, the courts, and related programs and services.

Thus, the authors of the report were able to inform different groups of participants about many of the significant issues emerging from the study by using a variety of reporting and communication procedures.

Audiences and Purposes

As they construct their presentations, research participants should carefully identify their *audiences* and *purposes*. The major questions asked are, "What information should be presented?" and "How can we communicate most effectively with this particular audience?" In human service contexts, audiences of clients, professionals, family members, and administrators may require somewhat different presentations since different agendas will be relevant to the different audiences, each of whom may have a different part to play in actions emerging from the research process. All groups, however, will need to understand one another's perspectives so that they can work together to achieve their desired purposes.

Presentations, therefore, will vary according to the purposes to be achieved. Short, informal presentations assist participants to communicate the progress of activities to each other, enabling progress to be monitored effectively and ensuring that all are working in unison. These types of presentation will be very different from more carefully structured and planned presentations required at key points in the research process. If participants wish to inform a key stakeholding group—administrators, funding body representative, supporters—of issues emerging from their inquiries to garner support for actions they wish to take, then more detailed and carefully structured presentations may be necessary.

Presentations will also be affected by desired outcomes. If research participants wish to generate a clear or deeper understanding of people's experience, then participants will prepare evocative presentations designed to achieve that effect. Such presentations will be multidimensional, providing a clear picture of the significant event, the context in which it occurs, and its impact—rational, physical, emotional, and spiritual—on the lives of participant stakeholders. This is a more emotive presentation seeking to engender understanding of the dynamics and complexities of people's experiences and perspectives. If participants wish an audience to focus on more practical issues for planning purposes, then the presentation will take a more didactic form, emphasizing the key features and elements of the issue under investigation. Presentations that keep people informed of activities in progress but that require no action on their part will differ from those presentations requiring decisions, inputs, or actions on the part of the audience. In the latter case, the presentations themselves must be structured to make provision for audience participation at appropriate points.

> ***Ernie:*** In recent years I was involved in the initiation of a community development project in a poorer suburb of a large city. Preliminary research with prospective participants and associated stakeholding audiences identified the purposes of the program. These provided the basis for continuing developments, including program organization, staffing, facilities and equipment, budgeting, and so on.
>
> As we worked through the developmental processes, different means were employed to inform the different audiences of program details. A chart summarizing the focus areas was used to talk about the emerging program with other prospective participants. A flowchart assisted the planning team to work through organizational issues and communicate with people from associated agencies. A series of short reports provided relevant information to a variety of other stakeholders, including local organization committees and a community advisory group.
>
> These forms of presentation enabled stakeholding partners and participants to maintain a clear picture of the program as it developed and ensured wide acceptance within the community. Lengthier, more detailed formal reports were prepared for funding agencies who contributed to the project.
>
> A related collaborative study at a local school prepared short reports for teachers, administrators, and parents. These were presented verbally to the principal, to a meeting of school staff, and to a meeting of parents. The project was marked by high degrees of participation by parents, and enabled school staff to contribute to the project. The combination of written and verbal presentations provided the means to reach a wide range of participants.

Planning Presentations

Well-planned presentations ensure that stakeholding audiences are well informed, enabling them to maintain clarity and to gain deeper insights into the issues investigated. In planning presentations, research participants should use similar processes to those used for report writing (see above), defining:

- **Audiences** Who are the audiences to whom we wish to present?
- **Purposes** What are our purposes in presenting to these audiences?
- **Understandings** What do we wish our audiences to know or understand?
- **Content** What information or material will assist us to achieve this purpose?
- **Format** What presentational formats might best achieve this purpose?
- **Outcomes** What do we wish to achieve? What outcomes are desired?

Steps in Planning

- Identify the *audience* and *purpose.*
- *Identify participants* whose experiences and perspectives are pertinent to the presentation.
- *Review the data* for each of these participants.
- *Review the categories and issues* emerging from analysis of the data for each participant.
- Use categories to *construct a framework* of headings.
- *Write a script,* using units of meaning and elements within the data.
- *Review and edit* the script, checking for accurate rendering of participant perspectives and appropriateness to the audience.
- *Member-check* by having participants read the script.
- *Practice* the presentation.

The basic outcome of presentation planning is an *outline* or *script* that presents information in easily accessible form. An outline in bullet-points provides a script that guides presenters. The script may be complemented by additional material, including quotations from participants or documented information to be read verbatim to an audience. More formal presentations may be rehearsed to ensure presenters are clear about the material and to keep their presentation within allotted times.

Research participants therefore need to carefully prepare a script that has the following basic format:

- **Introduction**
    The focus of the project—the issue investigated
    The participants
    The purpose and desired outcomes of the presentation
- **Body of the Presentation**
    Previous and current activities: What has happened; what is happening
    Key issues emerging from research: What has been discovered; what is problematic
    Implications: What needs to be done (actions, next steps)
- **Conclusion**
    Review of the major points covered

Presentations should be carefully scripted and directed, so that each participant understands precisely where and when to speak and knows the material for which he or she is responsible. Practice provides both clarity and confidence, maximizing the possibility of an informative and effective presentation. This is especially important for people who are not used to speaking publicly, but their inclusion—the effect of people speaking for themselves in their own voice—dramatically increases the power of a presentation.

In only rare situations should people read from a written report. Though these types of presentation provide people with feelings of safety and accuracy, they usually detract from the purpose of the event. The written word is different in form and function from the spoken word, and people reading from a paper usually fail to convey the meaningfulness that is a necessary function of a presentation. We have all experienced forms of presentation, delivered in mournful monotone or excited exuberance, that rattle or drone on and on. Usually there is far too much information for the audience to absorb and little opportunity to process that information. Rarely do audiences in these situations gain appreciable understanding, and retention of information is limited. Presenting an address by reading from a prepared paper is an art that few possess.

> ***Ernie:*** I recently assisted members of a Neighborhood Collective to plan a presentation to a national academic conference. They were intent on communicating the outcomes of their research to the professional world, but were rather overwhelmed by the prospect of participating in what was, for them, a rather imposing setting. We planned carefully to ensure we were fully prepared. After carefully identifying the purpose of their presentation—the major message they wished to present to a largely academic audience—they carefully reviewed the material they had accumulated, identifying and assessing those features that appeared central to the research in which they had engaged.
>
> These features were ordered into a framework of ideas—headings and subheadings—that provided the outline for a script for the group's presentation. Individual group members were then allocated responsibility for presenting each of the various sections. They rehearsed their presentation a number of times, reallocating some material to different people or places in the report until the participants were clear on what they needed to say and when. Much of their presentation was in the form of a dialogue between members of the group.
>
> The presentation at the conference was very successful, providing the audience with a clear understanding of the power of community participation in a research process. The degree of engagement of the audience was evidenced by their rapt attention and the diversity of questions they asked. The participants were highly delighted by the success of their presentation, an event that further heightened their research skills and feelings of empowerment.

Enhancing Verbal Presentations: Audiovisuals

"Talk is cheap" is a common saying that has relevance to presentations. Though brief verbal presentations can sometimes be effective, it requires a skilled and practiced orator to hold an audience for an extended period. Interest and understanding are greatly extended when visual and auditory materials are incorporated into presentations, aiding in clarity and enabling significant quantities of factual information to be presented. Statistical summaries, numerical information, or lists of features and elements may be presented in chart form or as overheads. Charts have the advantage of providing a constantly available record of issues, but they suffer sometimes from problems of size. Overheads and other electronic means of displaying information have great clarity, but they can only be projected on one sheet at a time and thus place limits on the flexibility of a presentation.

A variety of visual aids complement and enhance verbal information. Diagrams, maps, concept maps, symbolic representations, figures, and so on, provide effective ways for presenting information and focusing attention. Whiteboards or chalkboards also enable the active construction of illustrations and diagrams to stimulate attention and enable the structured exposition of a wide range of subject matter.

These processes can be presented in a highly sophisticated form using electronic media such as audiotaping or videotaping or utilizing software such as PowerPoint. It is important to ensure that these are used in moderation since too much use of videos or other electronic media can be detrimental to a presentation, creating a passive audience and detracting from feelings of engagement. Judicious use of electronic media, however, can provide vivid illustrations or large chunks of information, greatly enhancing people's ability or willingness to participate in ongoing dialogue. As a stimulus they are sometimes unparalleled.

At each stage, therefore, we need to ask how to best achieve the types of understanding we desire. Presentations can be greatly enhanced by using:

- Maps
- Charts
- Artwork
- Concept maps
- Lists
- Figures
- Overheads
- Audiotapes
- Videotapes
- Electronic presentations

Ernie: For some years, Aboriginal colleagues and I provided workshops on cultural sensitivity for a variety of audiences. The intent was to assist workshop participants to investigate ways of modifying their professional work practices to ensure greater effectiveness in cross-cultural contexts. These sessions included short segments of a video film showing Indigenous people presenting accounts of their experiences.

One segment popular with audiences presented an old man talking of the time that police and welfare officers came to take away his children. Moved to tears, he talks about how he was prevented from taking any action as his children were driven away. Returning the next day he tells how he placed a piece of old tin over the sole reminder of his children, their footprints in the sand.

This segment, used many times in workshops and presentations, never failed to evoke rich and sometimes intense discussions. It provides keen insight into the way past events continue to affect community life. Sometimes a picture *is* worth a thousand words.

For some audiences, presentations may take on an almost concertlike appearance. Creative presentations may incorporate a variety of materials and performances (see below), providing a rich body of factual information and authentic understandings of people's lived realities. Presentations, constructed from materials derived from the analysis of data, use key features and elements as the basis for a script, incorporating "quotes" from the data to highlight important information. Presenters may incorporate tape-recorded information derived from participant interviews, they may read from reviewed materials, or they may include segments of video or aural recordings, poems, songs, or role plays. The rich variety of possibilities enables children, youth, and adult participants to fully express the ideas with which they have been working.

Interactive Presentations

Presentations are more effective when they are interactive. It is difficult to stimulate interest or involvement in a research process when the audience is passive and uninvolved. Where there is no provision for audience participation, people are likely to feel left out or disregarded, as if their perspectives and issues are less important. Wherever possible, presentations should provide opportunities for all participants to interact with the material. At regular intervals, audiences should have opportunities to participate in the unfolding presentation, commenting on issues, asking for clarification, or offering their perspectives on issues presented. As part of a "hermeneutic dialectic"—meaning-making dialogue—these processes not only enable people to extend and clarify their understanding, but also increase their feelings of inclusion and ownership in the project at hand.

Presentations may also include small-group work, enabling participants to explore issues in greater depth by engaging in dialogue or by perusing related documents or materials. Feedback from small-group discussions provides a further means to gain greater clarity and understanding, especially about points of contention or uncertainty. This points to the need for flexibility, to allow participants to take advantage of opportunities arising in the course of presentations. It is possible to turn a presentation into a workshop or focus group, so that audiences become active participants in the ongoing development of the investigation. In these circumstances time may be allocated for this purpose to allow audiences to take advantage of the ideas emerging from their work together.

Ernie: When I work with research groups, I often instruct them to chart the key elements of their recent activities. Group members then speak to their charts, reporting on their progress and any issues arising. The audience can then comment or ask questions to clarify or extend the presenter's comments. This not only informs the audience clearly, but assists presenters to extend their thinking about the issues raised—an integral part of the process of researching.

Performances: Representing Experience Artistically and Dramatically

Performances add to the possibilities for providing deeper and more effective understandings of the nature of people's experiences. They present multiple possibilities for entering people's subjective worlds to provide audiences with empathetic understandings that greatly increase the power of the research process. Performances enable participants to "report" on their research through:

- Drama
- Role play
- Song
- Poetry
- Dance
- Visual art
- Electronic media

By engaging their work performatively, research participants use artistic means to enable audiences to take the perspective of those whose lives are performed, to enter their experience vicariously and understand more empathetically their life-worlds. Using artistic and dramatic media, researchers can capture and represent the deeply complex, dynamic, interactive, and emotional qualities of everyday life. They can engage in richly evocative presentations comprehensible to children, families, cultural minorities, poor people, and other previously excluded audiences.

Poetry, music, drama, and art can create illuminative, transformative experiences for presenter and audience alike, stimulating awareness of the different voices and multiple discourses occurring in any given social space (Denzin, 1997; Prattis, 1985). They provide the means to interrogate people's everyday realities by juxtaposing them within the telling, acting, or singing of stories, thus revealing the differences that occur therein and providing the possibility of therapeutic action (Denzin, 1997; Trinh, 1991). While performances fail to provide the certainty required of experimental research, or to reinforce the authority of an official voice (Atkinson, 1992), they present the possibility of producing compassionate understandings promoting effective change and progress (Rorty, 1989).

This is clearly a postmodern response, making possible the construction of evocative accounts revealing people's concrete, human experience. Performances provide the means of complementing or enhancing reports and presentations by:

- Studying the world from the perspective of research participants
- Capturing their lived experience
- Enabling participants to discover truths about themselves and others
- Recognizing multiple interpretations of events and phenomena

- Embedding experience in local cultural contexts
- Recording deeply felt emotion—love, pride, dignity, honor, hate, envy—and the agonies, tragedies, triumphs, and peaks of human experience embedded in people's actions, activities, and behavior
- Representing people's experience symbolically, visually, or aurally in order to achieve clarity and understanding

> *Ernie:* In recent years I have been privy to some stunning performances that have greatly extended my understanding of people's experiences. I have seen project evaluations include poetry, song, role play, and art which provided deep insights about my work practices. I have seen the powerful artistic work of children provide wonderfully illuminative representations of their experience. I have sat in the audience, deeply moved by a teenage group's dramatic presentation of their experience of sexual harassment. I have been surprised by the depth and extent of my responses to these performative presentations, feeling deeply "touched" by what I have seen and heard, and more sensitive to the nature of the performers' experiences and how the issues represented sit in and affect their lives.

Planning Performances: Developing a Script

Performances are built from the outcomes of data analysis, using similar techniques to those used to fashion reports and presentations. Research participants work creatively to construct a performance, using key features and elements evolving from analysis. *Poems, songs,* and *drama,* as well as *symbolic and visual art,* may be used to represent their experiences and communicate their perspectives. As with written and other forms of representation, performances need to be conducted with a clear understanding of the *purpose* they wish to achieve with a specific *audience.* Participants should ask: "What do we wish this audience to know or understand? And how might we best achieve that knowledge or understanding through our performance?"

- Identify the *audience* and *purpose.*
- *Identify participants* whose experiences and perspectives are to be represented.
- *Review the data* for each of these participants.
- *Review the categories and issues* emerging from analysis of the data for each participant.
- Use categories to *construct a framework* of the key features of the experiences and perspectives.
- *Write a script* using units of meaning and elements within the data.
- *Review and edit* the script, checking for accurate rendering of participant perspectives and appropriateness to audience.
- *Member-check* by having participants read the script.
- *Rehearse* the performance.

Producing Performances

As with any script, there will be decisions to be made about who will perform which *roles,* how the *setting* will be designed, what clothing or *costumes* will be worn, and who will *direct* the staging of the performance (i.e., take responsibility for overall enactment of the performance).

Rehearsals are an important feature of performances, enabling participants to review the quality and appropriateness of their production and providing opportunities to clarify or modify the script. People will also become familiar with their roles, sometimes memorizing the parts they need to play, though readings may be used effectively where people have minimal time for preparation or rehearsal.

Sometimes action research requires research participants to formulate on-the-spot performances, so that role plays requiring minimal preparation provide an effective means for people to communicate their messages. For this mode of performance, participants should formulate an outline of a script from the material emerging from their analysis, ad-libbing the words as they enact the scene they wish to represent. Role plays are especially powerful when participants act out their own parts, speaking in their own words and revealing, in the process, clear understandings of their own experiences and perspectives.

Video and Other Electronic Media

Although live performances provide effective ways to communicate the outcomes of research, video and other electronic media offer powerful and flexible tools for reaching wider audiences. Not only do video productions provide possibilities for more sophisticated performances, but they enable the inclusion of people whose personal makeup inhibits them from participating in live performances. The technology now available enables video productions to be presented on larger screens, to be shown on computer screens, or to be incorporated into more complex online productions.

Dirk Schouten and Rob Watling (1997) provide a useful model for integrating video into education, training, and community development projects. Their process includes:

- Making a recording scheme
- Recording the material
- Making an inventory of the material
- Deciding what functions the material will serve in the text
- Making a rough structure for the text
- Making an edit scheme on the basis of the rough structure
- Editing the text

Although producing a quality video requires high levels of expertise and careful production, current technology enables even amateurs to produce short and effective videos. By recording events, agency workers, service and community practitioners, and client groups can provide engaging and potentially useful productions that extend the potential of their work. This type of recording enables people to dramatize their experience and engage in forms of research from which they were previously excluded.

Videotaping also provides research participants with methods for storing and presenting their material. Current possibilities include videotape, CD or DVD discs, or computers. In addition, these can be viewed or transmitted through a variety of media, including video and DVD players, streaming video, and community television. With these formats, it is possible to reach a wide variety of audiences and to achieve many effective educational purposes.

Examples of Performances

Case One: HIV Awareness

A youth group wished to provide information about HIV in their community. They wrote a script that captured the experience of a family whose son is diagnosed as HIV positive. The script incorporated dramatic dialogue about sexual behaviors that had resulted in the son acquiring HIV and steps that he might have taken to reduce the risk. It followed him through the experience of contracting AIDS, working through a medication regimen, and finally dying of the disease. Produced as a play and presented by an amateur theater group, the performance provided a graphic means for educating the broader community about HIV.

Case Two: Domestic Violence

Concerned about the levels of treatment provided by her agency to victims of domestic violence, the director of a local agency acquired funds for some of her staff to produce a local videotape about the issue. Incorporating the perspectives of victims, former perpetrators, family members, and agency staff, it traced the history of domestic violence in some of the families and the steps that could be taken by people suffering from domestic violence. It provided a very useful tool to inform people of the levels of domestic violence in their community and to explain the steps that individuals could take to deal with situations they confronted in their personal lives. For its sources, the video used material from recorded interviews and from role plays and reenactments of events.

Case Three: Community Needs Survey

A human service worker facilitated a community needs survey in a rural community. She realized that the formal report, written for the state welfare authority, would not be read by people in the town, and so she worked with people who had been involved in the study to consider how they might effectively inform the community. Using the key elements of the report, they wove the information into a variety of scripts and produced a concert featuring short verbal presentations, poems, songs, artwork, and short plays. In this way they communicated central features of the report to their local community.

Case Four: "Alcohol carousel [literature and artifact display] and children's school drawings as part of a community education strategy" (Allamani, Forni, Ammannati, Sani, & Centurioni, 2000)

As part of a Community Alcohol Action Research Project, 5,500 alcohol carousels were distributed during 1996 in the project's areas where they were freely available.

Consumer association members and school parents were surveyed using a questionnaire. Local key people were also interviewed using qualitative methods. In all circumstances the carousels proved to be understandable and useful and elicited discussions about alcohol issues. A 2-year training program in communication skills and alcohol prevention for 13 teachers in local preschools, elementary schools, and middle schools followed the research. Teachers then planned and implemented a health education program on alcohol and food issues. One outcome was nine drawings produced by the schoolchildren. The drawings were exhibited in some schools and supermarkets and were hung in city buses.

SUMMARY

This chapter describes three main formats for presenting the outcomes of research: *written reports*, *presentations*, and *performances*.

These can be used to provide evocative accounts enabling empathetic understanding of participant experience. They should:

- **Clearly and accurately *represent* participant *experiences* and *perspectives***
- **Be constructed to suit specific *audiences* and *purposes***

***Written reports* may take the form of *accounts, narratives, biographies,* or *ethnographies,* written as individual, joint, or collective accounts. They may take the form of *informal summary reports* for project participants, *formal reports* for professional and administrative audiences, or *academic reports* for research journals.**

***Presentations* may integrate *a variety of media,* including verbal reports, charts, flowcharts, maps, concept maps, art, figures, overheads, video and audiotapes, and other electronic presentations.**

***Performances* may include *drama, art, poetry, music,* or other formats. These may be stored, displayed, and presented in a variety of visual, aural, and electronic forms.**

Procedures for constructing *written reports* or *preparing scripts* for presentations and performances include:

- **Identifying *audience* and *purpose***
- **Selecting participant *perspectives***
- **Reviewing the *data***
- **Selecting the *key features* and *elements* of experience from the analyzed data**
- **Constructing a *framework* or *outline* using these features**
- **Writing the report or script**
- **Reviewing and editing the report or script**
- **Member checking for accuracy and appropriateness**

7

Taking Action: Passion, Purposes, and Pathways

RESEARCH DESIGN	DATA GATHERING	DATA ANALYSIS	COMMUNICATION	ACTION
INITIATING A STUDY	CAPTURING STAKEHOLDER EXPERIENCES AND PERSPECTIVES	IDENTIFYING KEY FEATURES OF EXPERIENCE	WRITING REPORTS	CREATING SOLUTIONS
Setting the stage			Reports Ethnographies Biographies	Action plans
Focusing and framing	Interviewing	Analyzing epiphanies and illuminative experiences	PRESENTATIONS AND PERFORMANCES	A helping process
Literature review	Observing	Categorizing and coding		Assessment and evaluation
Stakeholders	Reviewing artifacts		Presentations Drama Poetry	Organizational change
Data sources	Reviewing literature	Enhancing analysis	Song Dance Art	Community development
Ethics		Constructing category frameworks	Video Multimedia	Professional development
Validity				Strategic planning

Contents of This Chapter

This chapter describes the transition from data analysis to action.

The chapter begins by explaining the need to develop a culture of inquiry that engages people in the task of resolving their issues and problems.

The next section describes the development of an *action plan* detailing tasks and procedures for resolving issues.

Further sections describe how action research processes may be integrated into everyday human service activities, including:

- *A helping process* that assists participants to solve the problem that is the focus of the research
- Three different approaches to the *evaluation* of programs and services: Responsive evaluation, Open inquiry, and Audit review
- *Organizational and community change*, using two guiding frameworks—PREPARE and IMAGINE
- An *asset-based community development* process
- Development and implementation of a *professional development* program
- A *strategic planning* process that provides frameworks guiding systematic planning for organizations

Taking Action: Using the Outcomes of Inquiry

The "Action" phase of inquiry distinguishes action research from other forms of investigation, applying the knowledge and understandings emerging from inquiry for immediate practical purposes. Most research is completed when the data are analyzed, the report written, and recommendations presented. Action research, however, requires research participants to engage in activities that work toward resolution of the problem or issue on which their inquiries have focused. In this phase of action research, participants engage in the development of an action plan that stipulates the steps they will use to take action.

These processes are not separate from the regular work of human service practitioners, but rather, they are incorporated into everyday work routines. Thus the steps of the following intervention model might be seen as one cycle of an action research process:

Engagement (focusing and framing)
↓
Assessment (data gathering and analysis)
↓
Planning (reporting and planning)
↓
Implementation (action to be taken)
↓
Evaluation (next research cycle)

Action research processes may be integrated into everyday human service activities—case management, group work, program evaluation, community development, and so on.

It is important for a culture of inquiry to emerge so that people increase their research skills and capacities and apply them automatically to problems at hand. Research does not supply a quick fix for a long-standing problem, nor does it provide an add-on activity that intrudes into already taxing demands of professional or community life. As a "culture of inquiry," research becomes an integral part of the everyday lives of human service professionals and those with whom they work.

Engaging People's Passion

Effective and innovative research outcomes are likely to emerge when clients, groups, or program participants are actively involved in the development of solutions to their problems and issues. The success of a program, project, or intervention rests as much on commitment and ownership as on the skillful enactment of professional techniques. When people are truly invested in activities enabling them to take action on an issue about which they are concerned, they often do so with *passion* that enhances their capacity and willingness to invest themselves in the project at hand.

The possibility for this type of outcome is increased dramatically, therefore, when people actively participate in research tasks and processes. They get excited, energized, and motivated, willing to invest considerable time to enact activities or achieve goals they have identified.

> *Rosalie:* Our professional experience in agency and community settings demonstrates this feature of professional life. When individuals and community groups engage an issue with energy and enthusiasm, we provide them with support and assistance as they first investigate the issue, then formulate solutions. In many, many instances, we have seen people from the most disempowered sections of the community engage in highly successful activities, developing programs and services that not only provide for their individual needs, but often greatly enhance their capacity to contribute to the life of their community, family, or organization. The passion with which they engage issues that they are able to define in their own terms demonstrates the effectiveness of the principles embodied in a participatory action research process.

In the Action phase researchers continue to engage the working principles of action research presented in Chapter 1:

- **Relationships:**   Maintaining positive working relationships with all stakeholders
- **Communication:**   Informing stakeholders of ongoing activities
- **Participation:**   Providing opportunities for stakeholders to engage in activities
- **Inclusion:**   Including all stakeholders and all relevant issues

A key feature of this process is to ensure that primary stakeholders—those principally affected by the issue—are centrally involved in planned actions. If youth apathy is an issue, then apathetic youth need to be a major part of the process. When human service workers and administrators are concerned about the lack of involvement of families, then it is necessary to find ways to include uninvolved families in the research process. Though it may take more time to achieve initially small gains, the long-term benefits of engaging the passion of people are palpable. People's energy and enthusiasm are infectious, and the relationships developed provide the basis for ongoing actions that transform people's ways of thinking and behaving.

From Analysis to Action: Developing Action Plans

Sometimes solutions to the research problem emerge spontaneously, people seeing clearly what steps they need to take to work toward resolution of the issue they have identified. Often, however, effectively dealing with problems deeply rooted in the context requires careful and systematic planning. It is relatively easy to formulate plans with a client, a colleague, or other individuals in the workplace. At the family, community, or regional level, however, more comprehensive plans are sometimes required to ensure adequate input from and engagement of key stakeholders. The following sections first delineate a simple planning process and then provide additional frameworks to assist people engaged in larger or more complex issues.

Establishing an Action Agenda

At this stage, participants need to step back a few paces to scrutinize the information acquired thus far. Information available from previously completed processes of inquiry provides the basis for an action agenda. Reports, presentations, or performances articulate discoveries and understandings and identify key features or issues to be addressed. Derived from the framework of ideas and concepts emerging from analysis of data, these may suggest specific actions to be taken by participants. Often, however, they are merely a set of agendas to be dealt with, setting the stage for a planned course of action.

The first step is to review the purposes of the investigation in terms that lead to a solution. The issue or problem is framed as a question and then translated into an objective. For example:

- **Problem:** The family is failing to accomplish case plan activities.
- **Research Question:** Why are family members failing to accomplish their assigned activities?
- **Objective:** To find ways of enabling family members to accomplish their assigned activities.

The next step is to review the framework of features and elements constructed during the data analysis phase. These should suggest issues or agendas that could be pursued in order to accomplish the objective. In some cases a number of issues or agendas will emerge, and participants will list them in order of priority, so that the most important issues are engaged first.

If the research processes have been truly participatory, then it is likely that some of this work will have been accomplished as reports and presentations were prepared. If report writing has been the responsibility of an individual or small group, however, research facilitators should be wary of using report recommendations as the basis for action. Too often, reports written in isolation from stakeholders are not grounded in the concrete realities of the stakeholders' lives. They are sometimes written in abstract or generalized terms and recommend actions that are too generalized, overambitious, or unrealistic, and that fail to speak to actual possibilities for participants or to capture their interest. Effective action requires issues, agendas, and priorities for action to emerge from a truly meaning-making dialogue among participants.

In summary, research participants establish an action agenda with the following steps:

- Affirm the focus of the project, and state it as a *problem.*
- Frame a *research question* as a focus for investigating the problem.
- Formulate an *objective* suggesting the type of answer needed.

Couto, Stutts, and Associates (2000), in their study of a juvenile court system (see Chapter 9), identified recurring systemic problems, gaps in services, and several effective interventions. On the basis of this information they recommended the following *action steps:*

- Expand the evaluation component of all programs that serve children.
- Expand prevention and intervention services and funding for at-risk children with severe needs:
  - Child abuse and neglect prevention services
  - Truancy prevention services
  - Community-based intensive in-home services
  - Comprehensive outpatient and residential programs providing mental health, rehabilitative, and educational services
  - Specialized programming for at-risk teenage girls
  - Community-based school programs designed to provide early identification of and services for children with special educational needs
  - After-care services for children and youth returning to the community from foster care and other juvenile placements
  - Follow-up for juveniles released from probation
- Develop a coalition of service providers and others to advocate for systemwide coordination of services to children, youth, and families and to overcome funding and service deficiencies.

They also identified a list of targeted opportunities for philanthropic foundations that provided funds for related programs and services.

- Review the framework of *issues, features, and elements* emerging from data analysis.
- Select agendas requiring action from the framework.
- *Prioritize* the issues, distinguishing those to be subject to immediate action from those to be delayed for the medium or long term.

Creating Pathways: Constructing an Action Plan

Carefully formulated plans enable participants to envision the concrete steps they need to take to accomplish a desired outcome. Participants devise a plan of action for each issue identified as a priority in the action agenda. The plan includes:

- A statement of the overall purpose to be achieved (the *goal or purpose*)
- Desired outcomes (*objectives* that specify when people will know they have achieved their goal)
- A sequence of tasks that people will undertake in order to accomplish each outcome (*tasks* and *steps*)
- The *names of the people* who will carry out the tasks
- The *place* where activities will occur
- The *time* when each activity should be accomplished

Ernie: Some of my colleagues were involved in a project focusing on increased juvenile crime. Participants restated the issue as a goal: "To decrease juvenile crime." Reviewing the analysis from previous phases of research revealed objectives related to this goal. In a context where both parents were often engaged in the workforce, factors related to increased juvenile crime had included "lack of youth leisure activities," "poor school attendance," and "lack of after-school programs." These were restated as three objectives: to develop youth leisure activities, to improve youth school attendance, and to organize after-school programs. Teams of relevant stakeholders developed a plan for each issue and brought the plans to a combined planning session for discussion, modification, and endorsement of all stakeholders. In this case, each planning group included a member from each of the primary stakeholding groups. The issue "poor school attendance," for instance, had a team that included teachers, young people, school administrators, and parents.

A simple six-question framework—why, what, how, who, where, and when—provides a useful basis for systematic planning. Using the above example as the basis, it would look like this:

- **Why:** State the overall purpose of these activities—for example, to reduce juvenile crime. This *purpose or goal* statement describes the ultimate end point of the project.
- **What:** State what actions are to be taken in the form of a set of *objectives*—for example, to organize an after-school program for teenagers, to develop a youth center.
- **How:** Define a sequence of *tasks* and *steps* for each objective.
- **Who:** List the *people* responsible for each task and activity.
- **Where:** State the *place* where the tasks will be done—at a school, a community center, a youth club, people's homes, etc.
- **When:** State the *time* when work on each task should start and when it should be completed.

A planning chart may be used to articulate all facets of the work (see Figure 7.1). The chart clearly defines all dimensions of the project and allows people to see their place in the broader scheme of things. It also includes the resources required to complete the tasks and identifies the source of funds. It provides a concrete vision of the active community of which the people are a part, and it enables the participants to check on their progress as they work through the various stages of the project together.

Each of the tasks indicated in Figure 7.1 requires a number of steps or activities. These can be listed in a separate column or can be specified in a separate action plan for each task. Once details have been entered on the chart, participants can review the plan to check and clarify each person's responsibilities, the sequence of activities, and the materials and resources required for each task:

- Have we identified all needed materials and equipment? Who will obtain them? From where? When?
- Are funds needed? Where will they come from? Who will organize them? When?

PURPOSE (Why): What are we trying to achieve?							
OBJECTIVE What	TASKS How	PEOPLE Who	START When	FINISH	LOCATION Where	RESOURCES	FUNDS
1. Establish a youth center	a. Obtain permission b. Repair and renovate c. Plan organization	Ms. Jones Lions Club Students Volunteers	6.3.02	12.6.02	Unused church	Paint Timber Tools	$1,500 School district Town council Government grant
2. Organize after-school programs	a. Establish an art program b. Establish a sports program c. Establish a tutoring program	Mr. Whipple Jenny Bruce Jose Venus	1.5.02	4.4.02	Youth center	Art materials Sports equipment	$350 School district Fees

Figure 7.1
Planning Chart

- Do the people responsible have adequate time to accomplish their tasks?
- Should other people be involved? For what tasks? Who will ask them? How will they become part of the process? Who will describe the project to them? How can they become part of the community?

Each of these elements is included in the review of the plan, with objectives, tasks, and activities carefully defined and assigned. Larger or more complex issues may require monitoring an extensive array of activities, but smaller projects usually need only limited time and resources for planning.

Dealing with Difficulties

Sometimes planning procedures become bogged down because people begin to focus on the difficulties that might intrude. Statements that give voice to such difficulties might include: "What about. . . ," "Yes, but we can't do this because. . . ," "The father won't allow . . . ," "The parents can't . . . ," "Teens aren't capable of . . . ," "We haven't the time to . . . ," "The funds aren't available to . . . ," and so on. If these statements are left unanswered, people will soon become de-energized, and an air of futility will arise.

Each of these types of concern needs to be formally acknowledged, clearly recorded, and then incorporated into the planning process. It is essential that these types of issues are seen as problems to be solved, rather than reasons not to take action. Most such statements are easily resolved, but sometimes they need careful and creative thinking to enable effective action to continue.

Some of the above statements point to the need to bring other stakeholders into the project. If the father and teens, for instance, are included in the process, then their perspectives and agendas can be accommodated immediately. If not, then work needs to be done to ensure their perspectives and agendas are reflected in the plan, so that "What the father will allow" becomes part of the creative formulation of the plan of action.

Most issues arising in the course of planning can be accommodated immediately and relatively easily. Each needs to be reformulated from a *problem* to a statement of an *objective or task,* which is entered into the action plan. The problem "Funds aren't available," for instance, might be formulated as the objective "To seek an allocation of funds from . . . " or "To search for sources of funding for . . . from . . . " This objective would be extrapolated through *tasks and activities,* a *person* responsible for the tasks, and a *timeline* for beginning and completing the tasks.

Supporting and Monitoring Progress

It is important that someone has responsibility for monitoring the implementation of the plan. Whoever is delegated this role needs to ensure that people carry out the designated tasks in the time allocated. This may require the person to talk with participants informally from time to time, asking them how things are going and whether they need any assistance. It may be done through informal talks in homes, parks, fast-food restaurants, or other common meeting places or by phone messages or e-mail.

The person monitoring progress also must be willing and ready to offer personal support, especially to people working in difficult situations or carrying out difficult or complex tasks. Often, in these situations, the person merely needs to be a "listening ear," providing a means for participants to debrief, vent where necessary, or review and think through the work they're doing.

Progress should also be monitored at meetings of participants. The meetings should be regular enough to ensure that people remain committed to the project and to each other. Meetings should provide opportunities for people to report on their activities, to review the overall plan, and to make any modifications or changes in objectives and tasks if they become necessary.

SUMMARY: ACTION PLANNING

1. Affirm the focus of the project and state it as a *problem.*
2. Frame a *research question* as a focus for investigating the problem.
3. Reframe the question as an *objective.*
4. Review the framework of *issues, features, and elements* emerging from data analysis.
5. *Select agendas* requiring action from the framework.
6. *Prioritize* the agendas, distinguishing those to be subject to immediate action from those to be delayed for the medium or long term.

(continued)

7. For each agenda devise an action plan that includes:
   - A statement of overall *purpose* (why)
   - A set of *objectives* to be attained (what)
   - A sequence of *tasks* and *steps* for each objective (how)
   - The *people* responsible for each task and activity (who)
   - The *place* where the tasks will be done (where)
   - The *time* when tasks should start and be completed (when)

The Helping Process

The helping process can be thought of as a process of action research that assists people in resolving issues in their lives. Each of the phases of the helping process suggested by Hepworth and Larsen (1993) might be envisioned as a cycle of an action research process, the Look-Think-Act framework assisting clients and groups to gain mastery over their situation. As action research, however, helping is enacted as a participatory process of inquiry focusing on ways of constructing the situation from the client's perspective.

Phase I: Exploration, Assessement, and Planning
  - Explore clients' problems by eliciting comprehensive data about the people, the problem, and the environmental factors. (Look—data gathering)
  - Formulate a multidimensional assessment of the problem, the systems that play a significant role in the difficulties, and relevant resources that can be tapped or must be developed. (Think—data analysis)
  - Mutually negotiate goals to be accomplished in remedying or alleviating the problem and formulating a contract. (Act—action plans)

Phase II: Implementation and Goal Attainment
  Implementation
    - Review action plans. (Look—gather data)
    - Devise strategies to enact tasks. (Think—analyze)
    - Enact tasks. (Act—take action)
  Monitoring Progress
    - Review tasks and actions of clients. (Look—gather data)
    - Evaluate the effectiveness of actions. (Think—analyze)
    - Modify actions and tasks to increase the likelihood of success, enhance client motivation, and encourage progress. (Act—take action)

Phase III: Termination and Evaluation
  Termination
    - Review attainments. (Look)
    - Make decisions about termination. (Think)
    - Effect successful termination of the helping relationship. (Act)
  Evaluation
    - Review helping processes and outcomes. (Look)
    - Assess the effectiveness of processes. (Think)
    - Report on the effectiveness of processes. (Act)

Assessment

Assessment is another procedure that can be constructed as an action research process. The professional practitioner facilitates processes of inquiry in which clients gather, analyze, and synthesize salient data in order to remedy or ameliorate problems. As action research, assessment is a collaborative, participatory process leading to therapeutic outcomes. Hepworth and Larsen (1993) suggest:

> If you involve clients in the assessment process to the fullest extent possible, by inviting their views and responding to them with respect, they are likely to respond similarly to your views. On the other hand, if you attempt to impose your judgments on clients, they are likely to resist either openly or covertly. What we [advocate] is an open and mutual process that culminates in a synthesis of your own and your clients' views. The result of such mutuality is likely to be more accurate assessments and greater investments of clients in the assessments as well as in the planning and contracting processes. (p. 229)

Kirst-Ashman and Hull (2001) suggest a four-step assessment process:

1. Identify your client. Who exactly is your client? On whose behalf are you working?
2. Assess the client in the situation. Think about the client's situation.
3. Cite information about client problems and needs.
4. Identify client strengths.

O'Connor, Wilson, and Setterland (1998) see assessment as a process for formulating an understanding so as to effect a purposeful intervention, locating the processes that restrict or create problems for the individual or group. The following questions provide focus for the assessment process:

- Who experiences the situation as problematic or causing difficulties?
- How is the situation formulated by different persons and/or constituents?
- What aspects of the social arrangements are individuals or groups indirectly interfacing with? What influences the ability of these individuals to exercise control in their lives and resolve difficulties or tensions? What factors inhibit individuals (and groups) from controlling their own lives?
- How do the individuals or groups understand or construct these interactions? The purpose is to broaden their understanding of the situation.
- Where does the situation fit in the individuals' or groups' life stream—why now?
- How do the individuals' or groups' interactions with existing arrangements affect their ability to control their lives and develop equitable relationships?

Community Assessment

O'Connor, Wilson, and Setterland (1998) also suggest the preparation of a community profile as a form of assessment. An action research approach to assessment provides practitioners with an understanding of the context in which they are working, helps them identify significant resources, reveals the history of the situation, and helps describe the social environment. It clarifies the purpose (focus and framing), describes the community and its history (gathering data), and makes sense of this information (analysis). Assessment provides the means to plan solutions to problems and gaps. Questions providing focus for this form of assessment–community profile include:

- **Purpose:**   Why are we developing a community profile? How will it be used? Who will see it? (Focus)
- **History of the community:**   What has happened in the past? (Gathering data)
- **Description of the profile process:**   Who is involved? How was it put together? (Gathering data)
- **Description of the community:**   This may include boundaries, physical description, population description (including age, gender, ethnicity, household type, income, occupation, education, home ownership, etc.), services and resources, political representatives. (Gathering data)
- **Analysis:**   This section makes sense of the above descriptions—what and how the community is functioning, problems, gaps, etc. (Data analysis)

Evaluating Programs and Services

Evaluation is an inherent part of the Look-Think-Act (plan, implement, evaluate) action research cycle. Conceived as an action research process, it provides constructive insights into people's activities in agency, organizational, and community contexts. Evaluation may be applied to particular activities or to large projects, programs, and services.

This section presents three models of evaluation that are concomitant with participatory action research: **responsive evaluation,** derived from a process suggested by Guba and Lincoln (1989), and two orientations of action evaluation—**open inquiry evaluation** and **audit review evaluation** (Wadsworth, 1997). Readers engaged in the evaluation of large and complex projects would do well to consult these sources in detail.

The approaches to evaluation described are *formative,* insofar as they focus on ongoing activities, rather than describing or measuring a discrete set of outcomes, a *summative* process of evaluation. Formative evaluation, in other words, attempts to understand the more complex processes through which change takes place and to determine the types and qualities of change occurring, rather than solely measuring or describing client or organizational performance on a specific set of outcomes.

Responsive Evaluation

According to Guba and Lincoln (1989), evaluation is not primarily a scientific technical procedure, but is a fundamentally social, political, and value-oriented process of inquiry. Evaluation outcomes are not a description of "truth," "reality," or the "facts," but are constructions, largely shaped by the values of the constructors, that make sense to actors in a particular situation. These constructions are inextricably linked to the particular physical, psychological, social, and cultural contexts within which they are formed. Because of the inherently political characteristic of evaluation, there is a need to recognize, Guba and Lincoln suggest, how evaluations can be used to enfranchise or disenfranchise stakeholding groups.

Their responsive approach to evaluation is clearly aligned with the underlying principles of participatory action research revealed in this book. Their approach has an action orientation that defines a course to be followed and requires evaluators to interact with people in ways that respect their dignity, integrity, and privacy. This means that there should be:

- Full participative involvement
- Political parity of those involved (control)
- Consensual, informed, sophisticated joint construction
- Conceptual parity
- No perception that people are subjects or objects of study

Basic Elements of Responsive Evaluation

Two basic features of responsive evaluation make it the vehicle of choice for participatory action research. **Responsive focusing** determines what questions are to be asked and what information is to be collected on the basis of stakeholder inputs.

> Responsive evaluation . . . . signal(s) the idea that all stakeholders put at risk by an evaluation have the right to place their claims, concerns, and issues on the table for consideration (response), irrespective of the value system to which they adhere. It was created as the antithesis of preordinate evaluation, which assumes that the evaluator and client together possess sufficient information and legitimation to design and implement an evaluation completely, without the need to consult other parties. (Guba & Lincoln, 1989. p. 12.)

Responsive evaluation uses a **constructivist methodology,** assuming that it is not possible to formulate an objective view of reality, that views of reality are not independent of the observer. In speaking of a responsive evaluation, Guba and Lincoln (1989) note:

> Its exercise unites the evaluator and the stakeholders in an interaction that creates the product of the evaluation, utilizing an hermeneutic dialectic approach aimed at establishing that interaction and maintaining it within quality bounds. Moreover, the product of the evaluation is not . . . a set of conclusions, recommendations, or value judgements, but rather an agenda for negotiation of those claims, concerns and issues that have not been resolved in the hermeneutic dialectic exchanges. (p. 13.)

These features make responsive evaluation an especially pertinent tool in action research since the processes of evaluation not only are responsive to participant stakeholders views and perspectives, but become the basis for assessing action to be taken. The principal audiences of an evaluation are stakeholders, whom Guba and Lincoln define as:

- Those put at risk by the evaluation
- Agents who contribute to the evaluand (the "instrument" of evaluation)
- Putative beneficiaries that are expected to profit from the evaluation
- Secondary beneficiaries, e.g., client families
- Victims—those injured or deprived by the implementation of the evaluand

Guba and Lincoln speak of the need to provide stakeholders with insights about the roles they might play and questions they might ask, as well as informing them of their right to become full partners in the evaluation.

The Flow of Responsive Evaluation

Since action research incorporates participatory processes, much of the following activity has already been accomplished by participants. Sometimes, however, an external evaluator is a required part of funding. Where an evaluation is set up separately, evaluation facilitators will move through the following steps:

Contracting
- Initiating a contract with the client or sponsor

Organizing
- Selecting and training a team of evaluators
- Making arrangements for evaluation facilitators to enter the context
- Making logistical arrangements
- Assessing local political factors

Identifying stakeholders
- Identifying agents, beneficiaries, victims
- Mounting continuing search strategies
- Assessing trade-offs and sanctions
- Formalizing "conditions" agreements

Developing within-group joint constructions
- Establishing hermeneutic circles (focus groups)
- Making the circles
- Shaping the emerging joint construction
- Checking credibility

Enlarging joint stakeholder constructions
- Enlarging through new information and increased sophistication
- Making the circles again
- Utilizing documentary information
- Sharing interview reports
- Using evaluator's etic (outsider) construction

Sorting out resolved claims, concerns, and issues
- Identifying claims, concerns, and issues
- Resolving by consensus
- Setting aside as case report components

Prioritizing unresolved items
- Determining a participatory prioritizing process
- Submitting items to prioritization
- Checking credibility

Collecting information and adding sophistication
- Collecting information and training negotiators
- Utilizing further hermeneutic circles
- Gathering existing information
- Using new and existing instrumentation
- Performing special studies

Preparing an agenda for negotiation
- Defining and elucidating unresolved items
- Elucidating competing constructions

- Illuminating, supporting, refuting items
- Providing training
- Testing agendas

Carrying out the negotiation
- Selecting a "representative" circle from all stakeholding groups
- Making the circle
- Shaping the joint construction
- Checking credibility
- Determining the action

Reporting
- Providing reports on the above activities to stakeholding groups

Action
- Planning for action emerging from the evaluation process. (Although not stated explicitly, this is the final stage of an evaluation process.)

Guba and Lincoln's responsive evaluation process is very similar to the steps of an action research routine, though the terminology they use is somewhat different. Hermeneutic circles, for instance, comprise groups of stakeholders and are designed to enable participants to "make meaning" together, in similar fashion to those described for focus groups in previous chapters. Nevertheless, Guba and Lincoln provide a sophisticated process for enabling stakeholders to work together to assess the ongoing progress, accomplishments, and gaps in their work. Responsive evaluation provides the basis for evaluating programs and services and may be incorporated into the evaluation phase of a strategic planning process (plan, implement, evaluate).

Action Evaluation: Everyday Evaluation on the Run

Yoland Wadsworth provides another approach to evaluation implicitly consonant with the action research processes described in this book. Though its language and concepts sometimes differ in detail, the approach described in *Everyday Evaluation on the Run* (Wadsworth, 1997) engages similar processes of inquiry, presenting a conceptual framework that can be applied as two orientations to evaluation: open inquiry and audit review. Like action research, action evaluation works through reiterative processes of inquiry enabling participants to collaboratively explore their work, providing greater insight into their activities, and identifying ways to solve problems or enhance the outcomes they seek. Cyclical processes of inquiry assist participants to build or extend their common understandings of the worth of their activities, encouraging them to test the value of what it is they are achieving:

Reflection
- Observe our actions in the world.
- Think about what we are observing and experiencing.

Design
- "Name the problem."
- Set out to systematically answer the questions that are arising:
    Who or what will be researched?
    Who will do the research?

Who is it for? Whose lives will be improved (the critical reference group for whom services are provided)?

Who will provide the services, funds, etc., for the critical reference group?

Fieldwork
- Be sure all relevant parties participate in "finding out."
- Discover what different people think and value and what things mean to them.
- Observe, read, listen, interact, participate, question, and listen again.
- Reach effective understanding (of what people think, value, etc.).

Analysis and conclusions
- Identify themes, trends, or understandings.
- Synthesize new or better theories.
- Develop conclusions, explanations, and theories.

Feedback
- Check with those researched or evaluated that we "got it right."
- Check theories, conclusions, and explanations with the critical reference group—those for whom the services are provided.
- Check with those who provide services to see if they think the findings are understandable, plausible, and convincing.

Planning
- Consider options for changed and improved practices.
- Check to see that realistic, practical, and achievable "recommendations" are prioritized, agreed upon, finalized, planned, and put into practice.

The above general process may be interpreted in two ways: as open inquiry evaluation or as audit review evaluation. The differences are articulated in the following sections.

Open Inquiry Evaluation

The general thrust of open inquiry evaluation is indicated by a definition of the term "inquiry"—the act of seeking. The focus in open inquiry evaluation is on the operational processes of the organization or project. Open inquiry examines existing practices in the following ways:

Starting with general questions
- How are we doing? What are we doing? What's working? What's not? How do we know?

Asking problem-posing and problem-solving questions
- How could we improve things?

Asking what the community needs
- What is missing? Where are the gaps?

Repeatedly asking "opening-up" questions
- Why are we doing this? The idea is to build theory from diverse sources.

Starting with immediate problems

Revealing existing assumptions and intentions

Developing new and improved evaluative criteria

An open inquiry approach to evaluation, through its focus on identifying and solving problems, increases the chances of solving significant problems and improving programs, services, or organization. It enables innovative, creative, and dynamic ideas and perspectives to emerge and provides participants with a sense of enthusiasm.

For some people in some contexts, open inquiry is not sufficiently systematic and comprehensive, and it risks overlooking important matters. The uncertainty involved in the emerging construction of evaluation criteria and foci, with the consequent possibility of lack of clarity, disagreement, and conflict as different parties express apparently oppositional perspectives, is also seen as a weakness. Generally, however, the essentially anthropologic, interpretive approach inherent in open inquiry evaluation makes it particularly relevant to participatory processes of inquiry.

Audit Review Evaluation

Audit review evaluation uses a more focused approach, though people sometimes see it as complementary to open inquiry. The sense of this approach is signaled by the word "audit"—the act of checking. The audit starts with different questions and has different end points. The audit review focuses on:

Checking objectives
- Starts with questions based on an existing set of objectives: Have we done what we set out to do? What are the signs we have done this?

Finding gaps and irrelevancies
- Asks questions to uncover gaps and irrelevancies: What are we not doing? What are we doing that we shouldn't?

Identifying needs
- Assumes community needs are known

Distilling information
- Asks questions that "narrow down," that check activities on the bases of pre-existing understandings

Revealing problems
- Systematically problematizes all existing activities, i.e., checks to see if they are problematic

Reviewing practices
- Examines practices in light of existing objectives

An audit review has the advantage of checking all matters previously planned for, reassuring participants that much has been done and that matters not yet attended to will be attended to. The comprehensive nature of this approach is especially advantageous if the prior research base was strong, enabling participants to affirm previous agreements and strengthening a collective sense of direction. The fixed nature of the exploration also can feel very comfortable, providing a sense of stability and unity.

The audit review, however, does not always discriminate between still-valuable activities and those that have become outdated. It does not identify what needs to change or how changes might be accomplished. The attention to detail enabling a comprehensive review of activity may also be tedious and wastefully time-consuming.

An audit review provides, however, a useful approach to evaluation, an approach especially loved by those responsible for administering or funding projects, programs, and services. The sense of a fixed universe and clearly defined objectives provides an illusion of expertise and "best practice" often at odds with the complex realities of agency and organizational environments. In the end, however, it can provide more concrete evidence of the extent to which a set of objectives has been achieved, though lacking insight into whether those objectives are appropriate or relevant.

Organizational Change: PREPARE and IMAGINE

Although action research is presented in this book as a linear or cyclical process, in reality the various components interact more dynamically. This becomes evident when action research is applied to the processes of organizational and community change suggested by Kirst-Ashman and Hull (2001): engagement, assessment, planning, implementation, evaluation, termination, and follow-up. Two complementary frameworks are incorporated into this process. PREPARE provides the means to conceptualize assessment and planning processes, and IMAGINE assists the implementation and evaluation phases.

Each of these approaches may be considered as an operational component of an action research process. Research facilitators may work with individuals, families, groups, organizations, or communities and may address problems from a wide range of perspectives.

PREPARE: Assessment and Planning

The purpose of a PREPARE process is to evaluate whether the goal related to organizational change is potentially worth a macro change effort. It might be thought of as an *initial assessment*. Participants review the nature of the problem and judge whether they have the resources to pursue change through the following processes:

1. **P** Identify *problems* to address: Define and prioritize problems, translate problems into needs, and determine which needs are to be addressed.
2. **R** Review your *reality:* Evaluate the variables working for or against the change, as well as personal strengths and weaknesses.
3. **E** *Establish* primary goals: Define the ultimate goal that will fulfill the need or solve the problem.
4. **P** Identify *people* of influence: Identify individuals and groups within the organization or the community who can help make the changes.
5. **A** *Assess* potential costs and benefits: Estimate the financial costs and benefits, as well as the political costs and benefits to the organization.
6. **R** Review professional and personal *risk:* Weigh the benefits of the change process against personal and professional risks—possible effects on career and workplace interpersonal relationships.
7. **E** *Evaluate* the potential success of a change process: Evaluate the chances of success and decide whether or not to make a commitment to the changes.

Systematic processes of assessment, evaluation, and decision making provide a sound basis to proceed with a desired change process.

IMAGINE: Implementation and Evaluation

Once the decision is made to enact change, the IMAGINE framework guides the process of implementation:

1. **I** Start with an innovative *idea:* Identify and start with an innovative idea about the change to take place.
2. **M** *Muster* support and formulate an action system: Identify individuals or groups who can influence the change process and seek their support. Formulate an action system that designates the composition of the group facilitating change, their commitment to the purposes of the process, and their ability to work collaboratively.
3. **A** Identify *assets:* Identify available funding and personnel willing to engage in the change process.
4. **G** Specify *goals,* objectives, and action steps to attain them: Establish the major goals, the objectives that specify how each goal will be achieved, and the specific steps needed to achieve each objective.
5. **I** *Implement* the plan: Implement planned activities.
6. **N** *Neutralize* opposition: Communicate with decision-making administrators, understanding the change process from their perspective. Respond to critics, identify supporters, resolve conflicts, and beware of potential obstruction.
7. **E** *Evaluate* progress: Monitor and evaluate the progress of the change process.

Community Development

Action research skills and processes may be used to strengthen and enhance community development. Communities and groups may apply the methods of inquiry in a systematic way, gathering information, engaging in analysis, and planning their developmental work. Kretzmann and McKnight (1993) provide an approach to community development consistent with the assumptions of action research. Asset-based community development—ABCD—starts with the process of locating the assets, skills, and capacities of residents, citizen associations, and local institutions. The community-building process is based on the assumption that every community has a unique combination of assets upon which to build its future. Kretzmann and McKnight (1993) further suggest the need to recognize that all individuals are "gifted," especially those who often find themselves marginalized because a label—such as "old," "disabled," or "poor"—defines them in terms of a perceived deficiency.

Characteristics of Asset-Based Community Development

Kretzmann and McKnight's model of community development is characterized as asset-based, internally focused, and relationship-driven:

Asset-based
- The process begins by identifying the assets present in the community—individuals, associations, organizations, institutions, the physical environment, and the local economy.

Internally focused
- Strategies focus initially on building agendas and problem-solving with local residents, workers, associations, and institutions.
- The model stresses the primacy of local definition, investment, creativity, hope, and control.

Relationship-driven
- One of the central challenges is to build and rebuild relationships between and among individuals, associations, institutions, the physical environment, and the local economy.
- Relationships are based upon the strengths and capacities of the parties involved, never on their weaknesses and needs.

Asset-based community development mobilizes the hidden capacities of all individuals and groups within the local community. Thus community development may commence with any local group, but it may be enhanced when people in local institutions—parks, libraries, schools, police, hospitals, and so on—enter into strong community partnerships with each other and with local residents and citizen associations.

Community Assets

Positive aspects of a community may be identified within five asset categories: *individuals, local clubs* and *associations, organizations* and *institutions,* the *physical environment,* and the *local economy.*

Individual assets: Every individual has capacities and personal gifts. Strong communities are places where the assets represented by each person are identified and valued.

Local clubs and member association assets: The basic community entity for empowering individuals and mobilizing their capacities and gifts is the local club or member association. This may include a group such as a choir or a youth group within a larger organization such as a church or community center. A local club or member association is an amplifier of the assets each person represents.

Organizational and institutional assets: In addition to individuals and associations, every community hosts some combination of more formal public, private, and nonprofit organizations and institutions. Organizations and institutions are complex entities, incorporating a range of assets such as buildings, equipment, programs, and relationships.

Physical environment assets: Every community is situated in a physical space that includes both natural and built environments. Land and open space, buildings, infrastructure such as transportation and utilities, water, and location are all aspects of the community's physical environment assets.

Local economy assets: All the activities that take place in a community related to the monetary value of people, places, or things are part of the local economy. The local economy represents a community asset in the way money flows within and through it, along with the benefits that accrue to local people as a result.

Community–Building Processes

Kretzmann and McKnight describe a community-building process that has five key features. These do not represent a blueprint for development, but they do identify some of the major challenges facing community developers and suggest a path to follow:

Mapping capacities and assets
- **The capacities of individuals:** The gifts and talents of local people.
- **The gifts of "strangers":** Marginalized, alienated, or ignored groups.
- **Associations of citizens:** The mostly voluntary groups in which citizens express and act upon their interests, commitments, and beliefs.
- **Local, private, and nonprofit institutions:** The local institutions, businesses, and not-for-profit organizations.
- **Physical assets:** Locating and mapping the physical assets of a community—land, buildings, streets, transport, infrastructure, and so on.
- **Capacity finders and developers:** Locating and building a team of community leaders.

Building relationships
- The community becomes stronger and more self-reliant when local residents link with each other.
- People are linked in the process of mapping local assets.
- They build strong ties by solving problems and taking on tasks together.

Mobilizing and information sharing
- **Developing the local economy:** Using the assets of individuals, associations, and institutions to contribute to the neighborhood economy.
- **Strengthening a neighborhood's capacity to shape and exchange information:** Validating, strengthening, and expanding current places where information is exchanged—newspapers, hair salons and barbershops, churches, clubs, taverns, street corners, and so on.

Developing a vision and a plan
- Begins by asking questions like "Where would we like our community to go in the next 5, 10, or 20 years?"
- Seeks to develop a commonly held identity and shared vision.
- Uses consensus-building processes as the basis for community-based planning.
- Includes three commitments that attract and coordinate local capabilities:
  1. Begin with local assets.
  2. Expand the table to include the full range of leadership, including those not normally thought of as community leaders.
  3. Combine planning with problem solving to connect strategies with current purposes and strategies.

Leveraging outside resources to support locally driven development
- Outside resources are leveraged only when local capacities, developments, assets, and other capacities have been engaged.
- Assistance and funding from outsiders, including government and philanthropic sources, should support and enhance, rather than drive, local initiatives.

Action research processes incorporated into each aspect of an assets-based approach to community development would enhance the capacities of individuals and groups to gather, analyze, and use the large bodies of information they acquire. Examples of complementary community development processes and projects may be found in a wide range of sources, such as Medoff and Sklar (1994).

Professional Development

One of the keys to successful and creative human service work is the ongoing development of the professional capacities of workers. They require the continued self-renewal emerging from processes enabling them to enhance and extend their skills and capabilities and to share the accumulated wisdom of others working in similar arenas. Professional development is acknowledged as a key feature of processes aimed at service or program improvement. Other professions historically have acknowledged the need for ongoing professional development and have well-instituted processes to ensure the continued upgrading of the skills and knowledge of their memberships.

Professional development, however, has a spotted history. Although many human service workers have profited from well-planned and thoughtfully articulated programs, too many have been subject to poorly developed, ad hoc arrangements focused largely on administrative matters only peripherally relevant to true professional development. Too often a worker's time is taken up by passively listening to the latest legislative requirements, or the changes in policy instituted by new administrators. For many, "in-service" has become a dirty word.

> *Ernie:* One worker told me with disgust of an in-service program instituted in her district. It consisted of a 45-minute videotape on the topic of working with bilingual families, a presentation resulting from a legislated mandate in that state that all workers would receive instruction in that topic. As a means of preparing workers to deal with the complexities of working with bilingual families, it was singularly simplistic and insultingly ineffective. The contempt in the worker's voice as she told me of this event spoke volumes.

The need for quality professional development clearly acknowledges:

- Professionals are committed to clients and their well-being.
- Professionals best know their work and how to enact work practices.
- Professionals are responsible for managing and monitoring client progress and well-being.
- Professionals think systematically about their practice and learn from experience.
- Professionals are members of learning communities.

Meeting ambitious social goals put into place over the last decade requires new innovative theories and methodologies. A new paradigm of professional development is required in which professional workers are provided with support and resources to develop a community of practice, embedding developmental activities in their everyday work and being resourced by outside experts where appropriate. A sound professional development process enables human service practitioners to engage in thoughtful, conscious decision making to create, implement, reflect on, and modify their work practices.

Action research provides a framework for human service workers to design and implement a program of professional development. Using the framework in this book, they may cycle through iterations of the research process to:

- Identify professional development needs
- Identify issues related to those needs
- Set goals and objectives for professional development
- Plan strategies of professional development
- Implement and evaluate professional development strategies

A systematic process of inquiry will enable human service workers to plan for sustained and substantive learning opportunities to be built into their ongoing professional work by tapping their collective wisdom and gaining access to other sources of expertise. Through processes of reflection and dialogue inherent in action research, they may work with colleagues to map out:

- Their current strengths
- Problematic issues in their work
- What they need to learn
- How they can acquire that learning
- What support systems are needed

Planning processes outlined in the first sections of this chapter provide the means to articulate a coherent, systematic program of development. Those processes are best accomplished in cohorts, though workers and administrators in city, regional, or state agencies and organizations may accomplish this collaboratively.

Human service workers need time and support to map out a plan for a program of continuing professional development that includes:

- What is to be learned by whom?
- How will these things be learned?
- Who will facilitate and support the learning process?
- Who will provide expertise?
- How will time and resources be allocated?
- How will new learning be supported, reinforced, and extended?
- How will new learning be assessed and reviewed?
- What financial resources will be allocated?

Where mandated administrative requirements are seen to be part of this process, they may be incorporated into the program as required, without setting up isolated and isolating sessions that often serve only to antagonize people. In these circumstances, administrative or legislative requirements may be incorporated into a more holistic picture that makes more sense to the participants. Professional development programs also are enhanced if they are aligned with program and service planning processes in agencies or organizations.

Strategic Planning

Action research may be used effectively at the agency, family, group, community, or regional level. It is useful not only as a way to assist in the solution of specific problems, but also as a means of enhancing the effectiveness of traditional human service activities such as case planning, organizational planning, community development, and policy making. Action research may also be used to assist organizations to plan systematically to ensure that they operate efficiently and effectively. Often organizations start with good intentions or begin their operations with small and highly effective programs and services. As they grow, however, there is always a danger that they do so in an ad hoc way that ultimately may threaten the effectiveness of the organization itself.

Ernie: I have seen many situations where organizations have lost direction. One community agency, established to service the needs of disparate groups in the community, became controlled by one of those groups and organized the activities to provide services for that group only.

In another situation I saw staff in an organization working under high levels of stress because they had gone outside boundaries established by the funders. Staff were unable to cope with the apparently never-ending demands of their client group.

In both instances, these agencies were able to use action research processes to engage in strategic planning that enabled them to review their directions and activities and to formulate clear steps to develop effective services for their client groups.

As organizations grow and develop, systematic planning processes ensures that the programs and services they offer accomplish the ends for which they were designed and that they make the most efficient use of the limited resources available.

Sound organizational planning requires careful consideration of both immediate outcomes and long-term effects related to the quality of people's individual lives and to the quality of the social life of the community and the nation. Within a democratic, civilized, and humane society, people must have opportunities to have a harmonious, healthy family life in the context of a safe, supportive community. People in organizations need opportunities to develop a clear vision of the ways in which their organization can enhance the life of the community. Ultimately, they need a vision that enables them to look further than their immediate activities, so that they continue to grow and develop according to the needs of the people they work with.

Strategic Planning: Building the Big Picture

Most organizations have policies that broadly define their nature—what type of organization they are and what their purposes are—what they will try to accomplish. Policies provide the big picture of why an organization exists. An organization's policy may incorporate a social philosophy and/or a set of principles that speak to its values and the particular activities, services, and programs it offers.

As organizations grow in size and complexity, policy planning provides the glue that holds them together and keeps them on track. This kind of planning requires extensive investigation to incorporate the broad range of issues related to diverse groups of people in any social setting, as well as careful, systematic planning to ensure that an organization operates systematically and effectively, within the boundaries set by the financial resources available. A well-formulated policy provides a blueprint of the activities, services, and programs through which the organization will achieve its purposes.

Action research provides a particularly useful tool for strategic policy planning. It assists organizations and agencies to carefully articulate their policies by working systematically through the processes of inquiry described in previous chapters:

- Framing and focusing
- Gathering data
- Distilling or analyzing data
- Reporting
- Planning, implementing, and evaluating

The beauty of action research is its ability to be applied as a tool at all levels of a system, providing the means for systematic development of plans for the integrated development of programs and services. It may also be used, however, very locally, offering small groups the means to tackle specific issues and problems affecting the operation of services or relationships with constituent community groups.

The following sections present a strategic planning process, each phase being informed by an action research cycle, where an organization, agency, or group will develop the following features of its operation:

- **Vision:** A statement of the long-term aspirations of the organization
- **Mission:** A description of the activities, services, and programs through which the organization will accomplish its vision
- **Operational and action plans:** A description of the ways in which those programs and services will operate

Creating a New Vision

A vision statement seeks to describe the broader intents and purposes of the organization. It is sometimes defined in terms of future goals that enable people to envision what they will have accomplished in the longer term. By looking to the future, members of an organization seek to look past day-to-day needs, activities, and administrative arrangements, to gain a clear understanding of the long-term intent of their work together.

The development of vision statements can be a dynamic process, providing opportunities to gain inputs from a wide range of stakeholders. A vision is often constructed in an ongoing way, incorporating ideas from many groups who explore and articulate their image of the future. Research questions enable participants to "think big" about their family and community situation. The questions may include the following types:

- What type of organization do we want? What should be the qualities of that organization?
- What type of community would I like (my children) to live in? What are the qualities and characteristics of that community?
- What is the purpose of the organization?
- Why will people participate in the activities/services/programs of this organization?
- What do we wish our clients to accomplish?

These types of questions assist people to formulate statements about the purposes of the organization and to explain how it will provide for the needs of individuals, groups, or the community.

Developing a vision often enables organizations to move past the more mundane and repetitive features of organization or community life, to engage the underlying purposes of their work and in the process to rethink—reenvision—what they wish to accomplish. A vision statement based on collaborative research provides people with the energy and purpose to work together.

Organizations have traditionally incorporated a vision of their values in policy statements, presented as *vision* or *mission* statements or as *principles*. Usually they incorporate broad statements of *purpose*, together with statements of *value*. For example:

Purpose
- All people have an inherent right to a lifestyle that will enable them to reach their highest possible potential.
- The responsibility of organizations in a democracy is to make it possible for all citizens to work together, so that they can live effectively in a world of expanding experiences and constant change.

Value
- All people are treated with dignity and respect.
- Lifestyle is unique to each individual.
- Clients are partners in the delivery of services.

The problem with such principles or philosophies is that they are likely to drift into the background and become meaningless "mom-and-apple-pie" statements with which no one would disagree but which no one takes seriously. Two conditions are required to provide the impetus for ensuring that vision statements are actualized in an organization's programs and services. First, all stakeholders—clients, administrators, families, and so on—should be involved in their construction so that the stakeholders both understand the statements and take ownership of them. Second, there is a concerted effort to articulate those statements through all levels of the organization, so that the principles and values described in the policy document are enacted in the ongoing work of managers, administrators, professional staff, client services, and so on.

From Mission to Action

A well-organized institutional context provides strong degrees of association between broad policy statements and particular services and programs. Broad vision statements, which are essentially philosophical in nature, need to be specifically linked to particular programs, services, and activities. Carefully articulated links at each level of planning provide guidance for those responsible for implementing the policy or plan—from *vision*, to *mission*, to an *operational plan* describing the ways in which programs and services will be developed, and to action plans detailing how these programs and services might be instituted.

An organization may construct a vision for a program that:

- Includes the provision of services for all clients, regardless of race, ethnicity, class, gender, or sexual orientation
- Ensures that those services provide for the emotional, physical, and social well-being of all client groups

The organization's mission, enabling this vision to be achieved, might be to:

- Provide youth and parent support programs in all districts served by the organization
- Design appropriate services and activities
- Provide special facilities (buildings, materials, equipment, and so on) in support of those services and activities
- Supervise and monitor programs and services
- Provide funds and personnel to implement programs and services

Each branch or office of the organization articulates an operational plan, using a set of objectives related to the above mission. These might be to:

- Organize and coordinate the ongoing operation of each program or service
- Provide supervision and support for those programs
- Provide resources—equipment and materials—and special services in support of programs, services, and activities
- Evaluate the effectiveness of the programs
- Link the programs and services effectively to relevant groups in the community

Action plans enact the *mission* established in conjunction with the *vision*. Program planning derives from activities emerging within operational plans and incorporates philosophical guidelines delineated in the organization's vision statement.

Organizations always run the risk of becoming atrophied, and of their provision of services becoming highly ritualistic and mechanical so that activities become stale,

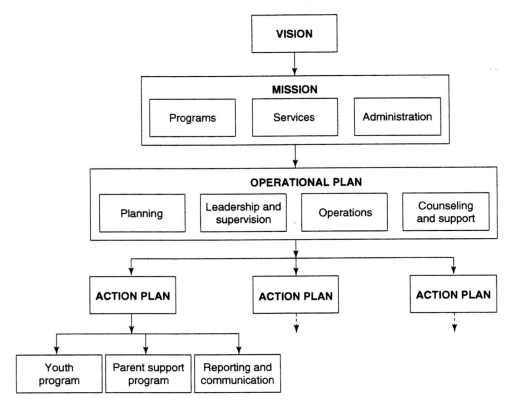

Figure 7.2
Strategic Planning Process

repetitive, and stressful. Moreover, narrowly prescribed procedural rules, sometimes related to specific budgetary or political pressures, often threaten the creative and effective implementation of an organizational vision. Opportunities for stakeholders to review and reenvision their work frequently provide the impetus for thinking outside the box to maintain a focus on the real purposes of their endeavors, thus maintaining and enhancing their organizational life.

The strategic planning process depicted in Figure 7.2 is a nominal version of an actual planning process. It shows the levels of planning that need to occur and signals the interconnection among the different sections. Different people—senior administrators, workers, and clients—would have responsibility for establishing detailed plans at each level. The figure illustrates, however, that what happens in program and service delivery is linked to larger issues and agendas. Action research processes provide the means for organizations to acquire and analyze the complex array of information systematically, as a basis for coherent, effective programs and services.

SUMMARY

This chapter describes the transition from analysis to action.

It first describes processes for developing *action plans* related to the problem or issue studied.

It then describes a number of everyday human service activities that may be enhanced by the use of action research processes:

- **The helping process**
- **Assessment**
- **Evaluating programs and services**
- **Organizational change: PREPARE and IMAGINE**
- **Community development**
- **Professional development**
- **Strategic planning**

Action Research Toolkit

8

Introduction

The distinctive feature of action research is that it is interactive. Unlike the unobtrusive and objective stance of experimental and survey research, action research sometimes engages participants in complex and diverse activities that require individuals and groups to work together. Since change is often an outcome of an effective research process, participants may experience difficulties in negotiating the diverse agendas that confront them, as well as the multiple and sometimes conflicting roles they must play. As they juggle the competing demands placed on them by a changing work or social life, participants must also keep track of all the steps required to develop and sustain the outcomes they desire. This chapter provides a toolkit to assist researchers to keep track of their activities and to work systematically through difficulties they may experience.

This toolkit of techniques and processes is not meant to provide fixed recipes or rigid step-by-step procedures that *must* be followed. Rather, the techniques and processes recommended here are akin to mind maps that assist people to understand where they are in the action research process and how they might move forward. They are suggestive rather than prescriptive, and they are presented in summary form. Those in need of more detailed guidance can go directly to the sources cited to obtain the information needed to enact the procedures successfully. There are many variations for each, so that researchers can seek sources that most clearly fit their situation or that are more readily available in their context. The toolkit includes:

- Conflict management
- Stress management
  - Sources of stress
  - Guidelines for managing stress
  - Time management
- Social action
  - Campaigning
  - Social activism

- Surviving bureaucracy
- Working with groups
  - Principles of group work
  - Group processes
- Meetings

Conflict Management

Conflict is a normal part of human interaction, and often a necessary part of a change process. When people with different backgrounds, histories, agendas, and personalities work together, conflict easily arises and needs to be dealt with openly and constructively. The major task in managing conflict is to ensure that differences in perspective and purpose are resolved through processes of negotiation. These processes should enable the different parties to come to a mutually acceptable arrangement that enables the action research project to continue to evolve. When issues are left unresolved, conflict often erupts into heated outbursts, personal attacks, and the undermining of project activities. The art and craft of working with people is to create conditions that minimize conflict and to resolve issues that arise before they become major impediments.

For action research, negotiated agreements are the best means of resolving conflicts, creating conditions for people to work together productively and harmoniously. When resolution of issues occurs by the exercise of power or authority, the power of the process is diminished considerably. Conflict may be resolved by the following means:

1. Acknowledge conflict—do not assume that it will go away.
2. Discuss, describe, and define the issues related to the conflict as a group, not within cliques or in private conversations.
3. Listen to all points of view. All voices should be heard and be given equal weight.
4. Use open-ended questions to focus on participants' actual experience and their interpretation of events (see Chapter 4, Questioning Techniques).
5. Employ active listening skills. Record and read back participants' own words to ensure that their perspective or position has been adequately and accurately recorded.
6. Clarify perspectives, issues, and positions when they are unclear.
7. Examine discrepancies between different participants' experience and their interpretations of events. Focus on what actually happened.
8. Include both emotional and objective features of participants' experience—how they felt as well as what happened.
9. Begin by focusing on areas of agreement and common ground.
10. Avoid win-or-lose situations. Seek compromise solutions based on consensus rather than power-mediated solutions decided by vote.
11. Work for cooperation, and not competition.
12. View differing positions as complementary perspectives rather than competing alternatives.

Stress Management

> **Ernie:** I was once involved with the development of an organization that provided multiple services to agencies across the state. In the early days of the organization, with few staff and too many tasks to be completed, I often felt overwhelmed by the situation. Many people would visit the office to talk through issues, the funding authority required quarterly reports on progress, and we seemed to be constantly involved in meetings—planning meetings, consultation meetings with clients, crisis meetings, and so on. Paperwork seemed to cover my entire office—desk, chairs, shelves, cupboards, and even the floor held piles of correspondence, reports, training materials, procedures manuals, and so on. It was not unusual as I sat at my desk writing reports and dealing with administrative matters to have people regularly interrupt to confer on an issue or for me to sign a document. Through all this activity the phone rang so constantly that I rarely held an uninterrupted conversation.
>
> I began to feel increasingly stressed. I slept poorly, often waking in the early hours of the morning with work-related matters rushing through my mind, unable to return to sleep. Not only was I constantly tired, but also anxious about the huge pile of urgent matters that seemed to pile higher and higher around me. My weight rose rapidly as I nibbled my way through snacks, and had a few drinks in the evening to relax after a very demanding day at the office or in the field. Nothing helped with the constant feeling of being weighed down, of feeling unable to make headway, or of feeling any sense of accomplishment, despite our obvious success. I felt constantly depressed. My fellow workers suffered similar experiences, and despite our commitment, relationships started to break down and angry clashes became increasingly frequent.
>
> Eventually I took extended leave to recuperate, but I've since learned the importance of finding organizational and personal ways to minimize stress in my workplace, and I've learned a number of techniques to deal with stressful situations. In these days of economic rationalism and "downsizing"(which means, usually, less people to do the same amount of work), stress management is a crucial part of professional life.

Sources of Stress

Human service professionals often confront highly sensitive issues, very demanding work contexts, and a wide range of diverse and complex agendas. In these circumstances, stress can easily become an ongoing feature of the situation and sometimes threaten the efficacy of the work or the success of a project. It arises from the increasingly complex responsibilities, the large amounts of paperwork, and the complicated needs of diverse clients and client groups that are a common part of professional life. Stress may manifest itself:

- **Physiologically**—High blood pressure, sleeplessness, stomach upsets, illnesses, headaches, rashes, other physical conditions
- **Psychologically**—Feelings of anxiety and depression, inability to concentrate, obsessive behavior, overuse of alcohol, drugs, and/or medication
- **Behaviorally**—Being argumentative or aggressive; exhibiting withdrawal, avoidance, or passivity

Stress may be associated with any of the following conditions:

- **Environment**—Crowded work environment, lack of privacy, lack of space to do the required work, noise, and so on
- **Urgent deadlines**—Constant demands to take action, to complete paperwork; lack of lead time
- **Heavy workload**—Too much work to do in the time allocated
- **Distractions and interruptions**—People interrupting your work with a question or request; the telephone ringing constantly
- **Poor interpersonal relationships**—Interacting with colleagues and clients with poor interpersonal skills; dealing with people who are argumentative, aggressive, passive, blaming, demanding, and so on; working with people whose personal style is dramatically different from your own (personality conflict)
- **Ambiguous roles and responsibilities**—Lack of clarity about who will do which work, who will be responsible for completing tasks, supervising activities, and so on
- **Lack of skills**—Not having the skills or experience to do the required work

Guidelines for Managing Stress

Stress is often so deeply embedded in a work situation that it requires systematic and conscious efforts to (a) reduce stress, (b) prevent stress, and (c) cope with stress. The following guidelines suggest some ways that human service professionals may manage stress in their everyday worklives. They may need to instigate measures to minimize feelings of stress, to learn ways of interacting with clients and colleagues that maintain harmonious relationships, to enact their professional duties more efficiently, and to evaluate the appropriateness of the way work is organized in their agency or organization.

The guidelines do not provide a comprehensive program for managing stress, but they do point to issues that need to be addressed. It is worthwhile to review each of them from time to time to identify areas where time and conscious effort are required to systematically deal with problems that may be emerging or to resolve stressful situations that have entered the workplace. When high levels of stress are evident, an outside consultant or mediator may need to be used to take systematic, therapeutic or organizational action.

Personal

Living a healthy lifestyle provides the foundation for accommodating stresses in the workplace. Constantly monitor your personal well-being and:

- Consciously evaluate your lifestyle to ensure that appropriate provision is made for *sleep, exercise,* and a healthy *diet*

- Learn *relaxation techniques* that may be applied on a regular basis or used in times of stress—deep breathing, meditation, biofeedback, yoga, etc.
- Seek *professional help* when stress manifests itself significantly—visit a doctor, counselor, or therapist

Interpersonal

Maintain positive working relationships by:

- **Communicating:** Regularly inform the people with whom you work of your activities, and provide them with information they may require.
- **Listening:** Be sure to use active listening skills since they will assist you to "really hear" what people are saying and to acknowledge the worth of what they are saying.
- **Negotiating:** Don't stick rigidly to your own perspectives and agendas. Be ready to compromise and to accept alternative viewpoints.
- **Including:** Provide opportunities for others to work with you or to complete tasks you think of as "yours."
- **Sharing:** Share information, resources, materials, space, etc., where possible and appropriate.
- **Resolving:** Let people know when you are annoyed or disturbed at their actions and seek immediate resolution.

Professional

Minimize stress by ensuring that your work is well organized and that you carry out work tasks efficiently:

- **Allocation of time:** Minimize waste of professional time through time management techniques (see below).
- **Professional competence:** Do not take jobs that are well outside your level of professional competence, and monitor work activities to ensure you are not asked to engage in tasks far beyond your level of skills or knowledge.
- **Professional development:** Allocate time in your yearly schedule to refresh, replenish, or extend your professional skills and knowledge.

Organizational

Stress frequently arises because of the sheer volume of work. In some cases no amount of planning or organization will overcome the resulting stress. Often, however, efficient and creative use of people's time and energy enables workers to deal with temporarily stressful situations and to increase the effectiveness of their work in the process. Human service workers and administrators should consciously review the following features of their work:

- Work environment
  - There is adequate space to carry out work tasks.
  - There are no distractions.
  - Noise levels are not excessive.
  - People have privacy when engaged in sensitive work with clients or fellow professionals.

- The environment is clean and attractive.
- Offices and desks are tidy and well ordered.
  - Workload
    - Work tasks can be completed in the time allotted.
    - Tasks are, as far as possible, equally distributed across workers.
  - Task allocation
    - There is a practical system for allocating tasks.
  - Roles and responsibilities
    - Each person understands his or her roles and responsibilities—the type of tasks that the person will be assigned. This is especially important where organizations and agencies have associated consultative bodies, management committees, or policymaking boards.
  - Deadlines
    - Workers have adequate time to respond to requests or accomplish tasks.
  - Efficiency
    - Explore ways that work may be accomplished more efficiently, through planning, time allocation, rationalizing activities, and so on. The question to ask is, "How can we accomplish a task or activity as effectively using less time and/or resources?"
  - Funds
    - Review the use of funds and financial resources to ensure that maximum benefit is gained through their allocation.

Time Management

Making efficient use of time is one of the best means of minimizing stress. The following activities provide guidelines for this purpose:

- **List work tasks:**   List incomplete work tasks and activities.
- **Allocate time:**   Estimate and note the time needed to complete each task or activity (10 minutes, 3 hours, 2 days, etc.).
- **Prioritize:**   Rate tasks and activities according to their urgency—I (immediate), M (medium term), L (long term)—and then rank according to their importance—1, 2, 3, . . .
- **Rationalize:**   Set aside a block of time to complete minor tasks—completing forms, answering correspondence, etc.
- **Schedule a "phone time":**   Do not answer the telephone when it rings. Allow callers to leave messages on the answering machine, and set a time aside each day when you answer all calls.
- **Reduce distractions and interruptions:**   Minimize distractions and interruptions by letting people know when you do not wish to be disturbed. Put up a sign ("Do Not Disturb"), close the office door, inform people (nicely) when they are interrupting, arrange for messages to be taken—by office staff, and use a phone answering machine.
- **Review activities:**   List *all* activities in which you are engaged, to ensure you eliminate unnecessary or inappropriate actions. Each person should make sure he or she is not doing other people's work.

- **Monitor:** Over a period of a week, each worker should record daily all their activities and the time spent on each activity. A chart of activities with space for time use may assist this process. An alternative method is to name all activities for each hour of a working day for a week. Identify wasteful or inappropriate uses of time.
- **Plan:** Make a daily and weekly schedule of the activities you wish to accomplish. Use your prioritized list of activities to choose goals for each day. Specify tasks related to each goal and activity.
- **Rationalize:** Gather similar activities together, e.g., replies to correspondence, visits in the field.
- **Mark a calendar:** Use a calendar to schedule work, noting future appointments, meetings, and other times not available for planned activities.
- **Delegate:** If other people are available, delegate appropriate tasks to them.
- **Work systematically:** Keep track of your activities—use a wall chart, planning calendar, or other devices. Keep to your plan. Replan when emergencies or other exigencies intervene.
- **Avoid procrastination:** If you decide to put off an activity, be consciously aware of doing so. A general rule is to "Do it now!" since unpleasant or tiresome activities that have been avoided build easily to problematic proportions.

Social Action

The major approach to action presented in this book is through collaborative and participatory approaches to inquiry and development. Our experience suggests that where confrontation is used in early interactions, limited outcomes result in the long term. The fracturing of relationships, the development of antagonisms, and the polarization of positions arising from conflict-oriented approaches to implement social action are often not worth the price.

Having said that, there may be times when people in entrenched positions of power refuse to acknowledge the needs of groups or seem to work only in their own interests. When consistent efforts to engage such people in harmonious explorations fail, direct social or political action may be the only remaining option. In these cases it is expedient to engage in carefully planned procedures that maximize the possibility of an organization or social group acquiring what it wants.

Campaigning

Kelly and Sewell (1988) suggest that a campaign may be an appropriate response to a situation where decision makers fail to take account of people's needs or do not provide access to rightful resources. They suggest the need for careful planning, however, since people who rush into a campaign without careful thought and preparation can be very vulnerable. Kelly & Sowell describe five phases of a campaign:

1. **Focus:** Clarify the issue about which the change is sought.
2. **Mobilization:** Mobilize people who will support you, and marshal the facts and arguments that will enhance your position.
3. **Confrontation:** Confront those who are resisting change.

4. **Personalization:** Be prepared when people resisting change retaliate personally by threatening jobs, engaging in character assassination, or harassing friends and family of those participating in the campaign.
5. **Redefinition:** Take advantage of new possibilities that emerge.

Once a campaign is successful, conscious steps must be planned to repair relationships with those against whom the campaign was directed. To fail to accomplish this important step weakens the effect of the campaign and mitigates against future accomplishments. People may win a battle but lose the war.

Social Activism

Saul Alinsky (1971) was a strong advocate of militant social action. In *Rules for Radicals* he mapped out a revolutionary plan for social change that is uncompromisingly militaristic in its process and inherently Machiavellian in its focus—"how to create mass organizations that seize power and give it to the people."

Less dramatic perspectives on social activism suggest a more systematic approach to social change. Coover, Deacon, Esser, and Moore's *Resource Manual for a Living Revolution* (1985) provides a handbook of skills and tools for social change activists. Their comprehensive approach to activism focuses on long-term developmental strategies that include:

- The education and skilling of activists
- The development of a theory of change
- An analysis of the political economy
- A vision for a new society
- Strategies necessary to accomplish the vision

They present material to assist people to develop their understanding of working in groups to facilitate meetings, resolve conflict, and develop communities of support. The need for personal growth and consciousness raising, and the importance of education and training are also explored. These, they suggest, are important elements of social change since social process cannot change unless people change also.

They present a process of direct action that has the explicit goal of changing the structure or activities of an oppressive institution. Actions are highly visible and confrontational to make the situation public, to dramatize an unjust situation, to expose moral contradictions, and to influence change. The stages for a direct-action campaign include:

- Investigation
  - Define the goals of the campaign.
  - Describe the nature of the problem.
  - Acquire information.
  - Meet with interested parties.
  - Explore sources of resistance and support.
  - Investigate alternative possible solutions.
- Negotiation
  - Help parties understand each other and the reasons behind their actions.
  - Seek resolution of conflict.

- Establish ways to keep contact with the opponent.
- Recognize the limits of negotiation.
- Education (cultural preparation)
  - Make information available to bring about full discussion of the issues.
  - Provide an analysis of the situation.
  - Excite people with a vision of the future.
  - Create indignation.
  - Help people discover their own abilities and power.
  - Enter into dialogue with the groups and individuals most affected by the injustice.
  - Find ways to communicate with the public.
- Preparation
  - Plan preliminary strategy and tactics.
  - Pick an appropriate target for the action.
  - Indicate clear sponsorship.
  - List jobs to be done.
  - Inventory resources.
  - Develop a flowchart and a timeline.
  - Set up coordination and information centers.
  - Obtain permits.
  - Train participants.
  - Formulate decision-making processes.
  - Prepare for emotional and spiritual demands made on people.
  - Make legal provisions for arrests, bail, etc.
- Direct action
  - Test the strength and determination of opposing forces.
  - Change part of the oppressive structure.
  - Raise public consciousness.
  - Influence all people involved in the situation.
  - Choose the best actions to support the overall strategy.
  - Keep up efforts at persuasion.
  - Keep the initiative.
  - Overcome violence.
- Protracted struggle
  - Sustain action until goals are achieved.
  - Use nonviolent action.
  - Escalate action.
  - Provide alternatives.

Surviving Bureaucracy

Many human service professionals work in bureaucratic agencies, departments, or organizations. Bureaucracies are stable forms of organization that provide the means to coordinate activities of large numbers of people. The stability of a bureaucracy, however, comes at a cost, since rigid structures of operation are inherently controlling and often are not open to changes required by changing circumstances. Many organizations are oriented toward a form of management having the following characteristics:

- Decisions are made autocratically and hierarchically.
- The system is rigid and stable.
- Fixed procedures govern the rules of operation.
- The emphasis is on maintaining the status quo—changing the organization is difficult.
- Communication is from level to level of the vertical structure.
- The needs of the organization are primary; worker and client needs are secondary.

Kirst-Ashman and Hull (2001) characterize the operation of a bureaucracy as a:

specifically designed, formal structure and a consistent, rigid organizational network of employees [that] are most important for an organization to run well and achieve its goals. . . . Each employee holds a clearly defined job and is told straightforwardly exactly how that job should be done. . . . [A bureaucracy] calls for minimal independent functioning on the part of employees. Supervisors closely scrutinize all work. Efficiency is of utmost importance. Performance is quantified, . . . regulated, and measured. How people feel about their jobs is insignificant. Administration avoids allowing employees any input regarding how organizational goals can best be reached. Instead, employees are expected to do their jobs as instructed, as quietly and efficiently as possible. (pp. 126–127)

Kirst-Ashman and Hull suggest that these features of a bureaucracy often run counter to the needs of human service professionals, who need flexibility, creativity, and decision-making powers to be able to work effectively with their clients. They must carry out functions requiring highly personalized orientations to their work, where relationships and the feelings of clients are a necessary feature of the context. Quoting Knopf (1979), they provide a number of tips to assist workers to best survive some of the conditions imposed by bureaucratic forms of operation. These include:

- Identify your own needs or client needs, and use a problem-solving approach that explores a wide range of solutions.
- Learn how the particular bureaucracy is structured and how it functions (who does which work, which people and positions have greater authority, etc.).
- Treat bureaucrats as people with feelings, and treat them with the respect and interest you offer clients.
- Do not go to war with the bureaucracy.
- Limit the changes you seek to make in the operation of the bureaucracy—you cannot change everything.
- Seek clarity about your job expectations.
- Continue your professional development.
- Do not take on responsibilities well beyond your level of competence.
- Learn how to control counterproductive emotions.
- Use a sense of humor to take the edge off difficult situations.
- Learn to accept your mistakes with good grace.

- Develop a support system among your colleagues.
- Give in sometimes on minor matters. You are not always right.
- Keep physically fit and mentally alert.
- Leave your work at the office.
- Socialize occasionally with fellow workers and with organizational seniors.
- Do not seek ego satisfaction from the bureaucracy—it is largely a depersonalized system.
- Accentuate the positives when talking with people about the agency.
- No matter what your seniority, maintain some direct service contacts.
- Identify career goals, and determine whether they can be met within the system.

As a general rule, human service workers can survive, and even thrive, in a bureaucracy if they apply to their colleagues, including organizational superiors and inferiors, the same helping processes and skills that are part of their professional repertoire. "Leading from behind" is as important a function, though not usually organizationally recognized, as any other set of skills applied to face-to-face work with clients and client groups.

Another means of surviving bureaucratic organizations is to review the approach to the management and operation of the organization. Barker (1999, p. 488) suggests that a "total quality management" orientation would improve the functioning of organizations. This he defines as "an orientation to management of organizations, including social services agencies, in which quality, as defined by clients and consumers, is the overriding goal and in which client satisfaction, employee empowerment, and long-term relationships determine procedures." A more participatory approach to management that takes account of both client and employee perspectives in formulating goals and the practices through which the organization attains its goals may be more appropriate for human service delivery. In this case, the organization itself should take responsibility for reviewing its approach to management and instituting a thorough restructuring process that reviews not only the policy of the organization, but also its operational plans (see Chapter 7).

Working with Groups

Ernie: Over the years, I've worked with many community and professional groups. I've discovered that they provide a context in which people can work together to accomplish powerful ends, and to set in motion actions that sometimes result in powerful social and political change within organizations, agencies, or the community.

Working with people to effect change is not always straightforward or easy, however, and facilitating the activities of a group has been described to me as akin to "herding cats!" I've worked in groups where personality conflicts have resulted in harshly antagonistic exchanges between individuals, where strong-willed individuals have threatened to dominate and control the proceedings of the group, or where constant, whining complaints have threatened to disempower the people involved.

Over the years, I have realized that working with groups of people requires carefully planned activities, and skillful facilitation to ensure that maximum benefit is attained by marshalling people's strength and resourcefulness. Skill in working with groups comes through careful learning of the art and craft of group work, and is honed through continued experience. The following notes provide reminders of basic issues that need to be taken into account to enhance the possibility that a group of people may work together efficiently and effectively.

Principles of Group Work

Human service professionals often work with groups of people. Whether it involves working with colleagues on a larger project or working with community groups on issues for which they have responsibility—employment, drugs, domestic violence, and so on—group work provides an effective means of initiating action or developing a project, program, or service. Working with groups of people, however, is not always a straightforward process, especially when sensitive issues are at hand and diverse people are involved.

Relationships

One of the features of strong group life is harmonious relationships. Without this, people have difficulty in working together and maintaining the life of the group. A key feature of group life, therefore, is to develop processes that provide the means for people to attain and maintain good working relationships. People do not necessarily have to like each other, but they do need to respect and trust each other to maximize the possibility of working cooperatively to attain group goals.

Communication

Open and respectful communication is a fundamental ingredient of a successful group. Members must know what is going on and what activities people are engaged in, and they should have access to all information affecting group activities. Lack of information breeds misunderstanding and distrust.

Participation

Successful groups maximize opportunities for members to be actively engaged in activities related to the work of the group. When an individual takes on too much responsibility, through a sense of self-importance or a desire to make sure "it's done right," the energy of the group is likely to decline.

Group Processes

Johnson and Johnson (1997) provide a useful analysis of group work. They suggest that groups work effectively when:

- The group has clear goals that are relevant to all members.
- Communication is clear and accurate.
- Participation and leadership are shared.
- Appropriate decision-making procedures are used.
- Power and influence are shared.
- Controversy is accepted, and creative problem-solving is encouraged.
- Conflicts are resolved constructively.

The following features of group life assist in managing these issues:

- **Task accomplishment:** Tasks are accomplished promptly.
- **Leadership:** Leadership is shared according to interest, expertise, and personal qualities.
- **Power and influence:** No person or group dominates. All voices are heard equally.
- **Conflict:** Conflicts are minimized, and they are resolved constructively when they occur.
- **Decision making:** Decisions are made by consensus after sufficient discussion of relevant issues, and they are clearly recorded.
- **Goals:** Goals of the group are clearly stated, and they represent the perspectives and commitments of all group members.
- **Communication:** Group members are fully informed and can communicate with each other openly and honestly.
- **Rules:** There is a clear set of ground rules about the operation of the group to which all members are committed.

Meetings

> ***Ernie:*** I learned much about meetings from a colleague who chaired a University committee I attended regularly. Meetings started and finished on time, worked smoothly through an agenda, and participants engaged in healthy and informative discussion about complex issues. I took the efficiency of these meetings for granted until an occasion when Brian was absent and another person was chair. The one-hour meeting stretched into three, and people with important inputs were forced to leave to attend other duties. Debate on relatively minor issues, sometimes marginally associated with an agenda item, stretched on without resolution. Exchanges sometimes became acrimonious, and the chair would move on to other items when things became too uncomfortable. "Well, I can see we're not going to reach a resolution to this item, so I'd like to move on to the next item of the agenda. We'll come back to that next meeting!"

I left that meeting feeling tired and dissatisfied, with a much greater respect for the efficient and effective manner in which the meeting was usually chaired. The artful chairing we usually experienced enabled us to accomplish complex and important business with a minimum of fuss.

Meetings vary in size and degree of formality. In the earlier stages of an action research project, people may meet informally in small groups to exchange information, plan activities, or resolve problems. As the size and complexity of a project grows, meetings may increase in length and formality and need to be carefully planned to ensure that they operate efficiently and effectively. Especially when sensitive issues are being explored, or when people's lives and work are affected, meetings can easily deteriorate into hostile arenas of combative behavior or become so monotonously ritualistic that they become a waste of time. The task of those responsible for organizing and conducting meetings is to provide a safe environment in which people can work together harmoniously and efficiently. The following points are not rigid rules to which people should adhere at all costs, but issues that need to be taken into account:

- **Plan ahead:**   All arrangements for meetings should be carefully planned well in advance.
- **Clarify purposes:**   People should be clear about why they are meeting.
- **Select participants:**   Participants should include relevant stakeholders—those affected by the issues and purposes of the meeting.
- **Inform participants:**   Participants should be informed well in advance of a meeting so they can fit it in their schedules. They should also receive an agenda, together with any major reports or other information related to issues on the meeting agenda.
- **Choose a suitable time:**   It is important to make sure that meetings are held at times when all stakeholders are able to attend. Not only do individual schedules need to be taken into account, but meeting times should also accommodate institutional, organizational, and public schedules—public holidays, religious observances, operational schedules, etc.
- **Give thought to the choice of meeting place:**   Organizers should be sensitive to the effect of surroundings on the participants' sense of well-being. A community center or a person's home may, in some instances, be more conducive to effective communication than an agency office. The location should be comfortable and free from distractions.
- **Prepare an agenda:**   The agenda should list topics to be addressed in order of priority, and be made available to participants prior to the meeting. Participants should help shape the agenda, which may in some circumstances best be formulated at the previous meeting. "So we are agreed that when we next meet we will discuss the following issues. . . "
- **Make meeting materials available beforehand:**   Copies of relevant materials, including the agenda, any written reports, or other information, should be

provided to participants before the meeting so they have sufficient time to read and digest the material.

- **Ensure necessary equipment is available:** Equipment can include tea- and coffee-making facilities, chart paper and pens, whiteboards, and so on, according to the nature of the meeting and the needs of participants.
- **Keep on schedule:** It is important to state the ending time at the beginning of the meeting and then end at that time, except under special circumstances and with the agreement of those present.
- **Ensure that everyone can participate:** All people should be equally able to express their views. Discussions should be carefully managed so that "loud voices" do not dominate. Take special care to make sure that less powerful voices are heard.
- **Keep on target:** Whoever chairs the meeting should keep the group on target. Allow open discussion, but ensure that participants do not lose their focus.
    - Set aside new problems or items of interest that cannot be resolved quickly, and place them on the agenda for the next meeting.
    - Periodically summarize the discussion.
    - Avoid discussing topics not relevant to a specific agenda item—if necessary, set them aside for later discussion, or place them on the agenda for the following meeting.
    - Discuss lengthy issues and documents item by item, rather than allowing people to jump between sections of a lengthy report.
    - Refer contentious items to a subcommittee composed of people with differing views. The subcommittee should report back at a later meeting with suggested recommendations or with the issue clarified.
    - Keep reports brief.
    - Place a time limit on oral reports.
    - Place a time limit on any agenda item—"This is becoming time-consuming. I'll allow another 5 minutes of discussion and then put it to a subcommittee if we can't resolve it today."
- **Make decisions by consensus:** It is better to attain consensus than to put a decision to a vote. This encourages people to work cooperatively rather than engage in power politics in order to get their way. Attaining consensus often takes more time initially but is much more productive and effective in the long run.

Conclusion

The processes of action research are both naturalistic and interactive. Research facilitators and other participants sometimes have to engage in complex social interactions that are usually not seen as part of a research process. Action researchers need to learn or further develop skills that will build their capacity to work effectively in groups, communities, and agencies. This toolkit provides but a few of the many processes and skills that enable people to accomplish their work capably and confidently.

Case Studies in Action Research

9

Introduction

Examples of action research projects in human service agencies and community organizations are proliferating rapidly. The extent of interest in this form of investigation is demonstrated both by the expanding audiences at action research sessions at conferences and by the increasing number of reports in professional journals. It is becoming a recognized tool of social workers and other human service professionals, as well as a regular part of preservice preparation and in-service professional development.

The following case studies represent only a few of the creative and productive ways professional practitioners, clients, organizations, families, and community groups have applied action research in their agency, organization, and community contexts. As real-life studies, they provide some indication of the diversity of forms of participatory investigation and, particularly, applications of frameworks similar to those described in this book. They differ in style and quality and do not necessarily represent "best practice" in report writing. They do represent, however, the diverse means authors use to communicate information to different audiences, according to the purposes they wish to achieve. Studies include:

1. Young Offenders: From Casework to Capacity Building
2. Developing a Family and Neighborhood Center
3. Mending Broken Promises: Justice for Children at Risk
4. Hewson Community Cottage—A Service in a Fluctuating State of Turmoil
5. Action Research and Community Development

1. Young Offenders: From Casework to Capacity Building

This account is based on a series of interviews with a social worker and illustrates how action research can be applied to developmental processes. By starting with a single problem and working through a number of cycles of investigation, participants involved in this project increased the scope of their work to construct effective ways of dealing with a complex problem.

BUILDING THE PICTURE: THE GRACEVILLE CONTEXT

Graceville is a large town that suffers many problems common to rural communities in modern times. Despite a recent upturn in industries associated with the area, economic conditions are not conducive to a prosperous or healthy community. The rural downturn of past decades has left a large population of unemployed, who continue to struggle to maintain a semblance of an orderly family and community life. Chronic unemployment is associated with drug and alcohol abuse, petty crime, and disorderly conduct, especially amongst older children and teenagers.

THE PROBLEM: YOUTH AND CRIME

This latter group constituted particular problems for town authorities and relevant agencies, since continued occurrences of burglary, petty theft, vandalism, and drug and alcohol abuse were prevalent, especially amongst young males. Frustrations for police officers were exacerbated when arrests were followed by either warnings, community service orders, or short detentions that had young offenders back on the streets almost immediately. Reoffending youth provided continuing frustrations of time-consuming paperwork and court appearances associated with the almost monotonous routine of arrests. As one police officer stated, "It's a revolving door. Kids offend, we arrest, they go to court, then they're back on the streets. We take them home from detention and there is often no adult there, or the parents are drunk or spaced out. In some of these houses there is just no responsible adult we can hand the kids back to. Sometimes the kids are barely back home when we have to pick them up again for exactly the same thing!" Attempts to have parents control their children's behavior met with little success, many suffer-

ing similar problems themselves, or able to exert little control on their offspring. "What you want me to do?" one mother asked when approached by a police officer, "He won't do nothing I tell him."

CASEWORK AND CONFLICTING PERSPECTIVES

This continuing cycle of juvenile offending created problems between agencies within the town. Police blamed welfare workers for not placing greater restrictions on the children and their parents, criticism echoed by teachers at local schools who criticized welfare workers for their failure to ensure that children attended school regularly. Welfare officers, in turn, criticized schools for failing to provide an appropriate education for all children, and the police for merely dumping recalcitrant youth on their doorstep.

Police finally took legal action against a number of offenders. They applied to the courts to have them removed from their families and placed in the care of the state. Social workers within the welfare agency actively fought this approach, being adamant that legal requirements associated with wardships would not only increase their already unmanageable workload, but actually inhibit their ability to act effectively. "You can't imagine the paperwork associated with the legal requirements of placing a child, and monitoring their situation. We'd have less time to deal constructively with these kids than we have now!!"

STRONGER FAMILIES: COLLABORATIVE COMMUNITY WORK

It became evident that dealing with the children as individual cases was failing to have an impact. A coalition of workers from Graceville human services agencies decided to seek a systematic and collaborative solution to the problem and met to develop a plan of action for dealing with a situation that had reached crisis point. Participants at the meeting built a picture of the situation, noting the apparent poverty of families of repeat offenders, lack of parental supervision or control, and lack of leisure and sporting facilities, especially for youth. As one person at the meeting said, "They have nothing to do with their time but get in trouble."

Participants in the meeting focused on a number of areas in which they could take action. They decided, firstly, to take action at the level of the family. Further inquiries revealed useful family networks and resources that were available in the local community, including aunts, uncles, grandparents, brothers, sisters, and cousins of repeat offenders. Meetings with family groups were held to build a picture of the situation with them of each relevant young person, analyze the problematics of his/her situation, and explore possibilities for action. Police and agency workers focused on the need for family supports to stop kids from reoffending, and to deal with underlying issues such as drunkenness in the home. They also investigated possibilities for protective behaviors for young people confronted with potentially harmful situations, including the identification of a number of "safe houses" where kids could take temporary shelter. In addition, social workers helped identify ways that family members providing care and protection to the young people could receive some welfare benefits to assist them in their work.

In a variety of ways, therefore, participants in this process worked with families and youth to ensure that they had a clear picture of the situation and an understanding of the immediate and long-term harm likely to arise from its continuation. Their collaborative analysis of the situation enabled them to devise actions at the family level to begin alleviating the issues.

BUILDING COMMUNITY CAPACITY

Part way through this process, however, it became clear that these family-focused activities were only partial solutions to the problem. Some families lived in isolation, or suffered a history of drug and alcohol consumption, or were in other ways alienated from attempts to collaborate with authorities. The monthly interagency meetings that had resulted in work with families were broadened to include community leaders, including some from disaffected groups in the community. Further discussions enabled this group to extend the picture and the analysis, taking into ac-

count the history of the situation, the low levels of education of both adults and young people, and the limited opportunities for employment related to limited economic development in the region. They were also able to identify many assets, particularly the skills and experiences of many of those within the community including what were considered "at risk" families. Using these assets as a basis, participants in the group commenced a series of activities that is still expanding.

Today they organize regular social events and functions that provide the means for family members to both participate in and contribute to specific events, and by extension, to community life. They have commenced a series of programs for kids that provide leisure time activities, while at the same time enabling young teens to develop their own capacities to improve their situations. Programs regularly include activities designed to increase problem-solving skills, raise self-esteem, enhance self-confidence, and teach practical life skills. Youth are also rewarded for good behavior by gaining entry to special events organized by local police officers—movies, camps, and so on.

The outcome not only has been to engage youth in positive activities, but also contribute to the development of a community spirit in these sections of the town. As people come together proactively, they are developing their capacities to deal with related issues in an ongoing way. Further, these meetings and activities have assisted agency workers, teachers, health professionals, police, and others to increase their knowledge of the place and the people. They have developed deeper relationships that have made a significant contribution to their collaborative efforts and to their ongoing professional life. It has, as one worker commented, made their work a lot easier. Moreover, there is a much greater awareness of the need for people in these agencies to work collaboratively and holistically to create positive and healthy changes for the young people involved. Casework, family work, and community development activity combine effectively to start to make inroads in what is a historically complex situation.

2. *Developing a Family and Neighborhood Center*

This narrative is based on a series of interviews with Margaret Auld, coordinator of the South Lake Family and Community Center. It describes how Margaret and community center staff developed vibrant family- and community-based services and activities by systematically acquiring information and communicating with local stakeholders. It illustrates ways that action research processes can be applied to the development of community services.

INTRODUCTION

South Lake is a relatively new suburb on the outskirts of a growing metropolis, populated largely by young families in lower-income groups. Though many of the houses are quite new, the general environment by a number of accounts (Auld and O'Neil, 2002) is uninspiring and somewhat run-down. Like many newer housing areas, the history of development is somewhat spotted. Families have often lacked access to many of the services and resources available in more established areas, including health, child care, services for the aged, and so on. Moreover, the sheer newness of the population meant that many, especially young mothers or unemployed people, had yet to develop networks of friends and social contacts that support everyday family life and help people work their way through problems and crises.

A government-funded Family and Neighborhood Center was established in South Lake as a community resource, but initially failed to attract people from the area. Despite very evident needs in the community, few people contacted or used the facilities and resources available. Human service professionals offered a variety of services, including such programs as formal parent training courses, but people in the area failed to take advantage of them.

LISTENING TO THE PEOPLE: GATHERING INFORMATION AND ANALYZING THE SITUATION

When she was first employed as the Center coordinator, Margaret Auld was puzzled by the little use being made of what she thought could be a thriving community resource. The services at the Center were poorly used, and few people attended activities organized by staff. She determined to take steps to revitalize and energize the Center into a real resource that would contribute significantly to the life of the South Lake community.

As a first step, Margaret talked with those people who did come to the Center to find out why they were there, and gradually began to build a picture of what was happening to people in the community. She also began to visit local shopping centers, observing carefully the different groups going to stores and engaging in informal conversations, talking with people about what was happening around them and eliciting comment from them about their lives in this new community.

In these and other ways she was able to develop a more complete picture of the community and the people who lived there. She acquired an understanding of the different groups inhabiting the area, and where and how people were experiencing difficulties and problems. By listening carefully to what people were saying, Margaret identified some of the areas where a neighborhood center could provide services and activities that would enhance the lives of people in the community. These initial ideas became the basis for establishing services and programs that were relevant to the expressed needs of the people in South Lake.

By developing her relationships with existing Center participants, Margaret enlarged her network of contacts, established working groups around particular issues, and with them, began to plan activities related to the needs expressed by people with whom she had talked. A Center committee provided ongoing support for these activities, offering advice and support, and extending the Center's network of contacts.

COMMUNICATING WITH STAKEHOLDERS

Margaret prepared monthly reports that provided the means by which committee members were kept informed of all developments and activities. These reports were the basis for discussions around problematic issues, or the carefully planned development of services and activities. The Center was also expected to provide a six-monthly report to its major funding agency. Careful recording of information provided the means for constructing these reports, which acted also as a means for reviewing Center activities. In this way the committee was able to demonstrate that the objectives outlined in the service specifications related to funding criteria were met.

Margaret also established links with other agencies in the area, inviting social workers, child health nurses, and other workers to the Center and introducing them personally to people involved in Center activities. Clear procedures were also established for answering phones or talking with people, so that staff could acquire information about who had called or visited, why they had called or visited, and what they needed. Visitors were offered a cup of tea, informed about the resources and activities of the Center, and referred to other organizations or services if their needs could not be met. In this way staff continued to build an understanding of the people in the community and the directions that they might take in further development of the Center.

Other forms of communication included widely distributed pamphlets that informed people of the services and activities available at the Center, and a newsletter, sent out regularly to interested people, that reported on past and future events. The Center also provided journalists with stories that were printed in the local newspaper. In addition, the Center held regular community days for the public—social events that included food and entertainment and attracted sometimes 200–300 people. Over time the Center was able to ensure that its programs and services became widely known to members of the community and to communicate effectively with its constituency.

TAKING ACTION: DEVELOPING PROGRAMS, SERVICES, AND ACTIVITIES

Initiating new programs and services was not an easy task, and required patient and careful work over an extended period. People in the district were somewhat wary, and it was obvious that they did not want programs imposed on them by people in positions of authority. Margaret therefore worked directly with local people, but also sought the advice and assistance of state agencies in the area. She also encouraged local groups to use the Center as a base for their activities, and this broadened support for the Center.

Many families had recently moved to this housing development, with many young mothers experiencing loneliness and isolation. Their issues were among the first to receive attention. Most of this group did not want to put their young babies and toddlers into child care, but needed a break from the constant demands of parenthood—to have time out from their children. They also needed somewhere to meet other parents and socialize. A mothers' group was formed, met with a community nurse for a few weeks, then continued to meet independently. A play group for young children was established and soon attracted a large group of participants. Parents could bring their children to a play group and have time to talk with each other, sharing information, talking through issues related to children, family, and community life. It became a popular program that provided the basis for a wide range of services and programs that now characterize the ongoing life of the Center.

Today, the rooms of the center are abuzz with the busy chatter of children as they happily play with the equipment provided, under the supervision of staff and parents. Apart from play groups for babies and children of mixed ages, it also offers "Family Fun Time," where parents and their young "under-five" children can get together for stories, songs, and other activities designed to develop children's social skills. Other activities include a Teenage Parents Group, a Mothers and Toddlers Group, a Sewing Group, a Social Support Group for mothers recovering from drug addiction, a Men's Group, an Arts and Crafts group, and a Women's Time Out Group. Resources at the Center include counselling for women; a social worker available on a weekly basis; and a Toy, Book, and Puzzle Library for young children. In addition to its own activities, the Center is also used by other community groups as a meeting place. A wide variety of interests includes a Breastfeeding Association, a Bahai faith group, a local Christian church, and Alcoholics Anonymous.

CONCLUSION

Human service professionals often make the mistake of assuming they know the needs of people in the community. In doing so they merely imprint their own vision of the situation into activities and often miss the real issues confronting people. By providing people with opportunities to express their thoughts, needs, and wishes, Margaret was able to help formulate appropriate solutions to problems confronting people in that community. She assisted local people to establish an active and vital Center that continues to add to the quality in life of the community. The programs, services, and activities of the Family and Neighborhood Center clearly meet the needs of specific community groups, and provide a place where they not only use the resources available, but can develop a network of friends and social contacts.

Source: Auld, M. and M. O'Neill (2002). *The Community of South Lake: Measuring Social Capital and Community Pride.* Fremantle: DeVos O'Neill: Research and Evaluation.

3. Mending Broken Promises: Justice for Children at Risk

Richard Couto, Nancy Stutts, and Associates (2000).[1]

This report is drawn from a study commissioned by the Richmond Juvenile Court in Virginia that sought to assess gaps in court services and to evaluate the needs of at-risk children and their families. College faculty and their students used action research processes to interview court staff, social service agency staff, and detained juveniles.

In 1999, the Richmond, Virginia Juvenile Court marked the Centennial of America's juvenile court system. As part of its observance, the Court asked its Citizens' Advisory Council and the Jepson School of Leadership Studies to collaborate on a study of the gaps in Court services and the needs of at-risk children and their families. This report represents the research and findings of that collaborative study. The report identifies services that could strengthen the Court's ability to impact those at risk in the community and suggests targeted opportunities for philanthropic organizations to assist the Court to accomplish its goal. In addition, the report models a method of cooperation—among the Court, agencies serving the Court, community leaders, and higher education—to address serious problems and to propose steps to address them.

METHODS

Participatory action research distinguishes this report from others. Interviews with judges and clerks; officers of the Richmond Juvenile and Domestic Relations Court; Court Services Unit staff; law enforcement personnel; secure-detention staff; social service agencies personnel; educators; prosecutors and defense attorneys; and private bar attorneys and *guardians ad litem* directed the study. In addition, the report includes detained juveniles and other youth as part of the research team and not subjects of the study. Forty-three college sophomores interviewed youth in the Richmond Detention Center, the Richmond City Jail, and the Boys and Girls Club. The children's honest insight, as expressed in the words and artwork, adds inestimably to the report.

---

[1] Taken from the executive summary in the book of the same name. Reproduced with permission of the authors.

FINDINGS

Efforts to "get tough" on juvenile offenders often ignore the underlying causes of problematic behavior such as poverty, racism, unemployment, "war-zone" neighborhoods, mental impairment, school failure, and child abuse and neglect. Get-tough policies ignore adult and social delinquencies, and may even express some of these delinquencies as well.

Juvenile Court attempts to balance the following parameters in individual cases:

- sanctions and services;
- causes and consequences;
- retribution and reformation; and
- social control and social justice.

Obviously, Juvenile Court's intervention occurs after an offense is committed. Less obviously, when youthful offenders come before the Court, it applies the law and attempts to mend a battery of "broken promises." In doing so, the Court becomes part of a new set of promises. Juvenile Court provides "tertiary" prevention, which is the provision of interventions to prevent juvenile offenders from continuing or escalating law-breaking behavior.

Primary and secondary interventions, provided to youth before they get into trouble with the Court, are more cost-effective than later preventive measures or punishment. A RAND Corporation study found that early intervention programs recoup four times their cost of the time a child in a high-risk family reaches the age of 13. Punishment costs a lot.

- In FY 98 combined federal, state, and city funding for Richmond's juvenile justice system exceeded $7 million, averaging $600 per case.
- Detention services represent 43 percent of the budget; approximately $3 million annually averaging a per bed cost of $50,000, excluding education costs.

The Court also has to deal with the harm that others do to children. Too often, juvenile offenses come from adult and social delinquency toward them.

- Richmond City spends over $10 million annually in serving abused and neglected children.

- Of 142 Richmond children identified as requiring extraordinary services, the annual average cost of care was $57,250.

Program experience and evaluative research provide insight into effective programs that prevent juvenile delinquency. Research substantiates three primary focuses for intervention with youth: family, neighborhood, and school.

Family—Many of Richmond's at-risk children have experienced a series of traumas from "adult delinquency" such as parental abandonment; physical and sexual abuse and neglect; domestic violence; and parental addiction and substance abuse.

Neighborhoods—Poverty and risk factors are concentrated in specific census tracts of Richmond:
- African-Americans comprise 94 percent of the population of high at-risk, "war-zone" areas.
- The poverty rate of Richmond families is about four times that of surrounding counties.
- Over half of Richmond families with below poverty incomes are single-parent, female-headed families.

Schools—Richmond Public Schools in war-zone neighborhoods have lower student outcomes than other schools of the city.
- Not one student outcome measure of Richmond's public schools reached or surpassed those of surrounding counties or the state.
- Only one of 52 outcome measures of schools serving "war-zone" children exceeded the Richmond public schools' average.
- Eighty percent of detained juveniles have below expected literacy levels.

BARRIERS TO EFFECTIVE INTERVENTIONS

The juvenile justice system in Richmond has *too few resources* that impacts the programs and their intended outcomes adversely.

- Probation officers carry an average caseload of 60 juveniles; almost twice the recommended rate of 35.
- Richmond detention center is chronically overcrowded, operating between 50 and 100 percent over capacity.
- There is a shortage of placement options for teenage girls in the Court's care.
- Average foster care caseload is 28; state recommended levels range from 18 to 20.

The juvenile justice system in Richmond has *too little coordination and evaluation* among existing resources and programs.

- The Richmond Juvenile Justice Service Continuum has 12 to 15 separate programs provided by public and non-profit agencies as well as volunteers.
- Each program conducts its own evaluation of its youthful clients and develops a specialized service plan for them.
- There is little communication between the programs and some assessment work is duplicative.
- Continuum programs open and close without planning and coordination based on solid evaluation.

Too few resources and too little coordination *undermine programs' effectiveness*.

- There is no routine follow-up once the child is returned home from foster care.
- There is no systematic evaluation of programs serving children and families involved in maltreatment and domestic violence.
- Only 11 percent of juveniles placed in one of the continuum services have "graduated."
- Sixty-nine percent of the juveniles who enter the continuum will become repeat offenders.
- Fifty-two percent of these juveniles recidivate.

CONCLUSIONS

There are recurring systemic problems.
- The system is overburdened.
- Coordination of services is inadequate.
- There is not sufficient advocacy for resources and coordination to overcome funding and service deficiencies.

There are gaps in services.
- Insufficient prevention services designed to prevent both child maltreatment and juvenile crime;
- Insufficient funding to purchase community-based, intensive, in-home services for children who need them;
- Insufficient funding for services designed to keep families together and prevent further youth crime;
- Insufficient funding to purchase comprehensive mental health services for seriously emotionally disturbed children and parents designed to prevent hospitalization, incarceration or institutionalization;

- Insufficient number of residential programs providing intensive mental health services, especially for teenage girls, and funding for programs;
- Insufficient services to address children's literacy and education deficiencies;
- Insufficient funding for after-care services related to foster care, residential or juvenile correctional facilities and designed to support the successful and permanent return home of children and juvenile offenders; and
- A lack of individual advocacy services designed to overcome funding and service deficiencies to meet individual children's special needs.

There are several effective interventions.

- The Court Improvement Project streamlined docketing and case management for more efficient and effective administration of child abuse and neglect cases.
- Community policing improves neighborhood conditions by increased police presence and involvement in the community.
- Second Responders coordinates crisis intervention and immediate referral of domestic violence cases to police and social services.
- Drug Treatment Courts increase judicial involvement and provision of treatment services. A model for introducing new services based on evaluation, research, and planning.
- Curfew and Truancy Center provides coordinated service response to status offenders.
- CHIP (Children's Health Involving Parents) and Families First provide intensive home-based visiting programs of family support.
- Boys' and Girls' Clubs provide structured recreational and educational programming to at-risk youth.
- Al's Pals, a program at Virginia Commonwealth University, helps teachers and parents prevent aggressive behaviors in children ages 3–8.

ACTION STEPS

Expand the evaluation component for all programs, which serve children.

Expand prevention and intervention services and funding for at-risk children with severe needs.
- Child abuse and neglect prevention services.
- Truancy prevention services.

- Community-based intensive in-home services.
- Comprehensive out-patient and residential programs providing mental health, rehabilitative, and educational services.
- Specialized programming for at-risk teenage girls.
- Community-based school programs designed to provide early identification and services for children with special education needs.
- After-care services for children and youth returning to the community from foster care and other juvenile placements.
- Follow-up for juveniles released from probation.

Develop a coalition of service providers and others to advocate for system wider coordination of services to children, youth and families and for overcoming funding and service deficiencies.

TARGETED OPPORTUNITIES FOR PHILANTHROPIC FOUNDATIONS

Hold agencies that propose programs accountable to principles of effective practice.
- A broad spectrum of services which have the flexibility to cross traditional and bureaucratic boundaries.
- Flexible programming adaptive to individual needs.
- Care and respect for clients.

Require and adequately fund a comprehensive evaluation component for currently funded programs and new applicants.

Target funding to programs serving neighborhoods at greatest risk for poverty and crime.

Require and provide incentives for service coordination and program collaboration.

Invest in the vocational training and development of families and neighborhoods.

Provide technical assistance to aid funded programs to become stable community resources and to reach their established goals.

Promote the convening of public, private, non-profit agencies, citizens, and juvenile justice officials to improve and increase effective community collaboration designed to meaningfully resolve systemic problems and service barriers.

Require and adequately fund a comprehensive evaluation component for currently funded programs and new applicants.

4. Hewson Community Cottage—A Service in a Fluctuating State of Turmoil

By Ken Andrew

This previously unpublished study reports on an action research project undertaken by the manager of a team of support workers providing services to people with intellectual disabilities. It describes how the manager worked with major stakeholders to identify specific ways to improve the functioning of the services and the work conditions of service staff.

INTRODUCTION

> Community based action research seeks to enact an approach to inquiry that includes all relevant stakeholders in the process of investigation (Stringer, 1999, p. 38).

This report addresses the issue of services provided by a team of Direct Support Workers who provide accommodation and lifestyle support to a household of four people, each having an intellectual disability and varying degrees of challenging behavior. Key stakeholders in the study include the families of the residents, who play an integral role in their lives and therefore have an impact in regard to the service they receive. Other key stakeholders include the household staff, five permanent employees who work a rotating roster that provides a twenty-four hour service, seven days a week. These services and the team of support workers are often in a state of turmoil, with staff at loggerheads with each other and also with various family members. The stakeholders and the researcher will engage in an action research process to work towards acceptable and attainable solutions to this problem.

RESEARCH DESIGN

Background

Hewson Cottage is a four-bedroom home in a rural community with four residents who are all clients of the Disability Services Department (DSD). The residents include:

- Clive is a 25-year-old male who has some challenging behaviors.

- Olive is a 35-year-old female who now has long term health problems.
- Ingrid is a 25-year-old female who has very challenging behaviors.
- Ilsa is a 25-year-old female who has very high support needs and very challenging behaviors.

The regular staff of five workers attached to the cottage have been embroiled in many conflicts over the years, with each other, other direct support workers in the Department, and also with various local managers within the Department. They include:

- Jenny and Zena who are the longest serving members of the team.
- Zena has been on stress leave at least twice in the last four years.
- Gloria has been part of this team for two years.
- Owen has a long history with the Department.
- Arthur is the newest member of the team and has worked in this location for approximately one year.

The team at Hewson Cottage usually function in the best interest of the residents and during the last year have introduced some innovative ideas and even shown some creative brilliance. The competition between them is fierce and this has contributed to their vigor. However, the staff generally do not function very well as a cohesive team and often come into conflict with each other, and with the differing perceptions and ideals of the families of the residents. The task, then, is to establish what works, what doesn't and where to go from here.

DATA GATHERING

Interviews

Interviews were arranged with each member of staff and the parents of the clients, to enable them to tell their stories. Unfortunately, due to the nature of their profound intellectual disabilities, the clients could not be included in the interview process. However, in their daily routines the clients make their feelings known through their behaviors and interactions. Each person interviewed was given an outline of the process and asked to tell their stories relating to the service and their perception of it. Interviewees were also advised that their responses would be recorded (by way of note-taking) and their responses summarized in order to find some common ground. No one objected to this process and many were pleased to be asked for "their stories." As Stringer (1999, p. 28) notes: "Community-based research seeks to develop and maintain social and personal interactions that are non-exploitive and enhance the social and emotional lives of all people who participate."

Artifacts

Artifacts inspected and studied included:

- Previous correspondence between the service provider and families for the period January, 2000 to current
- File Notes on residents' files (from January 2000)
- Daily Communication book held at Hewson Cottage (from July 2001)
- Minutes of Monthly Staff Meetings (from July 2001)
- Minutes from Annual Planning Meetings for each resident in which each parent is involved (2000 to current)
- Minutes from Annual Team Planning days for staff (2000 to current)
- Results of Consumer Satisfaction Survey (Conducted by DSQ in 2001 with families)
- Results of Service Standards surveys (1999—conducted by DSQ with families)
- Performance Plans for staff (2000 to current)
- Learning and development plans and training records for staff (all records held)

ACCOUNTS[2]

The Staff

Owen: Owen has been a support worker for 6 years. During this time he has been involved in many conflicts with other staff members and as such feels vulnerable to the moods and opinions of others. He feels that past managers of the service did not support him

---

[2] A sample of individual perspectives derived from interviews is provided for illustrative purposes. The perspectives of each person interviewed were included in the original report.

enough and he is still wary of the current managers. He goes to extraordinary lengths to ensure that his "butt is covered" and that he is not left out on a limb. As a result he finds his time at work very stressful and even though his manager has told him that all of that is in the past, and he should move on, he cannot. He also realizes that the old school has gone and these are all new players, however, he still cannot relax. If and when a family member criticizes any aspect of the service, he feels that they are targeting him and he gets defensive. He realizes that his attitude brings him into further conflict with his fellow team members and rather than providing a quality service, he is always mindful of the impact, possibly negative, that things may have on him.

Owen thinks of managers as "necessary evils," he has seen so many come and go, he doesn't really care who it is. He has always fought his own battles in the past and will probably have to do it again. He believes that managers always take the side of the family and that they try and please them at the expense of the staff.

He feels that families often get in the way instead of letting people get on with their jobs. Families never notice the good things that you do but they are always quick to complain if something doesn't go their way. Owen knows that he does not have a particularly good relationship with any family member but he does try.

He doesn't see that this process will make any difference—it is just rehashing old stuff and nothing will change. He is willing to participate in the hope that parents will acknowledge how hard people work.

Jenny: Jenny has worked for the Department for almost twelve years. She has been with this particular service for seven years and feels at home there. She also feels in a rut and is getting tired, though she would rather be tired there than any other service the Department has. She has also been embroiled in many conflicts, though in the past they were mostly with management.

She is also a union delegate and has had to lock horns with management to support other workers and at times has felt that this has caused her more problems than it should. After all, she was only fulfilling her role and felt that she had been penalized for this in the past. She acknowledges that things have changed and the new management is far more conciliatory than the old school. She also acknowledges that in her union role she sometimes has to support staff even though they "deserve everything that happens to them." However she has a role to fulfill and this causes her personal dilemmas.

She has also been in conflict with many family members as they "don't have to actually work with their kids, so they don't know what it is really like." She does try to see it from their side; however, their perspective is often skewed as many think their children are "perfect," and yet they cannot look after them themselves.

Jenny is very cynical of what others do, and is a constant combatant with Owen. She indicates that the current managers are good—"At least you can say what you think and if they don't agree they'll tell you and you can argue back." In the past it has always been one-sided.

The Families

Clive's Mother: Mary thinks that her son gets a very good service from the staff. She gets a bit worried about Owen at times as he seems to get too involved in processes instead of looking after Clive. Jenny and Zena are great and she knows they ensure Clive has a lot of opportunities. They are always organizing activities or holidays for him.

She knows that she can ring the manager if she has concerns and speak her mind, and she does. The current manager is always available and follows up on everything she asks. This was not the case in the past and she was disregarded which made her very angry. Nowadays people are upfront and honest with her and that's the way she likes it. She has noticed many improvements over recent years, though some staff seem to have highs and lows. Basically she likes them all and feels happy that they support Clive. She acknowledges what a tough job it is and feels that she gives them support also.

She feels that she is relatively well informed about what happens and that if she wants to know more, she only has to ask. She is pleased that people take the time to ask her what she thinks, instead of her just telling them anyway and wondering if they are listening.

All she wants for her son is that he has the same opportunities as everyone else his age and the best life that he possibly can.

Specific Service Issues (for Clive's mother): Unsure of all "care" plans in place for Clive. Not exactly sure of what his role is in the house. Are his skills being monitored and maintained? Have seen the fire evacuation

plan, but are all casual staff familiar with this? Haven't seen his latest financial budget yet, but prepared to supplement if necessary. Get a bit worried about staff relationships at times—sense that things are not quite right.

Ilsa's Parents: Ilsa's mother, Betty, felt that they had to visit the house regularly to ensure that their daughter was not being neglected. She has been to the Minister on many occasions and felt that this was the only way that she could ensure that an acceptable standard was maintained. Ilsa's father, Doug, agreed that there were times that the level of service was far from adequate.

They feel that every time they visit the house they have to check on everything to ensure their daughter's health and well-being are not being compromised. They were extremely upset recently when her weight dropped and nobody noticed. They feel that staff do not persevere when feeding her and that she was starving. After all, Ilsa is just a child and needs constant monitoring and assistance. They do acknowledge that the staff, at times, do a wonderful job; however this level of service is not consistent. They feel comfortable about ringing the manager with their concerns as they are always followed up. But why does the manager not notice these things in the first place? They trust Jenny and Zena, but are wary of the others. They feel that Owen lies to them at times and Arthur is too inexperienced to understand Ilsa's complex needs. They have little faith in Gloria's ability to cope also.

They have recently bought a new house closer to the service in order to keep a constant eye on things. That's not to say they expect the worst, they just like to make sure their daughter is OK. They can't take her out very often as her behaviors can cause a problem for them as they both have their own health issues. Doug acknowledges that after all of these years that he still feels guilty that they had a child who was less than perfect, and as he has a nursing background, he knows how she should be cared for. If it wasn't for their own health issues, they would have her home again where they could look after her properly.

Betty and Doug do not wholly blame the staff for their inadequacies; they blame the Department for not training staff to look after their daughter correctly. He realizes that there are three other clients living there, but they don't have the complex needs that Ilsa has.

Specific Service Issues (for Ilsa's parents): They only receive information after the event. How regularly are plans in place for her health and well-being monitored? The house could do with a good cleaning and also needs a few repairs. They hope Ilsa doesn't have to participate in chores as she is too fragile. Does Ilsa get to choose when she wants to go out or stay home? How well are staff trained? They don't think anyone really listens to, or understands, their concerns. They get different stories from different staff.

Documentary Information

It was interesting to note that throughout the relevant documents, there was a general feeling that, from the staff's perspective, the majority of all crises were caused by members of the family's misunderstanding of events, overreaction to events, or interference in the service. On the other hand, families noted that any crises were caused by staff activities, or rather inactivity, and inaction by the Department to respond to the resident's or family's issues.

DATA ANALYSIS

A variety of significant issues emerged from analysis of stakeholder interviews and were categorized according to the following schema:

Relationships
- Between staff
- Staff and families
- Staff and clients

Information sharing
- Written
- Verbal
- House meetings
- Recruitment
- Social events

Skills
- Assess/record
- Reviews
- Participation

Family Input
- Plans
- General
- Outcomes
- Significant events

Confidentiality
- Consent

Environment
- House maintenance
- Personalization
- Health and safety issues—first aid, fire safety

Other
- Food preparation
- Diet

ACTION

The Next Phase

The next step will be to gather all parties together and revisit the process, share their perspectives (Stringer & Genat, 2004), and work collaboratively toward some solutions to increase both the provision of service to clients and the effectiveness of communication between all parties. While a culture of distrust is apparent, it may be initially difficult to break down these barriers and work toward a positive journey forward for all parties.

For the staff, another team planning day is being arranged to specifically address their issues and conflicts. Armed with their interviews and the analysis drawn from them, there will be specific issues to address as well as an overarching team rebuilding exercise. It should be an interesting day. Without the team working cohesively, the issues with families will never be able to begin to be effectively resolved.

Due to the geographical distances between families, a joint meeting of all parties cannot be convened until closer to Christmas, when there is more likelihood of everyone being in one place. This meeting can then serve as a forum to further discuss issues identified and work toward some common goals. It may also provide an opportunity to arrange an informal social gathering for residents, their families and the staff to celebrate Christmas and relax. As Stringer (1999, p. 29) notes: "The type, nature and quality of relationships in any social setting will have direct impacts on the quality of people's experiences and, through that, the quality of outcomes of any human enterprise." Through this exercise, relationships can begin to mend, and the impact on the service can be a positive one.

In the meantime, a draft action plan to address specific service issues that have been identified will be sent to all stakeholders for comment and any changes deemed necessary will be incorporated, before a final version will be sent for signing off by all parties. Once agreement on how to move forward is reached, and actioned, the job of monitoring and reassessing will be ongoing. A copy of how the draft action plan might look is attached at the end of this report.

REFLECTIONS ON THE PROCESS

When I attended the workshop on Action Research I kept wondering if this process would address the issue of the team at Hewson Cottage. As most other techniques had failed, or rather not achieved a great deal of positive outcomes for the stakeholders, I decided to try this method.

My primary concern, however, was that the stakeholders would only go over the same "old stuff" and not move forward. In the first instance this did occur, they all regurgitated the same old issues. Then I realized that this had occurred, as had happened so often in the past, because the "old stuff" had never been satisfactorily addressed or resolved. People had only been paid lip service in the past and nothing concrete had ever been done to heal old wounds or mend damaged relationships.

By using the Action Research process, the stakeholders eventually realized that they had the power to do this from within, and the researcher's task was to help them identify the "whys" and "hows." As Wadsworth (1997, p. 10) notes: "It (action research) is not research or evaluation done by some people and followed by action by some other people—it is action which is evaluated and researched with a view to identifying both where it has 'worked' and what to do if it can be improved by those parties to that action."

While certain tasks were identified early in the process and some action has been instigated to address them, this will need to be an ongoing process to ensure that a mere tick on the action plan does not lead to complacency and the presumption that if an action occurs once, it will occur again as the need arises. The monitoring process will need to continue even for those tasks that we all agree have been satisfactorily completed.

All of these identified tasks are essentially service delivery and service process related and are not intended to fix the situation, merely work toward fixing some elements of the problem. It is only a first stage, and some immediate action will hopefully demonstrate a commitment to improving processes by all parties. This, however, will have an impact on other underlying concerns and even if the tasks only work toward improving communication channels and by simply sharing information, then that will have achieved a great deal.

The Action Research process to date has achieved more than previous processes as it has involved everyone in their lived world, rather than other people's perceptions of that world.

REFERENCES

Denzin, N. K. & Lincoln, Y. S. (Eds.). (2000). Entering the field of qualitative research in *Handbook of Qualitative Research*. (pp. 1–17) California: Sage.

Stringer, E. (1999). *Action Research*. California: Sage.

Stringer, E., & Genat, B. (2004). *Action Research in Health*. Upper Saddle River, NJ: Merrill/Prentice Hall.

Wadsworth, Y. (1997). *Everyday evaluation on the run*. Sydney: Allen & Unwin.

Draft Action Plan for Hewson Cottage

Recommendations	Steps/Tasks	Resources Required	Timeline	Accountable Person	Outcome/Comment
All families to receive a copy of their son/daughter's Lifestyle Plans and the individual plans that result ensuring that goals are realistic and achievable, and have a developmental focus for the service user.	Copy all documentation and send to families	Photocopies	ASAP	Unit Manager	Underway & ongoing
	Families to participate in planning meetings		Dates to be organized ASAP	Unit Manager & family members	All resident planning meetings to be held prior to 3/11/02
Copies of plans sent to families to include monitoring and review dates and responsibilities clearly documented.	Develop monitoring sheet to send to families for review & comment prior to planning meetings	Photocopies	ASAP	Unit Manager	Review of current procedures to be instigated
Staff to liaise with families when a consumer's behavior is changing to keep families up-to-date on how the behavior change is being investigated.	Regular contact to advise families		Ongoing	Team	This process occurs and is ongoing
House routines to be explained to families, particularly what activities consumers are engaged in, and how these build on the person's strengths/skills.	Update house routines and profiles		ASAP	RCOs	Completed
	Copies to families	Photocopies			Done

(continued)

197

Draft Action Plan for Hewson Cottage (*Continued*)

Recommendations	Steps/Tasks	Resources Required	Timeline	Accountable Person	Outcome/Comment
Review current skill base of consumers and record in Individual Plan to safeguard current skills and ensure they practice regularly and are not lost.	Update resident profiles to include skills assessment	Skills assessment schedule	ASAP	U/M & RCOs	Completed
All family suggestions to be recorded in the report book and consumer files. Unit Managers to monitor and Residential Care Officers (RCOs) record in important notes what action was taken and feed information back to families.	Agenda items at house meetings		1 month	U/M	Now occurs at house meetings. Informal feedback to families via RCOs or at meetings if families are in attendance
Regular Information Sheets to be sent to families with changes to department, families to be sent a letter/phoned when there are any changes to their son/daughter's daily activities/programs.	Regular contact with families by either letter or phone		Ongoing	Team	Ongoing process

Consumer participation in running Hewson Cottage to be recorded in consumer's file, plans to increase responsibility and participation to be written up in Individual Plans.	As above				Done
RCOs to review files to check consent forms are up-to-date, and provide a copy of pro-forma to families to let them know what is released to whom.	Ensure info is up to date	Checklist	ASAP	Team	Underway
House to have professional clean inside & out.—U/M to liaise with landlord re: repairs and maintenance schedule.	Arrange cleaner Contact Landlord		1 month	U/M	Done
Service users to have personal ornaments/items/photos on display in main part of house as required.	Consumer choices		ASAP	RCOs	Done as required
Staff to revisit medication storage procedures, and storage and preparation of food with families when they visit the house.	1. Ensure medication locked away 2. Ensure kitchen is kept clean and correct hygiene procedures are in place		ASAP	RCOs	1. Done 2. Ongoing Practice

199

Draft Action Plan for Hewson Cottage (Continued)

Recommendations	Steps/Tasks	Resources Required	Timeline	Accountable Person	Outcome/Comment
Staff to review fire safety practices at Hewson Cottage, check fire equipment, smoke detectors and review evacuation procedures.	1. Arrange Fire Dept. inspection 2. Redo fire evacuation plan	- New evacuation plan	ASAP	U/M	1. Done 2. Done
Staff to check the first aid kit to ensure it is appropriately equipped, and feedback to families.	Have first aid kit checked		ASAP	RCOs	Underway
Families to be consulted when individual resident budgets are reviewed, this will enable families to have input into the process.	Advise families of budget outcomes	Budgets	July/Aug	U/M	
Staff to complete a skills audit of consumers to identify skills that could be developed to enhance participation in recreational activities.	Undertake skills assessment		ASAP	Team	Done
Families to advise of any changes/events which could impact on their son/daughter e.g. births, deaths, celebrations, illnesses.				Family Members/ team	

200

Families to be invited to attend house meetings at least once every 6 months.	Unit Manager
Families to be included in general recruitment & selection processes for greater understanding of procedures (e.g. training requirements).	Unit Manager
Families, residents, & staff to get together for celebration at least twice per year. E.g. Christmas party.	Team & Families

I acknowledge the results of the Action Research Project
I have read the above recommendations as detailed and support the outcomes listed:

Jenny _____ Date _____

Doug _____ Date _____

Gloria _____ Date _____

Arthur _____ Date _____

Zena _____ Date _____

Owen _____ Date _____

201

5. Action Research and Community Development

For a course in community-based action research, Jacqui Hunt engaged in an action research project. She used action research to assist her community development team to review and clarify their work and to identify their future directions. The following report presents the outcomes of her research project.

Experiments with Community-Based Action Research

Jacqui Hunt

November 2002

1. INTRODUCTION

> *We are not looking for the truth because there is no truth. What we are looking for is for every person to hear their voice in the analysis.*
>
> *Ernie Stringer*

Three months ago, I was a member of a new and growing Community Development team with no articulated definition of our craft. Lacking an agreed and shared approach, our work was progressing, but not as effectively as it could have been.

With new members joining the team and the complexity of our work increasing, we decided to undertake a research project to clarify the understanding, approach, vision and aims of our team. Rather than engage in traditional scientific research, we opted for "a more democratic, empowering and humanizing approach . . . permeated by values at every step" (Stringer, 1999: xiii, 9). Thus, our Community-Based Action Research Project began.

Three months later, we are significant steps closer to understanding what Community Development is for us, how we do it and why. It has not been a quick process, but then one thing we *do* know about Community Development is that it takes time. It has taken time to get to know the new members of our team and it has taken time to hear and understand their stories.

Though the research project is incomplete, the purpose of this document is to outline our team's ex-

perience to date with Community-Based Action Research, tracing where we have come in the past three months, the issues that have been raised, and where we think we might be heading.

2. SETTING THE STAGE

> *The organisation listens to the community, the organisation hears the community; they plan, they research and they act upon that.*
>
> *Diane, Community Development Worker and Resident*

Outreach Victoria is a community-based organization working in the fields of homelessness and housing in Melbourne, providing crisis and support services, tenancy advice and advocacy, as well as opportunities for Community Development.[3]

Outreach's Community Development Program began in late 1999 on two public housing estates in outer-metropolitan Melbourne. Until early 2002, the program consisted of one worker and one manager. Over the past six months, however, the Community Development Program has mushroomed into three projects involving a team of four workers. In response to such rapid growth, the team has been struggling with issues such as:

- What are we trying to achieve?
- What is our collective vision?
- What are our individual roles and responsibilities and how do they fit together?
- What is Community Development?
- How do we fit into the organization (which itself is going through a major change process)?

In June, an attempt to address some of these issues was made during a meeting involving the Community Development Manager, Outreach Victoria's CEO, and the two Community Development Workers then employed. The outcome of this meeting was a document clarifying Outreach Victoria's vision, mis-

---

[3] In December 2002, Outreach Victoria merged with Argyle Housing Service to form HomeGround Services. More information on HomeGround is available at *www.homeground.org.au*.

sion, and values, as well as the Community Development team's goals and program framework.

Since the June meeting, this document has remained untouched. The intention had been to revisit and continue working on the document, however, as other pressures mounted, this was not done.

In September, some major changes occurred within the Community Development team. The Community Development Worker who had started up the program resigned from the organization and three new workers joined the team. In the midst of all these changes, the new team agreed to engage in a deliberate and purposeful process of inquiry to work out what we were doing, why, and how.

3. WHY COMMUNITY-BASED ACTION RESEARCH?

Community-based action research is not just a tool for solving problems; it is a valuable resource for building a sense of community.

Ernie Stringer

Our team needed more than simply a definition of Community Development or an evaluation of our work. For that, we could have hired a consultant or gone to a textbook or website and found a multitude of definitions and case studies from around the world. What our team needed was our own articulated understanding of Community Development in the specific context of our work on public housing estates in Melbourne's northwest.

Perhaps even more importantly, our team needed a conscious and meaningful relationship-building process. In the months prior to the project beginning, some tension had been growing in the team because we had not taken the time to get to know each other, let alone listen and hear each other's experiences and practice wisdom. With new members coming to the team, it was obvious we needed to stop and make time to understand each other, as well as our collective purpose, to ensure we worked as an effective team in the future. We also wanted to learn new skills. As a relatively young team we were keen to learn new techniques that might enhance the way we worked together and with residents.

With its focus on local understanding of local issues, Community-Based Action Research also challenges traditional ideas of who constitutes an authority on a particular issue. Bouma (1993: 3–4)

suggests we are often seduced by a person's position or popularity instead of considering whether they have the particular knowledge required for the research task. In Community-Based Action Research, local people with local knowledge are recognized as authorities on local issues.

4. THE PROJECT

With the research approach decided, a Project Brief was established.

4.1 Project Aim

The aim of the project is to clarify the understanding, approach, vision, and aims of the Community Development team—to:

- review our work
- work more effectively as a team
- document our model of Community Development
- identify future directions for the Community Development team

4.2 Stakeholders

Stringer (1999: 49) defines stakeholders as "people whose lives are affected" by the issues being explored. At this stage, the stakeholders in this project have been identified as Jacqui, Rael, Diane (Community Development Workers), Trevor (Social Work Student on Placement), Alan (Community Development Manager), Stephen (Outreach Victoria CEO), and Michael (Tenancy Service Team Leader).

Ultimately, the way the Community Development team works will also impact on the residents of the estates and community organizations who link to Outreach Victoria. In recognition of this, additional phases of the project involving residents and community organizations are currently being explored.

4.3 Timeline

The original timeline set for the project was August–November 2002. This is likely to extend until early in 2003, particularly as the range of stakeholders widens.

4.4 Methodology

Stringer's Community-Based Action Research framework has been adopted to guide the project methodology. It is important to note that although this framework is set out as five clear, ordered steps along an Action

Research path, in reality each step is not linear. Rather, the processes within each step are ongoing, spiralling and often revisited several times throughout the life of the project. The flexibility that this has allowed has been invaluable in adapting the project to the changing environment in which we work.

Project Design The project was initiated, negotiated and constructed through a series of meetings of the Community Development team. I sought permission to take on the role of researcher/facilitator and establish a Project Brief. Stakeholders were identified and ethical considerations explored.

Data Gathering Stakeholders (researcher/participants) have participated in two interviews scheduled 1–2 weeks apart. The interviews took 1–3 hours and aimed to explore "the taken-for-granted visions and versions of reality that make up people's day-to-day life worlds, bringing their unquestioned assumptions, views and beliefs out in the open and displaying them for inspection" (Stringer, 1999). The interviews were recorded verbatim by the researcher/facilitator. Data has also been (and continues to be) collected from websites, journals, textbooks, and guest speakers.

Data Analysis Data analysis will involve three processes: individual analysis, joint analysis (by the researcher/participant and researcher/facilitator), and collective analysis (involving all stakeholders).

Communication Often the communication of research falls into the trap of being "wedded to the written word" (Prosser, 1998: 100). In Community-Based Action Research, appropriate methods for presenting the project and its findings should be considered, including options such as art, drama, poetry, song or multimedia. Examples of how the Community Development project could be communicated could include the use of information technology to communicate with other Outreach staff members regarding the role of the Community Development team or a poster outlining the Community Development team's vision, values, and approach displayed in the community centers where we work with residents.

Action After exploring issues, collective action to address these issues is the critical next step in the Action Research process. Guided by what has emerged from the analysis, the action could be small or large but aims to make meaningful and positive changes to the lives of the stakeholders. An example of action

could be adopting a strategy within the Community Development team to present our newly-created model to other parts of the organization so as to improve their understanding of our role.

5. EMERGING THEMES

The project is currently in the process of data collection and individual or joint analysis. At this stage, no collective analysis of the information accumulated has yet taken place. With this in mind, it is important to realize that the emerging themes identified below reflect my interpretations and analysis, as researcher/facilitator, and may not be shared or further developed by the collective stakeholders.

There is an important ethical consideration at this point in the Action Research process regarding the researcher/facilitator's privileged position of being the only member of the team privy to all the information. This raises questions about how quickly stakeholders should be brought together, and the researcher/facilitator's obligation to respect the confidentiality and sensitivity of what has been shared.

To this end, only some of the emerging themes from the interviews are outlined below. These themes have been identified through a process which began by mapping key issues with individual stakeholders and continued as I began to link similar key issues into themes.

Relationship Building

I've befriended people. I've sat down and listened to people's problems and helped find solutions to their problems. . . . Building friendships. Trusting certain people. Getting people closer together.

Diane

We've got close to building a platform now. I don't think we've achieved community building . . . but we have a platform, a relationship. We have an interest in the communities.

Alan

I look at it [Community Development] as being a really slow process and a frustrating process because you actually have to build the relationships first.

Michael

These snippets of wisdom highlight the importance of relationship building as one of the most important steps in Community Development. Throughout the interviews, participants spoke of taking time, being there, listening, hearing, hanging out, building trust, making friendships, and bringing people together. These processes refer in "experience-near" terms to what Rabindrinath Tagore, one of the founders of community building method, referred to as bonding and banding (Kelly, Unpublished: 4). Though often overlooked because it seems so simple or natural, relationship building is a time and energy-consuming process that can make or break future efforts to build community. Indeed, the first two years of Outreach's Community Development Program were dedicated to relationship-building with the community and creating that fundamental "platform" of trust and commitment on which new initiatives could be based.

Long-term Commitment and Exiting a Community

They [residents] made it known they didn't want do-gooders trying to fix things. I effectively made a commitment that I wouldn't be there for a short time.

Alan

It's a different thing when it's a profession for us and it's their life. I think it adds to their perception that we are just there temporarily . . . and I think that's the truth.

Rael

How long do we stay in there? Ultimately, is it something we aim to withdraw from? Yes. It's about building a community that is self-sustaining . . . so that we can pull out, withdraw.

Michael

Building relationships, developing trust, identifying issues, nurturing potential, seizing opportunities, and enhancing skills have been recognized as processes which require time and commitment. The commitment must be long-term by all involved (including funding bodies). In most of the interviews, workers struggled with the idea of balancing such a long-term commitment with the need to withdraw at

some stage in the process and allow the community to "stand on their own two feet" (Michael).

This issue raised concerns among stakeholders of:

- professional arrogance—assuming residents "need" us
- dependency—whether the organization promotes development or fosters dependency
- narrow focus—the focus on two estates when many others might benefit from a commitment to Community Development

Opportunities, Information, and Links

[Community Development] is giving the opportunity to residents . . . to show me, teach me, link me with what I am best at. [It] is being provided with information as a resident. I don't mean to be lazy, but if I don't know where to get the information, it's good to have it come to me.

Diane

You link people into the community a bit better than they are. . . . It's about opportunities but it still needs to be about how do we actually get people to think about their own abilities and create their own opportunities.

Michael

I started to think there's no point reacting to people's problems. We should be trying to address them and link people into the community.

Alan

In every interview, the idea of the Community Development Worker as a link or bridge between people and opportunities was explored. This related to what was described as an important role of the Community Development Worker in recognizing potential, knowing of opportunities, and encouraging the two to come together.

The idea of the Community Development Worker as a source of local knowledge and opportunities, rather than a provider of all services, has become important in our recent work where, for example, we struggled with how to provide exciting and relevant recreational and social opportunities for young people during the September–October school holiday period.

Rather than provide a school holiday program ourselves, our role can now be seen as one of linking people into resources already existing in the community, such as established competitions or the city council's school holiday program.

Challenging Stereotypes and Perceptions

It was very depressing when even your local police station, when they found out you lived on [Tunbridge] Mews, they'd say "Scumbridge Mews." The Office of Housing, the police, they don't take the time to learn where you come from, to learn what sort of person you are. They just know you're one of those people—the "scumbags from Scumbridge Mews."

Diane

Throughout the interviews, the idea of challenging perceptions and stereotypes has been raised in two important ways. Firstly, it has been raised as challenging the labels residents give themselves and their estates, such as calling one of the estates "the Bronx." It has also been raised, however, in terms of what people external to the estates (the general public, Office of Housing staff, police and community/welfare workers) think of the estates and those who live there.

From her own experience, Diane offered a suggestion of how these stereotypes and perceptions could be challenged:

People come from all walks of life and as you get to know them, they aren't so bad.

By providing opportunities for links and relationship building between people "from all walks of life," a range of stereotypes could be broken down. An example of how this is being attempted at present is through the Ford Information Technology volunteers who meet and share skills and experiences with the residents enrolled in the TAFE computer course.

Breaking Generational Cycles of Poverty

The most important thing is actually breaking people out of this cycle so that they don't feel they are the underdog for the rest of their lives (I assume that's how they feel). So they actually have the ability to enjoy their lives. It's giving them the power to break the cycle. I think that's the most important thing.

Michael

If we don't have a crack at intergenerational poverty then the ability of these communities to keep building is jeopardized.

Alan

Intergenerational cycles of poverty not only encompass trends of unemployment, poor housing options, and limited education, but also generations of learned behavior and ingrained belief. To intervene in a positive way in such cycles requires long-term work with individuals (adults and young people), communities, and systems; creating opportunities, self-belief and hope.

Community Development in Transient Communities

What restricts community development is the transient nature of the community.

Rael

The transient nature of public housing and the impact of this on Community Development efforts was raised by a number of researcher/participants including Rael who began with the above statement, then probed and clarified it through the interview process and came up with the following:

There are always going to be "underdeveloped" sections of the community . . . so [Community Development] is not only building lifelong skills . . . but also building the ability to pass on those skills. That's what we have to think about if we want to be sustainable. It's not just helping the community, but helping the community to help the next community.

It is important to stress that the above attempt to code and categorize the information collected through the interviews is not exhaustive, nor intended to provide answers to issues. Rather, it is intended as a presentation of some of the emerging themes.

Further analysis of these and other themes will be considered during the collective analysis session. Following on from this session, other sources of information will be analyzed. For example, the process of collecting articles and books of relevance for a Literature Review (in late November–December) has already begun and an invitation has been accepted by a guest speaker (a Community Development academic) to come and speak to the team shortly after the collective analysis session.

6. FROM THEMES TO ACTION

The aim of the Community-Based Action Research project is that themes, understood and meaningful to stakeholders, lead to action that stimulates change in their lives. Although we are yet to reach the formal collective analysis stage of the project, action can occur at any stage within the process, highlighting the spiraling (as opposed to linear) nature of the Community-Based Action Research framework. Another change in the team that has resulted from engaging in the Action Research project has been an increase in the level of day-to-day critical reflection and "big picture" analysis of our work.

7. ETHICAL CONSIDERATIONS

In the initial phase of negotiating and constructing a Community-Based Action Research project and throughout the subsequent phases, ethical considerations play a major role in ensuring the equality, harmony, honesty, and sensitivity of this relationship-based process (Stringer, 1999: 42). The following examples highlight some of the issues requiring ethical consideration throughout the project.

7.1 Documenting the Action Research Process for Study

As project initiator and facilitator, one of my primary considerations was my own motivation. I felt it was important from the onset of the project to ensure all stakeholders were clear that one of my motivations for engaging in this process was to reflect on it formally for the purpose of post-graduate study. All of the stakeholders have given permission for me to reflect on the process for study. The boundaries around how I reflect on this process include providing a copy of my report to all stakeholders for consideration before it is submitted.

7.2 Making the Process Explicit and Seeking Permission or Approval

Given the basis of this process in dialogue, I have found it important to make the Community-Based Action Research process explicit to ensure all of those engaged in the project understand the purpose and path of any information that is shared, as well as the role of each of the researcher/participants, particularly in the interview phase. I also found it was important to ask for permission to facilitate this project and

to confirm this, as awkward or unnecessary as this sometimes felt.

7.3 Relationships with Colleagues

Another important consideration in the role of project facilitator has been that of the quality of relationships with colleagues. Knowing from the start that there was some tension within the Community Development team meant it was important to consider how this would impact on stakeholders' ability to engage honestly and meaningfully, particularly in the interview process.

Furthermore, this related to new members joining the team and allowing time for them to get to know each other and settle into the organization without feeling the depth of their Community Development knowledge was being quizzed in their first week at work.

The other realization from this process relates to effective teamwork. It occurred to me that if a deliberate process of listening was used each time a new person joined the team, relationships and understanding could be significantly enhanced.

7.4 Valuing Different Types of Knowledge

Though it was obvious our team would benefit from the marrying of different forms of knowledge, it was not until the interview stage that I realized, in honesty, that I had placed more value on academic knowledge than other forms of knowledge. This was an important lesson for me because it highlighted that formal study is not the only way to learn about Community Development. Though I knew this in theory, it was the practical experience of really learning from others through the interviews that highlighted this bias.

7.5 Duty of Care with Information

At this stage in the process, where information has been collected and some analysis has started to take place, I am conscious that, as researcher/facilitator, I have access to all the information and others do not. I am starting to see links between stakeholders (identified above as Emerging Themes), however, I am reluctant to push these links too far, out of fear of influencing others and discouraging their own analysis. As mentioned earlier, being in this position raises questions about how quickly stakeholders should be brought together and the ethics of confidentiality and care.

8. WHERE TO FROM HERE?

Where to? That's the harder [question] because you've got the practical "where to" and the philosophical "where to." I'm stuck to be quite honest.

Michael

In the past three months, our experiences with Community-Based Action Research have been time consuming, but extraordinarily worthwhile. As we move toward articulating a collective understanding or model of Community Development, we are taking time to think about what we are doing, explore it, and document it.

8.1 The Practical Where to

Following Stringer's framework, our Community-Based Action Research Project has several steps remaining. These include completing the interviews and the individual analysis and joint analysis before the collective analysis session planned for late November. In addition, it involves planning processes for the collective analysis session, documenting and communicating the outcomes, taking action and evaluating the Action Research process. "Where to" also involves extending the project to include residents and community organizations influenced by Outreach Victoria's Community Development work.

8.2 The Philosophical Where to

By the "philosophical where to," Michael indicated he was referring to the "big picture stuff." Philosophy, as a "reflective method of answering the moral questions about the nature and purpose" of our lives, is an important consideration for our team (Carr and Kemmis, 1986: 54). It goes to the heart of why we do this type of work and how. Considering this could lead to the development and sharing of personal practice frameworks by each of the team members. . . .

I feel it's a natural part of my life.

Diane

I thought it would be nice to work with people again.

Alan

Their aspirations are just like any other kids, but they don't have the support to do it.

Michael

It's a sense of belonging, a sense of having something to contribute to the group, as well as being able to ask other people within the community to help you.

Rael

Update: September 2003
The collective analysis session went ahead late in 2002. Following this, our understanding and approach to Community Development was documented in a report titled *Thriving Places*. The team is still evolving but the report gives us a base that can be easily presented to new members and other people as a way of explaining what we do, how, and why. This report was launched by the Victorian Housing Minister in August 2003 and is available from HomeGround (e-mail *alanw@homeground.org.au* for a copy).

REFERENCES

Bouma, G. (1993). *The research process.* Melbourne: Oxford University Press.

Bourke, L. (2002). *YAQ's Sunshine Coast youth action research project.* Brisbane: Youth Arts Queensland.

Carr, W., & Kemmis, S. (1986). *Becoming critical: Education, knowledge and action research.* London: Falmer Press.

Douglas, J. (1985). *Creative Interviewing.* Beverly Hills, CA: Sage Publications.

Genat, B., & Stringer, E. (2002). *Action research in health.* SWSP7348 Readings. The University of Queensland.

Gubrium, J., & Holstein, J. (1997). *The new language of qualitative method.* New York: Oxford University Press.

Kelly, A. (2001). *SWSP7113 Community-based training.* Course Notes. The University of Queensland.

Kelly, A., & Sewell, S. (1998). *With head, heart and hand: Dimensions of community building.* (4th ed.). Brisbane: Boolarong Publications.

Kelly, A. (Unpublished). *The gift of a method of work: Step by step.*

Kemmis, S., & McTaggart, R. (Eds.). (1988). *The Action Research Planner.* (3rd ed.). Geelong: Deakin University Press.

Prosser, J. (Ed.). (1998). *Image-based research: A sourcebook for qualitative researchers.* London: Falmer Press.

Stringer, E. (1999). *Action research.* (2nd ed.). London: Sage Publications.

Whyte, W. F. (Ed.). (1991). *Participatory Action Research.* Newbury Park, CA: Sage Publications.

Online Resources 10

Introduction

In the past few years, online resources to support action research in human services have proliferated. A reasonably superficial search will uncover a vast array of links that provide human service practitioners and community groups with access to resources specifically relevant to their action research activities. By judicious selection, research participants may link to the courses, project descriptions, organizations, resources, listserves, and papers most suited to their purposes.

Online Web Searches

Web searches may be conducted to acquire understanding of action research processes, to acquire data relevant to a particular topic or issue, or to extend a literature review. A broad search may be made using any of the standard search engines such as Yahoo and Altavista.

To conduct an online web search, researchers should:

- **Carefully define the topic:** A succinct definition of a topic aids clarity and precision. It ensures you get the type of information you require. A description that is too general or lengthy will not give sufficient focus to the search.
- **Identify key terms:** Key terms identify the type of information required. Select two or three terms that define the nature of the topic. If you were searching for information to assist a community group to build its capacity to develop a project, you might identify the terms "community," "capacity," and "building."
- **Log on to a search function:** Log on to a search engine (by clicking on the "search" icon and then selecting the desired search engine).
- **Enter key terms:** Enter previously identified key terms.
- **Refine the search:** Often an initial search will not provide appropriate sources. It may identify many sources only peripherally related to the topic investigated,

or it may fail to identify an adequate body of resources. The search may be refined by changing the key terms or by adding another term that locates the topic more precisely. For example, the terms "project" and "development" may be added to or substituted for the previous entered terms. It might also be possible to refine the search by identifying the years to be searched or by specifying the type of publication to be included in the search.

- **Evaluating sources:** Web searches may identify a large array of material, some of which is of questionable value. Researchers should evaluate the quality of material to ensure its adequacy or appropriateness to the study in which they are involved.

Useful Websites

The list below provides but a small sample of websites giving information about action research. There are some limitations to these materials, insofar as even new sites go temporarily offline, and some become superseded. In some instances those authoring the sites have no resources to update the information and they become outdated. Those limitations aside, however, there is a wide range of resources having the potential to greatly enrich an action research project by providing links with practitioners with similar professional or health interests.

The categories below differentiate between types of sites, but these are not mutually exclusive since some sites are linked to others or link to similar sources. A brief search, however, will provide researchers with an understanding of the range of sites relevant to their purposes and contexts. A rather simple but effective method of identifying action research sites is to enter "action research health" as descriptors to a search engine and review the sites presented. More focused searches using more specific descriptors will reveal sites with more relevant information.

General Website Resources

These websites are multidimensional sites, each providing access or links to a broad range of topics and resources related to action research. They include literature, links, classes, resources, papers, publications, and descriptions of projects.

Action Research

Literature and websites. A checklist for action research. A definition of action research.

http://www.ched.coventry.ac.uk/Taskforce/actionre.htm

Action Research at Queen's University

Provides excellent links to programs, conferences, sites. Resources, publications, and student and faculty reports related to action research.

http://educ.queensu.ca/~ar

Action Research Electronic Reader

http://www.behs.cchs.usyd.edu.au/arow/readers

Action Research Resources

University of Minnesota.

http://www.extension.umn.edu/~hoefer/educdsgn/actresrc.htm

Action Research Resources

An excellent list of links to many good action research sites.

http://www.trinityvt.edu/edsite/action.htm

/NRM_changelinks/action research resources

Lists links to many useful action research websites.

http://nrm.massey.ac.nz/changelinks/ar.html

Action Research Resources

Facilitated by Bob Dick at Southern Cross University, this website provides many useful resources including an online journal, an online course, and a number of useful papers.

http://www.scu.edu.au/schools/gcm/ar/arhome.html

Action Research Guidelines and Methodology

These sites provide specific guidance to those wishing to extend their knowledge of and skills in action research methods.

A Beginner's Guide to Action Research

A very useful and comprehensive guide to action from Bob Dick.

http://ousd.k12.ca.us/netday/links/Action_Research/begin_guide_action_research

Action Research Methodology

An overview of the methodological approach of action research.

http://www.web.net/~robrien/papers/arfinal.html

Alcohol and Drugs

U.S. National Clearinghouse for Alcohol and Drug Information

Informative research briefs focusing on the use of community action research related to the prevention of alcohol and other drug problems.

http://www.health.org/research/res-brf/

Capacity Building

Measuring Community Success and Sustainability

Performance-level indicators and baseline measures.

http://www.ag.iastate.edu/centers/rdev/Community-Success/sample/html

Community Capacity Index

Provides many links to community capacity-building web sites.

http://www.sph.uq.edu.au/cphc/comcapacity/index/html

Inclusive Community and Democracy

A schools-based community-building site containing useful sites and links.

http://www.coe.wayne.edu/CommunityBuilding/

Community Development

Asset-Based Community Development Institute at Northwestern University

The ABCD model of community development is strengths-based. Chapter 1 of the ABCD handbook, *Building Communities from the Inside Out* by J. Kretzmann and J. McKnight, can be downloaded from this website.

www.northwestern.edu/IPR/abcd.html

Community Partnerships Kit

This website has a workbook and toolkit for community action projects. It was designed for community groups working on illicit drug issues but is also relevant for people working with other important public health and well-being issues. It includes clear sections on knowing your community, collecting information, planning, and implementing and evaluating your projects. The web page includes useful "toolkits" in areas like publicity and handling the media.

http://www.communitypartnerships.health.gov.au/

Social Capital

The resources and links here provide an introduction to social capital and its measurement.
www.mapl.com.au/A13.htm

Community Mapping

Community Mapping Project

Includes objectives, updates, and participating communities in Ontario.

http://www.opc.on.ca/mapping/index.htm

Description of a community mapping project in Boston.

http://www.ctcnet.org/r981cor2.htm

Community Organizations

The Poverty & Race Research Action Council

A nonpartisan, national, not-for-profit organization convened by major civil rights, civil liberties, and antipoverty groups. Its purpose is to link social science research to advocacy work to address problems at the intersection of race and poverty. The site incorporates health-related links—health; diet and nutrition; and women, families, and children—and provides information on relevant articles, literature, and grants.

http://www.prrac.org/

Disabilities

CAREERS & the disABLED Magazine

Career-guidance and recruitment magazine for people with disabilities.

http://www.eop.com/cd.html

Center for Computer Assistance to the Disabled

Nonprofit offering help with assistive technology for computer access to the disabled.

http://www.c-cad.org/

Disabilities-R-Us Chat Network

An Internet chat site created by and for people with physical disabilities. Includes a chat room, community message board, online disability meetings, disability links, and FAQs.

http://members.tripod.com/~disabled/

DISABILITY Information and Resources

An excellent resource listing websites for a wide range of resources available to disabled people.

http://www.makoa.org/

Disabled People's International

This is a network of national organizations and assemblies of disabled people concerned with promoting the human rights of disabled people through full participation, equalization of opportunity, and development.

http://www.dpi.org

Evaluation

Project Evaluation

Provides a framework and tools for verifying achievement of project objectives.

http://www.worldbank.org/html/oed/evaluation/html/logframe.html

Outcome Mapping

Evaluation of processes that are hard to measure, e.g., community development. This International Development Research Centre site includes sections on theory, frameworks, examples, projects, and publications.

http://www.idrc.ca/evaluation/outcome.html

Government-Sponsored Sites

The Deutsche Gesellschaft Ttechnische Zusammenarbeit

A government-owned corporation for international cooperation that provides information about innovative approaches to reproductive health through peer education, a youth center, theater, action research, and community-based services.

http://www.gtz.de/srh/english/project/proj3-4.html

HIV

AIDS Education Global Information System

http://www.infoweb.org/

The Health Action Research Team

Provides programs and resources to enhance the quality of life for HIV-infected and affected youth through peer-based skill building, education, training, and support.

http://www.themeasurementgroup.com/resource/hart_broch.htm

HIV InSite

Comprehensive information on HIV/AIDS treatment, prevention, and policy. Includes global resources.

http://hivinsite.ucsf.edu

International Organizations

SHARED (Scientists for Health and Research for Development)

Uses Internet networks to share essential information on health research and devel opment for developing countries. It provides access to people, projects, organiza tions, electronic journals, other databases, networks, and groups.

http://www.shared.de/default.asp

The World Resources Institute

Concerned largely with environmental issues related to population health and human well-being. It provides information, ideas, and solutions to global environmenta problems.

http://www.wri.org/health/

Mental Health

ARA Mental Health Action Research and Advocacy Association of Greate Vancouver

Promotes direct advocacy services that encourage the balanced well-being of ind viduals in order to achieve a normal, productive life. The research division presen project reports focusing on a wide range of issues, including income assistanc housing, medications, employment, and crisis intervention. The site provides links to other mental health sites for Canada and the United States.

http://home.istar.ca/~mha_adv/

The U.S. National Institute of Mental Health

This home site provides a wide range of resources for the public, practitioners, and researchers. It includes mental disorder information, as well as research fact sheets, conference reports, research reports, funding opportunities, and patient education materials.

http://www.nimh.nih.gov/

Project Management

A Guide to the Project Management Body of Knowledge

A useful text produced by the Project Management Institute. Access copies from the following address:

http://www.pmi.org/publictn/download/2000welcome.htm

National Competency Standards

Useful guidelines for project leaders and team members about the tasks to be undertaken for sound project management.

http://www.opo-sasa.com/~aipm/PMGuidelines.pdf

Social Worker Associations

Social worker associations provide access to many useful human service resources. The following list includes national social worker associations, but many states and provinces also have social worker association sites.

National Association of Social Workers

http://www.naswdc.org

National Association of Black Social Workers

http://www.ssw.unc.edu/professional/NABSW

Hispanic Social Workers Association

http://www.members.aol.com/HispanicSWA

British Association of Social Workers

http://www.basw.co.uk

Australian Association of Social Workers

http://www.aasw.asn.edu

Irish Association of Social Workers

http://www.iasw.eire.org

Hong Kong Social Workers Association

http://www.hkswa.org.hk

University Programs

The Center for Action Research in Professional Practice at the University of Bath School of Management

The center provides a wide range of information on action research, including papers and publications, conferences and workshops, and related websites.

http://www.bath.ac.uk/carpp/carpp.htm

Community-Based Practice

A concentration within a master of social work program at Portland State University.

http://www.ssw.pdx.edu/pgMSW_CBP.shtml

Community Development Academy

A series of three courses called the Community Development Academy is offered by the University of Missouri Community Development Extension Program. The five-day intensive courses focus on community building, community empowerment, and creating capacity.

http://www.ssu.missouri.edu/commdev/cda/cda.htm

Community Economic Development

An M.A. program in community economic development at Royal Roads University in British Columbia.

http://www.royalroads.ca/Channels/for+learners/future+programs/ma-community+economic+development/maced+home.htm

Women's Issues

Feminist.com

This site includes health and sexuality resources.

http://www.feminist.com/about/

Youth Work

Youth Work on the Internet

Virtual community for young people and professionals using the Internet for learning.

http://www.youth.org.uk

Youth Worker Resources

Provides tools needed for quality youth work.

http://www.youthworker.org.uk/

Youth Work Links and Ideas

A useful and interesting site providing links to many different youth work resources available on the Internet. Includes sites on advocacy and prevention, health, stories, programs, and issues, as well as other highly recommended sites.

http://www.youthwork.com

References

Abbott, P., & Sapsford, R. (Eds.). (1997). *Research into practice: A reader for nurses and the caring professions.* Buckingham, United Kingdom: Open University Press.

Alinsky, S. (1971). *Rules for radicals.* New York: Random House.

Allamani, A., Forni, E., Ammannati, P., Sani, I., & Centurioni, A. (2000). Alcohol carousel and children's school drawings as part of a community education strategy. In "Substance Use and Misuse." Florence Health Agency, Integrated Alcohol Center, Florence, Italy. 35(1&2):125–139.

Altheide, D., & Johnson, J. (1998). Criteria for assessing interpretive validity in qualitative research. In N. K. Denzin & Y. S. Lincoln (Eds.), *Collecting and interpreting qualitative materials.* Thousand Oaks, CA: Sage.

Arhar, J., Holly, M. L., & Kasten, W. C. (2000). *Action research for teachers: Traveling the yellow brick road.* Upper Saddle River, NJ: Prentice Hall.

Atkinson, P. (1992). *Understanding ethnographic texts.* Newbury Park, CA: Sage.

Barbour, S., & Kitzinger, J. (Eds.). (1998). *Developing focus group research: Politics, theory and practice.* Thousand Oaks, CA: Sage.

Barker, R. (1999). The social work dictionary (4th ed.). Washington, DC: NASW Press.

Barthes, R. (1986). *The rustle of language* (R. Howard, Trans.). New York: Hill & Wang.

Bell, J. (1993). *Doing your research project: A guide for first-time researchers in education and social science.* Buckingham, United Kingdom: Open University Press.

Benner, P. (Ed.). (1994). Interpretive phenomenology: Embodiment, caring, and ethics in health and illness. Thousand Oaks, CA: Sage.

Benner, P., Janson-Bjerklie, S., Ferketich, S., & Becker, G. (1994). Moral dimensions of living with a chronic illness: Autonomy, responsibility, and the limits of control. In P. Benner (Ed.), *Interpretive phenomenology.* Thousand Oaks, CA: Sage.

Berge, B.-M., & Ve, H. (2000). Action research for gender equity. Buckingham: Open University Press.

Berger, P., Berger, B., & Kellner, H. (1973). *The homeless mind: Modernization and consciousness.* New York: Random House.

Berger, P., & Luckmann, T. (1967). *The social construction of reality: A treatise in the sociology of knowledge.* Garden City, NY: Anchor.

Bogdan, R., & Biklen, S. (1992). *Qualitative research for education.* Boston: Allyn & Bacon.

Bray, J., Lee, L., Smith, L., & Yorks, L., (Eds.). (2000). *Collaborative inquiry in practice: Action, reflection, and making meaning.* Thousand Oaks, CA: Sage.

Bruner, E. (1986). Experience and its expressions. In V. Turner & E. Bruner (Eds.), *The anthropology of experience.* Urbana: University of Illinois Press.

Carr, W., & Kemmis, S. (1986). *Becoming critical: Education, knowledge, and action research.* Philadelphia: Falmer Press.

Carson, T., & Sumara, D. (Eds.). (1997). *Action research as a living practice.* New York: Peter Lang.

Chambers, R. (1992). Rapid but relaxed and participatory rural appraisal. In N. Scrimshaw & G. Gleason (Eds.), *RAP Rapid assessment procedures. Qualitative methodologies for planning and evaluation of health related programs.* Boston, MA: International Foundation for Developing Countries.

Chirban, J. (1996). *Interviewing in depth: The interactive-relational approach.* Thousand Oaks, CA: Sage.

Cook, T., & Campbell, D. (1979). *Quasi-experimentation: Design and analysis for field settings.* Chicago: Rand McNally.

Coover, V., Deacon, E., Esser, C., & Moore, C. (1985). *Resource manual for a living revolution.* Philadelphia: New Society Publishers.

Coughlan, D., & Brannick, T. (2001). *Doing action research in your own organization.* Thousand Oaks, CA: Sage.

Couto, R., Stutts, N., & Associates. (2000). *Mending broken promises: Justice for children at risk.* Dubuque, IA: Kendall/Hunt.

Creswell, J. (2002). *Educational research: Planning, conducting and evaluating quantitative and qualitative research.* Upper Saddle River, NJ: Merrill/Prentice Hall.

Dedobbeleer, N., & Desjardins, S. (2001). Outcomes of an ecological and participatory approach to prevent alcohol and other drug "abuse" among multiethnic adolescents. In *Substance Use and Misuse,* University of Montreal, Montreal, Quebec, Canada. 36(13):1959–1991.

Denzin, N. K. (1989a). *Interpretive biography.* Thousand Oaks, CA: Sage.

Denzin, N. K. (1989b). *Interpretive interactionism.* Newbury Park, CA: Sage.

Denzin, N. K. (1997). *Interpretive ethnography.* Thousand Oaks, CA: Sage.

Derrida, J. (1976). *Of grammatology.* Baltimore, MD: Johns Hopkins University Press.

Dilthey, W. (1976). *Dilthey: Selected writings* (H. Rickman, Ed.). Cambridge: Cambridge University Press.

Dreyfus, H. (1994). Preface. In P. Benner, *Interpretive phenomenology: Embodiment, caring, and ethics in health and illness.* Thousand Oaks, CA: Sage.

Fals-Borda, O., & Rahman, M. (1991). *Action and knowledge: Breaking the monopoly with participatory action research.* New York: Apex.

Fink, A. (1995). *The survey handbook.* Thousand Oaks, CA: Sage.

Foucault, M. (1972). *The archaeology of knowledge.* New York: Random House.

Foucault, M. (1979). *Discipline and punish: The birth of the prison.* New York: Random House.

Foucault, M. (1984). *The Foucault reader.* (P. Rabinow, Ed.). Harmondworth, United Kingdom: Penguin.

Frus, P. (1994). The politics and poetics of journalistic narrative. New York: Cambridge University Press.

Fuller, R., & Petch, A. (1995). *Practitioner research.* Open University Press.

Garfinkel, H. (1967). *Studies in ethnomethodology.* Englewood Cliffs, NJ: Prentice Hall.

Genat, W. (2002). Aboriginal health workers: Beyond the clinic, beyond the rhetoric. Unpublished Ph.D. thesis, University of Western Australia, Perth.

Goodenough, W. (1971). *Culture, language and society.* Reading, MA: Addison-Wesley.

Graham, K., & Chandler-Coutts, M. (2000). Community action research: Who does what to whom and why? Lessons learned from local prevention efforts (international experiences). In *Substance Use and Misuse.* Centre for Addiction and Mental Health, Ontario, Canada. 35(1&2):87–110.

Greenbaum T. (Ed.). (2000). *Moderating focus groups: A practical guide for group facilitation.* Thousand Oaks, CA: Sage.

Guba, E. G., & Lincoln, Y. S. (1989). *Fourth generation evaluation.* Newbury Park, CA: Sage.

Hart, E., & Bond, M. (1995). *Action research for health and social care: A guide to practice.* Open University Press.

Heath, S. B. (1983). *Ways with words: Language, life and work in communities and classrooms.* Cambridge University Press.

Hepworth, D., & Larsen, J. (1993). *Direct social work practice* (4th ed.). Belmont, CA: Wadsworth.

Heron, J. (1996). *Co-operative inquiry: Research into the human condition.* London: Sage.

Hills, M. (2001). Using co-operative inquiry to transform evaluation of nursing students' clinical practice. In P. Reason & H. Bradbury, *Handbook of action research.* Thousand Oaks, CA: Sage.

Holder, H., & Moore, R. (2000). "Substance Use and Misuse," Prevention Research Center, Berkeley, California, USA. 35(1&2):75–86.

Holstein, J., & Gubrium, J. (1995). *The active interview.* Thousand Oaks, CA: Sage.

Horowitz, I. (1970). Sociological snoopers and journalistic moralizers. *Transaction, 7,* 4–8.

Husserl, E. (1970). *Logical investigation.* New York: Humanities Press.

Jackson, M. (1996). *Things as they are: New directions in phenomenological anthropology.* Bloomington: Indiana University Press.

Johnson, D., & Johnson, F. (1997). *Joining together: Group theory and group skills.* Boston: Allyn & Bacon.

Kadushin, A., & Kadushin, G. (1997). *The social work interview* (4th ed.). New York: Columbia University Press.

Kelly, A., & Sewell, S. (1988). *With head, heart, and hand.* Brisbane, Australia: Boolarong.

Kemmis, S., & McTaggart, R. (1988). *The action research planner.* Geelong, Australia: Deakin University Press.

Kirst-Ashman, K., & Hull, G. (2001). *Generalist practice with organizations and communities.* Belmont, CA: Wadsworth/Thompson Learning.

Knopf, R. (1979). *Surviving the BS (Bureaucratic System).* Wilmington, NC: Mandala press.

Kretzmann, J., & McKnight, J. (1993). *Building communities from the inside out: A path toward finding and mobilizing a community's assets.* Chicago: ACTA Publications.

Krueger, R. (1994). *Focus groups: A practical guide for applied research* (2nd ed.). Thousand Oaks, CA: Sage.

Krueger, R. (1997a). *Moderating focus groups.* Thousand Oaks, CA: Sage.

Krueger, R. (1997b). *Developing questions for focus groups.* Thousand Oaks, CA: Sage.

Krueger, R. A., & Casey, M. A. (2000). *Focus groups: A practical guide for applied research* (3rd ed.). Newbury Park, CA: Sage.

Kvale, S. (1996). *Interviews: An introduction to qualitative research interviewing.* Thousand Oaks, CA: Sage.

Lather, P. (1993). Fertile obsession: Validity after post-structuralism. *Sociological Quarterly, 35.*

Lewin, G., & Lewin, K. (1942). Democracy and the school. *Understanding the Child, 10,* 7–11.

Lewin, K. (1938). Experiments on autocratic and democratic principles. *Social Frontier, 4,* 316–319.

Lewin, K. (1946). Action research and minority problems. *Journal of Social Issues, 2*(4), 34–46.

Lewin, K. (1948). *Resolving social conflicts.* New York: Harper.

Lincoln, Y. & Guba, E. (1985). Naturalistic inquiry. Newbury Park, CA: Sage.

Lyotard, J.-F. (1984). *The postmodern condition: A report on knowledge.* Minneapolis: University of Minnesota Press.

Malinowski, B. (1922/1961). Argonauts of the Western Pacific. New York: E. P. Dutton.

Marcus, G. (1998). *Ethnography through thick and thin.* Princeton, NJ: Princeton University Press.

Mascarenhas, J. (1992). Participatory rural appraisal and participatory learning methods. Recent experiences MYRDA and South India. In N. Scrimshaw & G. Gleason (Eds.), *RAP Rapid assessment procedures. Qualitative methodologies for planning and evaluation of health related programs.* Boston, MA: International Foundation for Developing Countries.

McCracken, G. (1988). *The long interview.* Thousand Oaks, CA: Sage.

McNiff, J. (1995). *Action research principles and practice.* New York: Routledge.

McNiff, J., Lomax, P., & Whitehead, J. (1996). *You and your action research project.* Bournemouth, United Kingdom: Hyde.

McTaggart, R. (Ed.). (1997). *Participatory action research: International contexts and consequences.* Albany, NY: SUNY Press.

Medoff, P., & Sklar, H. (1994). *Streets of hope: The fall and rise of an urban neighborhood.* Boston: Southend Press.

Mienczakowski, J., & Morgan, S. (2001). Ethnodrama: Constructing participatory, experiential, and compelling action research through performance. In P. Reason & H. Bradbury, *Handbook of action research.* Thousand Oaks, CA: Sage.

Milgram, S. (1963). Behavioral study of obedience. *Journal of Abnormal and Social Psychology, 67,* 371–378.

Morgan, D. (1997a). *The focus group guidebook.* Thousand Oaks, CA: Sage.

Morgan, D. (1997b). *Planning focus groups.* Thousand Oaks, CA: Sage.

Morgan, D., & Krueger, R. (1997). *The focus group kit,* Volumes 1–6. Thousand Oaks, CA: Sage.

Murphy, B., & Dillon, C. (1997). *Interviewing in action: Process and practice.* Wadsworth.

Noffke, S. (1997). Professional, personal and political dimensions of action research. *Review of Educational Research, 22.*

O'Connor, I., Wilson, J., & Setterland, D. (1998). *Social work and welfare practice* (2nd ed.). Melbourne: Longman.

Oleson, V. (1994). Feminisms and models of qualitative research. In N. Denzin & Y. Lincoln, *Handbook of qualitative research.* Thousand Oaks, CA: Sage.

Oppenheim, A. (1966). *Questionnaire design and attitude measurement.* London: Heinemann.

Patton, M. (1990). *Qualitative evaluation and research methods.* Newbury Park, CA: Sage.

Petty, R. (1997). Everything is different now: Surviving ethnographic research. In E. Stringer (Ed.), *Community based ethnography: Breaking traditional boundaries of research, teaching and learning.* Mahwah, NJ: Erlbaum.

Prattis, J. (1985). *Reflections: The anthropologic muse.* Washington, DC: American Anthropological Association.

Punch, M. (1994). Politics and ethics in qualitative research. In *Handbook of qualitative research.* Thousand Oaks, CA: Sage.

Reason, P. & Bradbury, H. (2001). *Handbook of action research.* Thousand Oaks, CA: Sage.

Ricoeur, P. (1979). *The model of the text: Meaningful action considered as a text.* In P. Rabinow & W. Sullivan (Eds.), *Interpretive social science.* Berkeley: University of California Press.

Rorty, R. (1989). *Contigiency, irony, and solidarity.* Cambridge: Cambridge University Press.

Rubin, H., & Rubin, I. (1995). *Qualitative interviewing: The art of hearing data.* Thousand Oaks, CA: Sage.

Schmuck, R. (1997). *Practical action research for change.* Arlington Heights, IL: IRI/Skylight Training and Publishing.

Schouten, D., & Watling, R. (1997). *Media action projects: A model for integrating video in project-based education, training and community development.* Nottingham, United Kingdom: University of Nottingham Urban Programme Research Group.

Schutz, A. (1964). *Studies in social theory.* The Hague: Martinus Nijhoff.

Schutz, A. (1970). *On phenomenology and social relations.* Chicago: Chicago University Press.

Sieber, J. (1992). *Planning ethically responsible research.* Newbury Park, CA: Sage.

Smithbattle, L. (1994). Beyond normalizing: The role of narrative in understanding teenage mothers' transition to mothering. In P. Benner (Ed.), *Interpretive phenomenology.* Thousand Oaks, CA: Sage.

Spencer, S., Unsworth, J., & Burke, W. (Eds.). (2001). *Developing community nursing practice.* Buckingham, United Kingdom: Open University Press.

Spradley, J. (1979a). *The ethnographic interview.* New York: Holt, Rinehart & Winston.

Spradley, J. (1979b). *Participant observation.* New York: Holt, Rinehart & Winston.

Spradley, J., & McCurdy, D. (1972). *The cultural experience.* Prospect Heights, IL: Waveland Press.

Stake, R. (1994). Case studies. In N. Denzin & Y. Lincoln, *Handbook of qualitative research.* Thousand Oaks, CA: Sage.

Stringer, E. (1999). *Action research* (2nd ed.). Thousand Oaks, CA: Sage.

Stringer, E. (2004). *Action research in education.* Upper Saddle River, NJ: Merrill/Prentice Hall.

Stringer, E., & Genat, W. (1998, January). *The double helix of action research.* Qualitative Research in Education Conference, Athens, GA.

Stuhlmiller, C. (1994). Narrative methodology in disaster studies: Rescuers of Cypress. In P. Benner (Ed.), *Interpretive phenomenology: Embodiment, caring and ethics in health and illness.* Thousand Oaks, CA: Sage.

Tarnas, R. (1991). *The passion of the western mind.* London: Crown.

Taylor, B. (2000). *Reflective practice: A guide for nurses and midwives.* Buckingham, United Kingdom: Open University Press.

Toombs, S. (1993). *The meaning of illness: A phenomenological account of the different perspectives of physician and patient.* Boston: Kluwer Academic Publishers.

Trinh, T. (1991). *When the moon waxes red: Representation, gender and cultural politics.* New York: Routledge.

Van Manen, M. (1984). Practicing phenomenological writing. *Phenomenology and Pedagogy, 2*(1), 36–39.

Van Manen, M. (1990). *Researching lived experience: Human science for an action sensitive pedagogy.* London, Ontario: Althouse Press.

Van Willigan, J. (1993). *Applied anthropology: An introduction.* Westport, CT: Bergin & Garvey.

Wadsworth, Y. (1997). *Everyday evaluation on the run* (2nd ed.). St. Leonards, Australia: Allen and Unwin. Paul and Co. Publishing Consortium.

Wadsworth, Y. (2001). The mirror, the magnifying glass, the compass and the map: Facilitating participatory action research. In P. Reason & H. Bradbury, *Handbook of action research.* Thousand Oaks, CA: Sage.

Winter, R. & Munn-Giddings, C. (2001). *A handbook for action research in health and social care.* London: Routledge.

Wolcott, H. (1994). *Transforming qualitative data: Description, analysis and interpretation.* Thousand Oaks, CA: Sage.

Young, S. (1999). *Negotiating racial boundaries and organizational borders: An interpretive study of a cross cultural training programme.* Unpublished Ph.D. thesis, University of Western Australia, Perth.

Youngman, M. (1982). Designing and analyzing questionnaires. In J. Bell (Ed.), *Conducting small-scale investigations in educational management.* London: Harper & Row.

Index